FIGHTERS OVER
THE AEGEAN

Learn more about Fonthill Media. Join our mailing list to
find out about our latest titles and special offers at:
www.fonthillmedia.com

FIGHTERS OVER THE AEGEAN

HURRICANES OVER CRETE, SPITFIRES OVER KOS, BEAUFIGHTERS OVER THE AEGEAN, 1943-44

BRIAN CULL

FONTHILL

Author's Note:

For an overall picture of events in the Aegean in 1943, including the Dodecanese Islands, the excellent accounts that appear in *War in the Aegean* by Peter C. Smith and Edwin R. Walker and *Churchill's Folly* by Anthony Rogers are recommended as further reading. However, these two books tend to focus on the politics and military and naval operations of what was a major defeat for the under-strength British forces committed to capture and hold the strategically important islands of Kos and Leros. *Fighters Over The Aegean* covers the role played by the RAF and Commonwealth air forces in the eventual defeat of the Luftwaffe and German naval units and shipping ensconced amongst the Greek islands. Their contribution led to the achievement of Prime Minister Churchill's long-term ambition of a British victory in the Aegean and, ultimately, Greece.

The surrender of Italy gave us the chance of gaining important prizes in the Aegean at very small cost and effort.

– Winston Leonard Spencer Churchill, September 1943

Fonthill Media Limited
Fonthill Media LLC
www.fonthillmedia.com
office@fonthillmedia.com

First Published in 2012 in hardback
This paperback edition published 2017

British Library Cataloguing in Publication Data:
A catalogue record for this book is available from the British Library

ISBN 978-1-78155-044-1 (hardback)
ISBN 978-1-78155-632-0 (paperback)

Typeset in 10pt on 15pt Platino Nova.
Printed and bound by CPI Group (UK) Ltd, Croydon, CR0 4YY

Connect with us
 facebook.com/fonthillmedia  twitter.com/fonthillmedia

CONTENTS

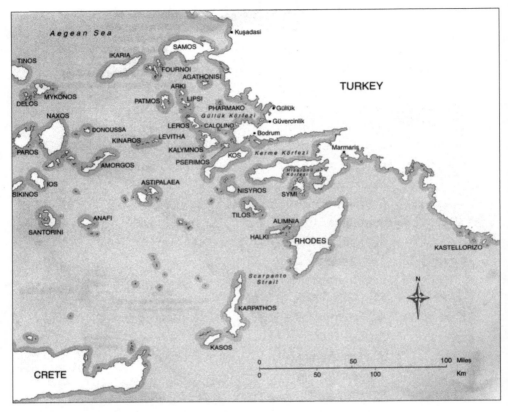

Map of the South-Eastern Aegean.

As with all my books, I prefer to let the veterans tell their own stories. Therefore, I make use of personal correspondence, memoirs, logbooks, official accounts, combat reports, and extracts from published (with due acknowledgement) and unpublished works to this effect.

The Situation in the Eastern Mediterranean and Aegean – Mid-1943

In November 1940, Italy invaded Greece. Britain, a close ally of Greece, came to her aid and after much bitter fighting Germany came to the aid of Italy. British troops were subsequently forced to withdraw to Crete and from there back to Egypt whence they came. Following the fall of Greece in April 1941 and the subsequent loss of Crete in May, mainland Greece and its many islands in the Aegean were rapidly occupied by Axis forces. With their mission efficiently and ruthlessly accomplished, German forces, particularly air units, began withdrawing to the Eastern Front, but even then the garrisons in Greece and Crete were far too strong for the British forces available to contemplate retaliatory action and so a *fait accompli* scenario prevailed for the next eighteen months. Notwithstanding, RAF bombers from North Africa carried out regular if infrequent small-scale nuisance raids whenever conditions proved suitable and aircraft available.

All was to change with the successful British and American invasion of Vichy-controlled North West Africa (Morocco, Algeria and Tunisia) commencing November 1942 (Operation *Torch*), culminating of the defeat of Feldmarschall Erwin Rommel and the Afrika Korps six months later. The war in the Mediterranean and Middle East had swung irretrievably in favour of the Allies who now turned their attention to the other side of the Mediterranean, most of which was under Axis control. With the fighting in Tunisia rapidly coming to its conclusion, there was earnest reorganisation taking place for the next step in the campaign to regain control of 'the soft underbelly of Europe'. For General Eisenhower, the Supreme Commander, Sicily was to be the focus for stage one of the invasion of Southern Europe, while the British commanders, geed on by Prime Minister Churchill, had their eye on regaining Greece.

However, the euphoria of victory clouded sensible decisions. The British Commanders-in-Chief (Cs-in-C) in the Middle East, Admiral Sir Henry

Harwood, General Sir Harold Alexander and Air Chief Marshal Sir Arthur Tedder, agreed that the greatest contribution that could be made in this theatre would be for neutral Turkey to come into the war, thereby reducing pressure on the Russians by forcing the Germans to maintain major units in Greece and the Balkans. Even if this were not to happen, they still believed that there was a good chance of being able to capture Rhodes and the other Dodecanese Islands[1] without the use of Turkish airfields, provided major operations in the Eastern Mediterranean were taking place elsewhere at the same time, thus keeping the Luftwaffe engaged. They knew it would be a gamble for the Germans had proved masters in being able to transfer air groups rapidly from one front to another across Europe. In conclusion, the Cs-in-C suggested resources required to those already in situ would be two auxiliary aircraft carriers, eighty-plus landing craft and ten squadrons of aircraft. Even though there was little chance of these requirements being met, this proposal was put to Prime Minister Churchill, who was then attending the Casablanca Conference:

> What do the Chiefs of Staff Committee think about this? I rather like it. I will discuss it with General Alexander.

However, the Americans soon made it clear that their main priority was the capture of Sicily from where an invasion of Italy could be launched. Nonetheless, Churchill charged the Cs-in-C with the task of planning and preparing for the capture of the Dodecanese, following which the Central Joint Planning Staff (CJPS) in Cairo published its findings:

> [The CJPS], realising that there was no hope of the required reinforcements being provided specifically for the Aegean operation until late in the year, were faced with the problem of what plans and preparations should be made. The degree and scope of operations in the Aegean would be governed largely by the demands of the forthcoming invasion of Sicily. The primary task would to be to stage some diversion in the Aegean as a help to the proposed invasion, but the final plan for that operation had not then been issued [it was not finalised until June 1943].
>
>   If the invasion of Sicily were successful, a favourable opportunity might arise for the seizure of islands in the Aegean, or even effect a landing in Greece. They examined the problem carefully and concluded that future operations in the Eastern Mediterranean might take some form of a diversion to the Sicilian invasion; or, secondly, large scale operations against Crete and/or Rhodes, as an alternative to Sicily, or as a counter to an unsuccessful invasion of Sicily; or, thirdly, the capture or occupation of Rhodes and other islands in the Dodecanese, or a landing in Greece as a result of a successful

invasion; or, lastly, the opening of the Aegean with Turkish co-operation for which plans would depend on the result of conversations with the Turks which we going to be held shortly.

It would be necessary to appoint a special commander and staff to plan any operations in the Aegean in general. In the meantime subversive and irregular activities, designed to lower the morale and reduce the resistance of the Italian garrisons were to be started in that area.

When General Sir Henry Maitland Wilson took over command of Middle East Forces from General Alexander in February, he received a directive from Churchill, which included the instruction that he was to prepare for amphibious operations in the Eastern Mediterranean. However, the Chief of the General Staff, Sir Alan Brooke, was highly sceptical about the venture. He wrote:

> He (Churchill) has worked himself into a frenzy of excitement about the Greek islands. He refuses to listen to any arguments or to see the dangers. The whole thing is sheer madness.

Nonetheless, with this goal in mind, Air HQ Egypt was disbanded on 5 March 1943 and replaced by Air HQ, Air Defences Eastern Mediterranean (ADEM), under the command of Air Vice-Marshal R. E. Saul. The command was composed of four new fighter groups, its day fighter squadrons equipped mainly with near-obsolete Hurricanes, which were unsuitable for operations over Sicily and were therefore practically redundant. By July, these new formations comprised:

209 (Fighter) Group commanded by Grp Capt. R. C. F. Lister, comprising 46 Squadron Detachment (Beaufighters) and 127 Squadron (Hurricanes/ Spitfires) operating from LG07, LG91, Misurata West, Berka III, Magrun North, Gardabia West, Gambut III, Beirut, LG8 and Ismailia.

210 (Fighter) Group (Tripolitania) commanded by Grp Capt. John Grandy, comprising 89 Squadron (Beaufighters) and 33, 213, 274 and 3SAAF Squadrons (Hurricanes), operating from Tamet, Misurata, Valdagno, Mellaha and Zuara.

212 (Fighter) Group (Cyrenaica) commanded by Air Commodore A. H. Wain, comprising 108 Squadron Detachment (Beaufighters), 80 Squadron (Spitfires), 94, 123, 134, 237, plus 7SAAF and 41 SAAF Squadrons (all with Hurricanes) operating from Menastir, Bu Amud, Gazala, Derna, Savoia, Bersis, Berka, Magrun and Marble Arch.

219 (Fighter) Group commanded by Grp Capt. The Hon. Max Aitken DSO DFC[2], comprising 46 Squadron equipped with Beaufighters and 74, 238, 335 (Greek), 336 (Greek) and 451 RAAF Squadrons, all with

Hurricanes, operating from Sidi Barrani, Mersa Matruh, El Daba, Dekheila, Idku, Bassandilla and El Gamil.

They would join 201 (Naval Co-operation) Group commanded by Air Vice-Marshal T. Langford-Sainsbury that was under the direct command of HQ ADEM, responsible mainly for the air defence of the North African coast east of Tripoli for anti-shipping operations, convoy protection and for containing the Axis forces in Greece and the islands in the Aegean. None of the squadrons within the groups were permanent and would be transferred from one group to another as need arose. 201 (Naval Co-operation) Group included in its current establishment 227 and 252 Squadrons with Beaufighter VIs and the newly formed 680 Squadron with PR Spitfires for operations over the Aegean and Greek mainland.

CHAPTER I

Hurricanes over Crete – Air Attack on Crete (Operation *Thesis*)

23 July 1943
Cretan Preamble

Following the hasty evacuation of Crete in May 1941 when assaulted by German paratroopers, many stranded soldiers remained on the run and were aided by Cretan resistance fighters or ordinary Cretan families[3]. Within months, British SOE (MO.4) operatives had arrived, some of whom were transported from Egypt by submarine, and set up a number of W/T stations in the mountains to provide help to both fugitives and the resistance. In two secret evacuations in May and June 1942, no fewer than fifty British and Commonwealth soldiers were taken safely back to Egypt.

Others made their various ways back to safety, including Sqn Ldr Edward Howell, who had been sent to Crete to take command of 33 Squadron just before the fall of the island in May 1941. During the few days that Howell was there he shot down three German aircraft before the paratroops' invasion. Severely wounded and left for dead, he was fortuitously found by German troops and taken to a makeshift hospital before being flown to Salonika where he joined other wounded airmen including Cdr George Beale RN who had been in charge of the Fleet Air Arm detachment, and one of his own pilots, Sgt Alan Butterick, whose leg was amputated. Before his own wounds had healed, however, Howell managed to escape from Salonika and with the aid of Greek civilians along the way eventually made his way to Turkey from where he was evacuated back to Egypt.[4]

The first commando raid against Cretan airfields took place during the second week of June 1942. The plan was to carry out attacks on Heraklion, Tymbaki, Kastelli and Maleme. Three of the groups came from the SBS (Special Boat Squadron) and the other from the SAS (Special Air Service). The date set for the simultaneous attacks was the night of 7/8 June, but the party tasked with the Maleme attack found the defences far too strong from them to penetrate, while Tymbaki was found to have been temporarily abandoned. The Kastelli raiders were more successful and managed to infiltrate the airfield where they placed charges on many aircraft, vehicles and fuel dumps. Five Ju 88s were destroyed (including one of 2.(F)/123) and twenty-nine other aircraft, mainly Ju 88s, sustained damage, while 200 tons of aviation fuel went up in flames. The party escaped unscathed.[5]

The Herkalion operation also met with success. The raiders eventually reached Herkalion on the night of 12/13 June but were unable to attack until the following night when they breached the defences during an RAF bombing raid. Charges were placed on the wings and tailplanes of sixteen Ju 88s, another on a Ju 88 preparing to take-off and one on a Fi 156 located nearby. All were believed destroyed or damaged, but it would appear that only two from 2.(F)/124 and one from 6./LG1 were destroyed, while six more from I/LG1 were badly damaged. Another from Stab I/LG1 was reported to have suffered 'motor damage' after take-off and may have also been a victim of the attack. The raiding party was betrayed during its withdrawal and one of the French officers was killed and the other three captured. In retaliation for the audacious raid, the Germans shot fifty Cretans including the former governor-general of Crete and the former mayor of Heraklion.

In September, the SBS carried out a similar raid on the Aegean island of Rhodes, an Italian stronghold that housed both bombers and fighters on its two airfields, Calato/Gaddura and Maritza. This was Operation *Anglo*, but it did not fare well since only two of the party of twelve returned safely; the others were captured and one of the two Greek guides was executed. Set against these losses were claims for at least thirteen Italian aircraft (SM.84s, Capronis and Mc.202s) destroyed or badly damaged.

The next commando raid against Crete's airfields was planned for June/ July 1943, codenamed Operation *Albumen,* which became known (with a touch of British humour) as the second annual raid. The raiding party arrived at Cape Kochinoxos onboard an MTB on the night of 22 June with Heraklion, Tybaki and Kastelli airfields the targets. All three attacks were co-ordinated for the night of 4/5 July. The aircraft destroyed at Kastelli included a Klemm KI 35 two-seat trainer and five Ju 88Ds of 2.(F)/123. The number of aircraft destroyed or damaged at Heraklion as a result of this raid is unknown. The overall estimate for aircraft destroyed/damaged at the two airfields was put at twenty-nine, but clearly this was on the optimistic side. In reprisal for the attack, the Germans executed fifty-two Cretan villagers including six Jews. This savage act was part of the reason for Operation *Thesis.*

The invasion of Sicily commenced on 10 July 1943 (Operation *Husky*). While the Americans flew mainly from bases in Tunisia and attacked the eastern end of the island, the RAF used Malta as the launch pad for its Spitfires, which housed many squadrons by the beginning of July to strike against the southern coast.[6] Following the successful but costly capture of Sicily and with the invasion of southern Italy underway, the Allies disagreed as to where to strike next. The Americans wanted to concentrate on pursuing the Axis forces in Italy northwards.

With the invasion of Sicily underway, various operations were put into action to thwart the German air units elsewhere in the region. An estimated 265 German and 180 Italian aircraft were based in Greece, Crete and the Dodecanese Islands at the time. Crete remained a major problem with its strong defences and airfields that housed Bf 109Gs of Stab/JG27 and Ju 87s of Stab, I and II/StG1, in addition to the reconnaissance unit 2.(F)/123 at Kastelli, which still had on its strength two high-altitude Ju 86Rs (with pressurised cabins) to add to its establishment of seventeen Ju 88Ds and four Bf 109G-4 reconnaissance aircraft. Suda Bay was the home to Ar 196 floatplanes of 4./126[7] that had recently been formed from the defunct 2./125. At least one ASR Do 24T was always on duty in the bay as were three Z506Bs of 288ªSquadriglia. The island's airfields were also used for aircraft in transit from the Greek mainland to Sicily. General Bruno Bräuer[8] commanded the German forces and General Angelico Carta[9] the Italian garrison.

Operation *Thesis* was the brainchild of Grp Capt. Max Aitken, OC 219 (Fighter) Group, who had at his disposal 100-plus virtually redundant Hurricanes including those available from 212 (F) Group. An official after-the-battle report (believed compiled by Grp Capt. Aitken) revealed:

> After the last convoy had disappeared out of the ADEM area, steaming for the beaches of Sicily, not a single shot had been fired. This resulted in a dangerous psychological situation which might have a disastrous effect on the morale of the squadrons and was none too good for other formations in the Command. It was therefore decided by the Air Defence Commander that a large-scale offensive operation employing most of the squadrons in the Command would produce the required tonic effect – and authority for a daylight attack on Crete by all available single-engine aircraft in 219 and 212 Groups, and certain aircraft of 212 (Naval Co-operation) Group, was given by the AOC C-in-C on 17 January. Taking part in such an operation, which was rendered highly dangerous by the longest sea crossing such a formation had ever undertaken, would be food for pride, thought and discussion in many messes long after the event was over.[10]

The plan was to carry out a massed raid aimed at destroying Crete's W/T stations and other communications with eight Baltimores of 454RAAF

Squadron providing the heavyweight punch while ninety Hurricanes were to strafe the W/T stations and targets of opportunity.

Thirty-six Hurricanes departed LG08 (Sidi Barrani), drawn from 74 Squadron (six led by Sqn Ldr J. C. F. Spud Hayter DFC), six from 451 RAAF Squadron led by Flt Lt E. K. Kirkman (KZ118), 238 Squadron (six led by Canadian Sqn Ldr Homer Cochrane DFC), Greek 335 (nine led by Flt Lt Georgios Pangalos and Flt Lt Nikolaos Volonakis) and 336 Squadrons – nine led by the CO Flt Lt Spyros Diamantopoulos (KZ370) and Flg Off. Ioannis Katsaros (KH927). They were led by two Beaufighters. Fifty-four Hurricanes took-off from Bu Amud and el-Gamil, drawn from 123 Squadron (nine led by Sqn Ldr Ken Lee DFC and including Yugoslavian Lt Ratko Jovanović), 134 Squadron (nine led by Sqn Ldr Bill Stratton DFC, a New Zealander, in HW533), 41SAAF Squadron with nine led by Major W. J. B. Chapman (HW775), nine from 237 Squadron led by Sqn Ldr John Walmisley (which included Greek-Cypriot/Rhodesian pilot Flt Lt Pancio Theodosiou), nine from 94 Squadron (Sqn Ldr A. V. 'Darky' Clowes DFM), plus nine from 7SAAF Squadron led by Major Corrie van Vliet DFC in KW752.

The leading Baltimore was the first to be shot down, all four crewmen surviving with serious injuries. All four aircraft of the second wave were shot down with just three survivors who were taken prisoner. In addition, a damaged machine made it back across the Mediterranean on one engine and ditched just short of the coast as it could not climb to the 500 feet of the airfield and was unable to land on the beach due to obstruction by ship wreckage. Next day a large search was mounted for possible survivors, without success.

Meanwhile, the Hurricanes had also fared badly. Sqn Ldr Ken Lee of 123 Squadron led the Bu Amud Hurricanes, flying KZ141.

Off we went at ground level, and we arrived right on schedule. We had long-range tanks which we dropped as we approached the coast. We went up a valley, but all we could see was beautiful scenery, full of olive trees. Not a soul was in sight. We were looking backwards and forwards, looking for something to shoot at. We got to the end of the valley, turned round and made the fatal mistake of coming down the same valley, by which time they were waiting for us. I was first in so I was supposedly in the safest position of them all.

As I came back out of the valley and then back over the beach I had a little check round the aircraft as we were going to be flying over the Mediterranean. To my horror my trousers were covered in oil, the oil line was spurting like mad. I glanced around, the oil temperature was way up as was the engine temperature. There was no way I was going to fly back across the Mediterranean like that. We had already decided on a plan as where to go and crash land, and be picked up by the Resistance. So I turned back and as I came over the coast the engine cut out. I supposed it overheated. I had to get down. I had been flying a Hurricane and other fighter aircraft every day for six years. I really could put an aircraft down on a postage stamp. I saw this little slot between the olive trees and went in there. When I was later interrogated the Germans didn't believe it, they thought it wasn't possible.

The drill was to try and set your aircraft on fire after you landed. I got out the little thermite bomb and set it off, put it on the wing and then headed for the bushes. I ran across an open space and after about fifty yards I felt a terrific blow in the guts. Someone on the ground had taken a shot at me and the bullet had gone through my webbing belt, through the buckle and out through the ammunition pouch on the other side. I was really lucky, a few millimetres over and it would have ripped my stomach open. Anyway, it knocked me flat and when I sat up someone was standing over me with the gun. He frightened me in a way. When we marched up this hill he was shooting my pistol off and I thought he was going to shoot me.

I was marched up to the local village when the German army officers were all having their breakfast, and they stood up and saluted, "Guten Morgen, Herr Myorr. Have you been wounded? Have you had your breakfast?" I had an omelette and a brandy with them. One of these fellows came to me and said, "Tell me sir, would you be kind enough, when you are interrogated, to say that it was one of my machine-guns on that hill that shot you down, and not those buggers over there?" A staff car came to collect me. As a squadron commander I was a comparatively rare object to catch and they wanted to know whether we were really going to invade.[11]

Sqn Ldr Lee was taken to headquarters at Heraklion before being flown by a Ju 52 to Athens where he met half a dozen other survivors of the raid. Two other members of 123 Squadron also failed to return: Flg Off. John Le Mare RCAF being killed in HW538, although Trinidadian Flt Sgt Fernand 'Fanny' Farfan (KW964) managed to evade capture and helped by Cretans and SOE to return to Egypt in September.

A second Bu Amud squadron, 238, lost two pilots though both Flt Sgt P. A. George RAAF (KZ130/J) and Flt Sgt Hilton Rayment RNZAF (HW483/ P) were both captured, the Australian pilot having not only survived a ditching but was machine-gunned as he swam for shore. 238 Squadron CO Sqn Ldr Homer Cochrane (HL657/D) was fortunate to get back with his badly damaged aircraft and landed safely at Bu Amud.

134 Squadron had similarly taken a beating with two pilots lost – Flg Off. William Manser (HW299), whose aircraft was seen to make a successful crash-landing, and Sgt David Horsley (HW372) were both killed – while two others returned were wounded: Flg Off. I. L. Lowen (HV905) with a

wounded leg and Flg Off. W. H. Wright (HW605) seriously wounded in a lung. Four other Hurricanes were damaged, one seriously.

The fourth Bu Amud squadron, 41SAAF, also lost a pilot with Lt W. J. K. Bliss SAAF failing to return. Major Chapman SAAF reported that he was strafing over Moires, near the south coast, when his aircraft was hit by a shell that passed through the port wing root, damaging the oil and glycol systems. Nonetheless, he was able to nurse his aircraft back to Bu Amud. On arrival the engine seized over the airfield but he was able to glide in and land safely. Lt Cyril George SAAF also crash-landed on the airfield when his engine seized owing to shell damage. Five others were damaged. Therefore, of the fifty-four Hurricanes from Bu Amud, eight failed to return (four killed, three POW, one evaded), plus two pilots returned wounded and at least further three Hurricanes were badly damaged.

The Sidi Barrani Hurricanes fared slightly better, although the two Greek units suffered four losses of whom only one survived. Wt Off. Eleftheriou Athanasakis of 336 Squadron flying BP232 lost one of his external fuel tanks on take-off, but despite the fact that he was made aware of the mishap by aircraft flying close to him, he refused to turn back in the full knowledge that he had not enough fuel for the return flight as recalled by Wt Off. Konstantinos Kokkas (a Cretan):

> I close to him and indicate him that his fuel tank is detached, he nods me that he realised it but he is not going to leave the formation. Another plane, also, nods him about the fuel tank, but Athanasakis insists...

After an almost three-hour flight, the Greek Hurricanes strafed the radar station in Ierapetra (south-eastern Crete) and many targets around the area (various military targets) despite heavy anti-aircraft fire. Over the area of Agios Nikolaos, Athanasakis reported a fuel problem and was going to force land. Kokkas continued:

> We hit camps, cars, cannon stations and every military target which was in front of us. Everywhere, though, the anti-aircraft guns respond. We pass through an open gorge and we reach the Agios Nikolaos plain. This is where I hear Athanasakis yelling that he is force-landing. Though, at the area he landed there was a German patrol, which pursued him. Athanasakis defended himself with his gun, trying simultaneously to escape. Nevertheless, the fight was uneven. Athanasakis' bullets run out, and as a result he fell dead by the enemy's gun fire.

Meanwhile, the remaining Greek Hurricanes continued their mission, flying to Heraklion and strafing a German camp where Wt Off. Sotirios Skantzikas' aircraft (KW250) was hit by flak and shot down. Kokkas:

The flak was ferocious but we gave as good as we got. I saw a German flag fluttering in a building on my right and sent a machine-gun burst into it. We were almost touching the windmills and the milk-white houses, while the Cretans were throwing their hats into the air and dancing with joy, waving their hands all the time. My classmate, Skantzikas, was flying next to my right and nods me with his thumb that he is hit. His aircraft is covered with oil, which reveals what is going to happen to my colleague. It was the last time I saw him...'[12]

Skantzikas also survived a crash-landing and was taken prisoner (see Appendix II), but neither of the two 335 Squadron pilots survived. Flt Sgt Vasileios Doukas was shot down near Kalo Horio Lasithiou on the south shore of the Bay of Mirabello. An intelligence source indicated that he had been taken prisoner. However, he was later reported to have been killed. Meanwhile, Flt Sgt Mauritius Laïtmer fell near Tymbaki. A pilot of 238 Squadron reported seeing a Hurricane bearing Greek markings crash into the sea a mile or so off Kasteliana. On return, Wt Off. Kountouvas (KZ314) of 335 Squadron reported having been attacked by a Ju 88 south of the island but escaped unscathed.

However, some pilots reported a relatively uneventful mission as Flg Off. Reg Sutton of 451 RAAF Squadron recalled:

Eighty Hurricanes [*sic*] were gathered and fitted with overload tanks. These were to be jettisoned on the Greek coast. The ground staff of the Greek squadron at Sidi Barrani spent all night painting messages on theirs. The Baltimores were to go in and bomb the aerodrome on the north-west of Crete; this they did and returned down the same valley. By this time every gun had been wakened and they had all been shot down [*sic*]. One of the pilots was a brother of one of our chaps.

The Hurricanes were led in by the Beaufighters, flying at wave top height to keep under the radar screen. We had been briefed about the island – where the targets were and where there was heavy flak. There were no targets where they were supposed to be and where there was not to be any flak, there was bags of it. I saw one aircraft strafe a small mountain – top shrine – and another have a quick burst at what appeared to be an ambulance. For the rest, nothing. I fired my guns on the way out just for the sake of firing them. We flew south and hit the North African coast to find the whole area covered in a tremendous dust storm. We were to land at Tobruk but quite a few aircraft were running low on fuel and had to put down along the road. I made the aerodrome, which one could only pick out because the sand was more intense, being easier to whip up, there being no ground cover. There was 10/10ths no visibility from 500 feet to the deck except for occasional eddies, which gave you a vague idea where the ground was. There had been two prangs on the aerodrome and one gathered oneself into a tight ball against the horrible rending crash of tearing metal, but all was well and a truck with its lights on found us and led us back to the flights. My time was 2¾ hours.

The two Beaufighters leading the el-Gamil Hurricanes, flown by Wg Cdr Russell Mackenzie (EL516/Y) and Flg Off. Wally McGregor RNZAF (JL619/X) encountered an Ar 196 at sea level as they approached the coast. Mackenzie made a full deflection attack and scored hits on its fuselage while McGregor followed with no apparent result before it escaped. A second Arado (or the same one) was seen a minute or so later and also attacked, but again with no tangible result. One of the following Hurricane pilots of 94 Squadron reported firing at an Arado, probably the same aircraft.

Of the twenty-seven Hurricanes from el-Gamil, one of 237 Squadron was damaged while 94 Squadron lost Sgt Bill Imrie (KW935/A) who was killed. Two other Hurricanes were slightly damaged. The CO reported:

07:15 Nine aircraft (of 94 Squadron) and others, led by two Beaufighters set off for Crete. Attacked barracks at Maleme and buildings at Alikianos, a dam on a river and a well-camouflaged camp. Sgt Imrie's aircraft hit by AA and he was heard to say that he was going down and other pilots saw him land neatly among some trees on the mountainside. Thought he was safe [sadly, he was killed]. Continuing sweep, flew along valley to Kastelli Sellinos and shot up W/T hut there. The route led them south-east of Gavdhos island, where the lighthouse, W/T unit and masts were attacked. On arrival back to base found that Flg Off Howley's aircraft had slight damage to prop and Flg Off Henderson's bullet holes in the fuselage.[13]

Capt. Harold Kirby of 7SAAF had a narrow escape when his aircraft KX961 clipped a high-tension cable, damaging the propeller tips and radiator. The mission report read:

Formation flew up the west side of Crete, about 6 miles off the coast, around Cape Spatha, attacked houses and staff car on coast before flying inland to the vicinity of Alikianos, where the power station on the lake and a transit camp were attacked. Numerous strikes were seen on the power station and Capt Kirby's aircraft hit a power cable. From Alikianos the squadron turned west to the Maleme-Sellinos Kastelli road and followed the road down to Sellinos. Very little was seen. One aircraft strafed houses at Kamhano … and the W/T station was attacked. There, some light AA was encountered. Formation left Crete for Gavdhos, expending the remaining ammunition on the lighthouse before setting course for home.[14]

All told, thirteen Hurricanes failed to return with eight pilots killed, four POW and one who evaded; two other pilots were wounded. Added to the loss of six Baltimores in which fourteen crewmen were killed and six taken prisoner, it proved to have been a poorly planned operation with disastrous results for very little return. One of the few positive actions occurred during the cover of the returning aircraft by Spitfires of 80 Squadron when Flg Off. J. C. R. Waterhouse (JK142) shot down a reconnaissance Ju 88 in flames into the sea. This was Ju 88D 4U+6K of 2.(F)/123 in which Uffz Friedrich Dieroft and his crew were killed.

MO.4 operatives on Crete were able to radio information back to Cairo regarding the effects of the attack. They reported that three Hurricanes flying low over the village of Souyia were subjected to machine-gun fire from the ground. They returned and swooped on the suspected gun site inflicting one fatality who happened by chance to be the quisling Tzimanokes who had betrayed at least seven British soldiers on the run. At Hag Nikolaos, bombs fell on an Italian army camp and killed four soldiers. Bombs killed twenty-one soldiers, three civilians and wounded thirty more soldiers at Ierapetra. At Pakhiano, a motor vessel was unsuccessfully bombed; however, a strafing attack killed one sailor and wounded two others including the captain.

So what went wrong? 454 Squadron's historian wrote:

> Certainly the concept of a feint across Crete was sound. In retrospect, there were a number of factors that led to failure. First, the planners at Group HQ had forgotten that although the Allies were on double summer time, the Axis were not. The plan assumed the German defences would be at breakfast and be caught unawares, but in Crete, breakfast was over and the Germans were already attending their daily duties. Second, the 120 fighters [*sic*] that were sent as escort took some time to co-ordinate and so the Baltimores consequently arrived over the island first. This alerted the island defences, anti-aircraft guns and enemy fighters. While the Allied fighters were small and nimble and flying at much higher altitude, the bombers were not. The defences would have been fully prepared and awaiting the low-level strike with the inevitable result.

The official (Aitken) report concluded:

> On the face of it, the material damage to the enemy was probably in no way commensurate with the total loss of 13 Hurricanes and five Baltimores, together with other aircraft casualties and damage. On the other hand it is undeniable that the unpalatable medicine administered to the enemy, couple with the fine tonic effect on 212 and 219 Group squadrons, made the operation a success on balance.

It seems unlikely that many of the survivors including those now incarcerated as prisoners on Crete or those who suffered injuries would have concurred with the sentiment. A few weeks later on 6 September, six Hurricanes of 336 Squadron led by Flt Lt Ioannis Katsaros carried out an attack on an Italian position near Koufonisi, on this occasion without loss.

CHAPTER II

Beaufighters over the Aegean – April-September 1943

The build-up of Beaufighter units for operations over the Aegean began as early as February 1943 when 252 Squadron was transferred to Magrun (Libya) on 21 February followed by the arrival of a new CO Wg Cdr Dennis Butler. 227 Squadron moved from Malta to Idku (Egypt) on 1 March. This unit began to equip with Beaufighter VIs fitted with bomb racks while Wg Cdr Russell Mackenzie DFC AFC was appointed CO shortly thereafter. 252 Squadron was tasked with carrying out armed patrols along the west coast of Greece, operating from Magrun, while 227 was to concentrate on the Aegean.

680 Squadron's B Flight, with its Spitfire PRIVs, had begun flying sorties over the Aegean from Cyprus checking for suitable targets for the Beaufighters and shipping activity in general. On 4 April, the unit suffered its first loss when BR663 failed to return. It transpired that Flg Off. Gerald Tozer's aircraft had developed engine problems and had carried out an emergency landing in Turkey where both pilot and aircraft were interned.

By mid-April, 227 Squadron was declared operational and moved to Gambut (Libya) for its first mission on 21 April when four aircraft carried out a sweep, which proved uneventful. Two days later, four Beaufighters departed Gambut at 08:15 for an offensive recce over the Aegean. Sgt David Warne RCAF (JL708/A) met and attacked an Ar 196, hitting its fuselage and wings. It was last seen diving away and was later reported (incorrectly) to have crashed with the loss of its crew. Nonetheless, first blood to the Beaufighters, but EL532/T was forced to belly-land at Derna with flak damage though neither Sgts Eric Havnar nor Denis Galley was hurt. On 26 April, Wg Cdr Mackenzie (JL531/M) led three Beaufighters to attack a large schooner reported off the eastern coast of the Greek mainland. This was set on fire but the aircraft crewed by Sgt Ron Harvey and Plt Off. Wally Fisher (JL639/O) struck the mast of the vessel and crashed into the sea with the loss of both crewmembers. A second Beaufighter (EL431/E) failed to return but the crew, Flg Off. Tommy Deck and Plt Off. G. W. Ridley, survived a ditching off the Turkish coast and were rescued and briefly interned (returning to Egypt on 8 June). Another Beaufighter (JL644/F) went down on 28 April, ditching off the north-east coast of Kythera owing to engine problems. The crew, Sgts J. H. Harrison and J. R. Sloper, managed to get into their dinghy and were rescued, but became prisoners.

Wg Cdr Mackenzie was at the head of four Beaufighters that attacked a small steamer on 1 May. Return fire from the 154-ton *Capri* hit the port engine of JL519/P, the aircraft crewed by Flt Lt Tom Freer DFC and Flg Off. Charles Holman. Unable to reach base they too headed for Turkey, escorted to the coast by Wg Cdr Mackenzie, where a successful forced-landing was made at Gaziemir/Izmir. Following a period of internment, the crew returned to Egypt towards the end of June. Two reconnaissance Ju 88s from the newly arrived detachment of I/Erg.FAGr. at Salonika/Sedes crashed and were destroyed while landing at the airfield. Six of the eight crew members were killed. Four days later, another aircraft from this unit – F2+LK off 2 Staffel flown by Uffz Johann Mödlhammer – failed to return from a sortie over the Aegean. The crew was lost.

Offensive patrols were carried out on a daily basis by 227 Squadron, caiques being destroyed or damaged on 4th, 8th and 9th May. Four Beaufighters of 227, now operating from Derna, carried out an offensive sweep on 11 May, Plt Off. Jack Phillips RAAF and Sgt J. Hawkes-Reed strafing two caiques which they believe sank after their crews jumped into the sea. The other pair, Plt Off. Cas de Bounevialle/Sgt Jim Scott in EL500/S and Sgt Bill Budd/Sgt Bob Jobling (JL514/R), sighted a Ju 52 floatplane that both attacked, Budd setting fire to its starboard engine whereupon it dived into the sea with no survivors. This was TF+BL of Seetrnsptstfl.1. Operations continued unabated over the Aegean where a number of small vessels and caiques were strafed and bombed during the month, but not without loss. Caiques were destroyed or damaged on 13th and 14th; on the latter date four Beaufighters attacked vessels in Syros harbour.

On 16 May, three Beaufighters on a sweep attacked two caiques but were approached by two Arados; an inconclusive combat witnessed the floatplanes depart. The Beaufighters continued to strafe the caiques only to learn that EL500/S, crewed by Sgt Eric Havnar from Southern Rhodesia and his navigator Sgt Denis Galley, was missing. Havnar had taken-off slightly behind the main formation so had carried on alone. It was later learned that EL500 had been shot down with only the pilot taken prisoner. Another crew was lost on 21 May when three Beaufighters encountered five Ju 52 floatplanes of Seetrnsptstfl.1 escorted by three Ar 196s near the island of Melos. The flight leader, Flt Lt James Atkins (JL514/R), was seen to attack an Arado head-on, the floatplane turning sharply to the right in an effort to get on the Beaufighter's tail, which it possibly did since Atkins' aircraft was shot down, he and his navigator Flg Off. Bob Wellington losing their lives. Plt Off. Phillips (JL533/K) attacked the same Arado and was able to open fire. A few seconds later it apparently crashed into the sea, 'Arado' wreckage being observed (probably Atkins' aircraft). However, it seems that the victim of the attack managed to return to Kalamaki badly damaged, its crew believing that Atkins' Beaufighter had collided with their aircraft before it crashed into the sea. Meanwhile, Sgt John Lewis (EL460/ U) carried out an attack on a Ju 52, from which he witnessed passengers firing from the windows with automatic weapons. The two surviving Beaufighters broke away when Arados attempted to engage.

Attacks on caiques was the order of the day for the Beaufighters. At least six were claimed sunk in addition to damage to a small M/V in three days before another aerial success was achieved on 27 May, when Wg Cdr Mackenzie (EL467/B) attacked Ju 88 3U+DV of 1./ZG26 and set its port engine on fire. Sgt Keith Thomas (JM235/W) followed in and knocked out its starboard engine whereupon it rolled over on its back and crashed into the sea. There were no survivors: Fw Erich Borner and his crew were killed. A second Ju 88 was seen and pursued, the CO scoring strikes on the rear-gunner's cabin but was hit in the starboard engine by return fire. The Ju 88 made off eastwards while Mackenzie headed for Cyprus where a safe landing was made.

Two days later (29 May), another Ju 52 seaplane fell to the guns of 227 Squadron pilots, C6+ES/7103 of Seetrnsptstfl.1 being the victim, onboard which one passenger (a marine) was killed and three crew wounded. Flg Off. Red Modera (EL460/U) led Sgts Keith Thomas (EL552/S) and A. D. Hay (JL708/A) on a stern attack while Plt Off. Jack Phillips (JL533/K) came in from head-on scoring strikes on its port engine and wing following which it alighted on the sea just as Modera (from Kenya) opened fire from astern. Thomas and Hay then carried out a strafing attack. The Beaufighters then turned their attention to an accompanying Ar 196, D1+IH of 1./126, flown by Fw Michalek. Plt Off. Phillips made the initial attack and scored hits, followed by the other three. The floatplane flew towards a nearby island, ditched in a bay on fire and the crew were seen running towards a village. The pilot survived unhurt but his observer died. The Arado was strafed until it blew up and the Ju 52 was seen to be burning fiercely. But for 227 Squadron the loss of six crews in four weeks was a rude awakening to its new role of running down German capacity to supply the Aegean islands by sea and air. However, six German aircraft had been shot down in return and a number of small vessels and caiques had been destroyed or damaged.

June's operations continued along similar lines although there was a lack of aerial encounters. An attack by Beaufighters on Stampalia harbour to the west of Kos on 4 June resulted in the loss of Sgts John Lewis and James Roff (EL460) due to heavy AA fire. However, this proved to be the only Aegean loss during the month that saw a switch to operations over the Ionian Sea, joining the Beaufighters of 252 Squadron in attacking shipping and harbours along the south-western Peloponnese coastline. These missions continued into July, 227 losing two more crews during that month.

On 24 June, thirty-five US B-24s and B-25s from Libya, with an escort of P-38s, paid Salonika/Sedes airfield a visit and proved to be a highly successful attack. Nine Ju 88s of II/LG1 were destroyed together with three auxiliary aircraft and at least forty mainly aircrew casualties including two killed. On 27 June, both Eleusis and Kalamaki airfields on mainland Greece were bombed by about fifty B-24s. Much damage was claimed by the Americans including three hangars, the runway intersection and administration buildings at Eleusis; fires and smoke were observed over whole area. Bf 109s intercepted of which three were claimed as destroyed and five as probably destroyed.

227 returned to Derna on 17 July and six days later led Hurricanes to Crete as part of Operation *Thesis*. The Beaufighters strafed radar and radio stations, guns sites and caiques, all returning safely. On 28 July, Wg Cdr Mackenzie led four Beaufighters to attack two vessels sighted near the island of Alimnia off Rhodes. Hits were scored on one of the ships, '...which gave out orange flames and black smoke before listing to starboard. The wreckage of this vessel was seen, with masts and funnel sticking out of the water when another attack was made on 30 July.'

46 Squadron had provided a detachment of Beaufighters for daylight operations in support of 227 Squadron and soon added to its scoreboard on 3 August four Beaufighters engaging Ar 196 7R+AK of 2./125 about five miles north-east of Chania (Crete). The Arado was shot down into the sea by Plt Off. W. Jenkinson (with Flt Sgt R. Kendall in V8766/U), taking with it Obfw Karl Steinkemeier and observer Ltn Wolfgang Zacharias, both of who were killed. It appears that the machine was erroneously reported to have been a Z.506B.

Beaufighter Operations from Cyprus

227 Squadron transferred to Cyprus on 16 August and was initially based at Limassol before moving to Lakatamia from where it would be better suited to operate over the Dodecanese. They were soon to be joined by 252 Squadron, which arrived on 9 September. For local defence a detachment

of 213 Squadron Hurricanes was based at Paphos and a detachment from 127 Squadron at Nicosia. Detachments from 46 and 89 Squadrons, both with Beaufighter VIs equipped with radar, also arrived at Cyprus and were based at Nicosia and Lakatamia respectively. Their main task was intended to be night intruder operations over and around Rhodes. A detachment of 680 Squadron PR Spitfires also arrived at Nicosia for operations over the Aegean. One of the PR pilots was an American from Massachusetts who had joined the RCAF, Flg Off. John Keller, who recalled:

> All of my missions were at 25,000 to 30,000 feet. One problem was the lack of adequate heat for the pilot at altitude. Bloody cold with half the heat ducted back to the cameras to keep THEM warm, for heaven's sake!! My longest mission was a 4-hour trip to Volos north of Athens. Further than any previous Spitfire trip. I was only targeted twice in 81 trips and would have been disappointed if the Nazis had not acknowledged my presence! I was one of the last to be allowed to finish my tour of 300 hours in a Spitfire. We were told that if we wanted to join the US Forces, we had to do it by a certain date or forever hold our peace. Those that did got dull jobs ferrying or training. I was glad I stayed with the British.

The previous month, on 22 July, Cyprus had received an unusual visitor. Four Hurricanes of 127 Squadron were scrambled from Nicosia at 19:00 to investigate an intruder approaching Limassol. Plt Off. Joe Pauley (BE331/C), Wt Off. Bex Asboe RAAF (BD930/H), Flt Sgt Tom Orford (BP224/J) and Flt Sgt Woody Woodward (BD880/G) were surprised to find a Ju 88 in colourful markings approaching the airfield. It showed no signs of aggression so the Hurricane pilots provided escort while it landed. It was a Ju 88D, NP+MK/White 1 of the Rumanian Air Force, flown by defecting pilot Serg.T.rez.av. Nicolae Teoduru of Esc.2. A few days later on 1 August, a flak-damaged B-24 of the 389thBG landed at Nicosia having participated in the disastrous Ploesti raid. The pilot had selected Nicosia to enable prompt medical assistance for a badly wounded crewmember. On 13 August, one of 46's Beaufighters (V8707) was attacked and damaged by Spitfires. The ever-vigilant Luftwaffe reconnaissance Ju 88s were soon snooping, the crews endeavouring to keep tabs on movements and reinforcements to the island.

396ªSquadriglia, part of 154°Gruppo based at Rhodes, received a number of Mc.202s and in September, two of these were detached to Kos. One of the Macchi pilots was Serg.Magg. Loris Baldi:

> When I was in the Aegean, a kind of mission which was regarded as very dangerous was to go on reconnaissance on the Cyprus coast. We had to

do that in the evening just before sunset to be sure that there weren't any convoys going to Rhodes. At that time, my plane was the Macchi 202. This aircraft could be filled with as much fuel as it was hardly enough to go and come back, so it was very important to save fuel. When we were in sight of the Cyprus coast, we could see the dust rising from the airport due to the leaving of the fighter aircraft which took off to defend their own territory. The Britains [sic] already got radar, but we didn't even know that such a device existed, so we had to get much nearer to get the information we needed. As soon as we did, we came back to the base, making a turning of 180 degrees and following the coast of Turkey...

227's first loss flying from Cyprus occurred on 2 September when four Beaufighters attacked a caique off Kos. JL552/Z struck the mast with its port wing, exploding on hitting the water. Four men were seen swimming near the wreck but it was believed they were from the caique since it was feared that the Beaufighter crew would not have survived such a crash. However, navigator Flg Off. Cyril Turner did survive and was rescued to become a POW, but his New Zealand pilot Flt Lt Wally McGregor DFC was killed.

CHAPTER III

Operation *Microbe* – British Occupation of the Dodecanese Islands

With the capitulation of Italy on 8 September, German forces in the Balkans moved quickly to take over Italian-held areas on mainland Greece and the Aegean. Crete and the nearby smaller island of Scarpanto were already under their control. At the same time, the British endeavoured to occupy the Dodecanese Islands chain. However, the Americans refused to assent to the British plans, arguing that this would divert attention from the main front in Italy. To emphasise their position, they refused to provide naval and air support, warning the British that they would have to go it alone. Thus, Operation *Microbe* was launched with only a faint chance of success, although the British hoped that the Germans would be too preoccupied with the Italian front to put up much of a resistance in the Aegean. They were to be proved sadly wrong.

The British planned to use the Dodecanese Islands as a base against German positions in the Balkans and as a means to pressure neutral Turkey into the war on the Allied side. The main prize, the island of Rhodes, housed 35,000 Italian troops and 7,000 Germans. The British hoped that the Italian Governor, Admiral Campioni, who was also Commander-in-Chief of the garrison, might be willing to seize control of the whole island, and to this end a three-man section of the SBS (Special Boat Service) was parachuted in from an RAF Halifax on the night of 9/10 September to meet with the Admiral. In the meantime, skirmishes between Italian and German troops had broken out on the island, specifically around Maritza airfield where German units began shelling Italian positions. Some Italian artillery units fought back, destroying the German guns before turning their fire on the airfield, destroying or damaging many of the Mc.202s, G.50s and CR42s of 154°Gruppo, and a few of the Z.1007s also based there. Others were later blown up by saboteurs.

On the night of 10/11 September, Lt-Col F. L. R. Kenyon, the newly appointed representative of III Corps, set off from Casteloriso in an RAF launch bound for Rhodes. He was accompanied by Grp Capt. Harry Wheeler.[15] They also hoped to persuade Admiral Campioni to join with the Allies. They also failed. Grp Capt. Wheeler instead went to Kos where he was to take command of the RAF element when it arrived. Rhodes therefore fell into German hands and within days the Luftwaffe would arrive in some force. The first of twenty Bf 109Gs of IV/JG27 arrived at Maritza on 17 September, three crash-landing on arrival three days later, all seriously damaged but without pilot injuries. IV/JG27 had formed at Kalamaki (Greece) in June, the Staffeln commanded by Oblt Gerhard Suwelack (10 Staffel), Oblt Alfred Burk (11 Staffel) and Oblt Dietrich Bösler (12 Staffel). The original Gruppenkommandeur was Hptm. Rudolf Sinner, but he had departed for the Eastern Front in July, his place temporarily taken by Oblt Bösler until the arrival of a new Kommandeur. Scattered between Rhodes, Crete and coastal Greece were thirty-four Ar 196s of SAG125 and SAG126.

With the failure of Plan A – the occupation of Rhodes with Italian co-operation – Plan B was put into operation, the occupation of Kos, sixty miles to the north-west of Rhodes from where the invasion would be launched. Leros, thirty-five miles further to the north-west, and Samos, forty miles to the north of Leros, were also occupied as were the smaller islands of Symi, Stampalia and Ikaria. Neither Leros nor Samos had an airstrip, so Kos was the key to any success that might be achieved. The invasion of Rhodes was intended to commence of 20 October, provided that Spitfires based on Kos would be able to provide short-range cover over the beaches and sea approaches to Rhodes. The immediate aim therefore became the successful occupation and equipment of Kos as a fighter base before that date. For this there was no real preconceived plan, although a wealth of detailed instructions had already been drawn up in previous plans for the occupation of Rhodes. It was necessary therefore to run the Kos operation on a day to day basis. Spitfires of 7SAAF Squadron were on standby at Nicosia ready to fly to Kos. A second squadron of Spitfires, 74 currently at Idku, was earmarked to follow.

The island of Kos is about thirty miles long and about seven miles wide. The only port is the town of Kos on the north-east coast opposite the Turkish mainland. The only airstrip was at Antimachia, some eighteen miles from the town. Based at Antimachia was a detachment of 396ªSquadriglia (154°Gruppo) commanded by Sottoten Giuseppe Morganti. He had at his disposal two Mc.202s, two G.50bis and three CR42s. Following the armistice, most of 154°Gruppo on Rhodes sided with the Germans, but the majority of Morganti's detachment sided with the British, albeit temporarily. The main Aegean seaplane unit, 147ªSquadriglia RM, had eight Z.506s and four Z.501s (of which three were based at Rhodes and three at Leros). On 11 September, one of these headed south and alighted off Dekheila and was towed in to harbour; more would follow, two Hurricanes of 451 Squadron providing escort to two a few days later. Meanwhile, it seems that the majority, if not all, of the Italian crews decided to side with the British.

On 10 September, Sottoten Morganti, flying a Mc.202 intercepted a He 111 or a Ju 88 near Rhodes and claimed it shot down. A Ju 88, 4U+HK of 2.(F)/123 captained by Ltn Klaus Delfs was reported missing near Rhodes, but reportedly on 13 September. On 11 September, the Luftwaffe from Rhodes carried out a reprisal raid on Antimachia airfield and destroyed on the ground two CR42s and damaged a G.50. One of the Italian pilots decided that he did not wish to fight the Germans and flew the remaining CR42 to Rhodes, presumably without authority (Macchi pilot Serg.Magg. Baldi was on leave, so missed the action). Apparently two of the remaining three fighters were flown to Turkey by Sottoten Morganti and Sottoten Carlo Berti to avoid a similar fate. Both pilots were temporarily interned.[16]

A detachment of SBS arrived from Casteloriso on 13 September, and at dawn a Beaufighter from 46 Squadron piloted by Sqn Ldr Bill Cuddie touched down at Antimachia airfield where it offloaded an RAF wireless team. A second Beaufighter flown by Flg Off. J. C. Atkins provided cover and both aircraft returned safely to Cyprus. The next arrivals were five Spitfires of 7SAAF Squadron that had departed Nicosia at 15:30. Each aircraft was fitted with a thirty-gallon jettisonable extra fuel tank. Two others had failed to take-off on time due to battery problems and, ten minutes late, were ordered to return to base. Under the command of Capt. Harold Kirby (JK466) the flight arrived at Antimachia at dusk, only to be greeted by inaccurate machine-gun fire from jittery Italian gunners. The other four pilots were believed to have been Lts 'Red' Taylor, Alex Cheesman, Ray Burl and Dennis Fisher. The Spitfires were followed by three Dakotas of 216 Squadron whose cargo included nine specially selected 7SAAF ground staff, escort for the Dakotas having been provided by six Beaufighters of 46 Squadron. Italian gunners also fired on the Dakotas by mistake, believing them to be German aircraft, Flg Off. R. R. Keiller's FD866 sustaining damage to its tail unit.

On the night of 14/15 September, seven more Dakotas of 216 Squadron arrived over Kos with 120 men of the 11 Para. The drop was successful with only one sprained ankle. The drop zone had been marked out by the SBS, Italian troops laying straw across the area before assisting the paratroops to remove their harnesses as soon as they had landed. At first light on 15 September, a standing patrol of two Spitfires of 7SAAF was maintained over Kos to give cover to the transport aircraft and ships bringing stores and reinforcements. Among these were the first troops of the RAF

Regiment. More Dakotas arrived with members of No.2909 Squadron of the RAF Regiment equipped with nine 20-mm Hispano cannons for airfield defence. They would be joined by No.2901 Squadron two days later.

On the ground, the Allied force now comprised the 1st Battalion, Durham Light Infantry, 120 men from A Company, 11th Battalion Parachute Regiment, and a number of men from the SBS and RAF personnel under the command of Lt-Col Kenyon. The force totalled approximately 1,600 British, although only 1,115 were combatants, 880 army and 235 from the RAF Regiment, and about 3,500 Italian servicemen from the original garrison. The SAAF pilots were appalled at the lack of not only radar, but even a reliable, basic reporting system:

> Italian observers' posts encoded reports of enemy aircraft and transmitted them to the post office for decoding before being telephoned to the landing ground, where they were marked in German in metric distances. By the time everything was cleared up, the enemy had long since come and gone.[17]

The five Spitfires flew protective patrols for incoming Dakotas, but only two operated at any one time. Four more Spitfires arrived under Maj. Corrie van Vliet DFC, with two spare pilots aboard one of the Dakotas, while Beaufighters of 46 Squadron again provided escort. The new pilots were Lts Allan Turner, 'Spud' Kelly, 'Gus' Ground, Peiter 'Pik' van Deventer, Arnold 'Bassie' Basson and 'Issy' Seel.

The enterprise got off to a bad start when Grp Capt. Harry Wheeler, Senior RAF officer at Kos, was seriously injured in a motor accident, suffering a fractured skull leading to his death six days later. Maj. van Vliet, who had only just arrived at Antimachia suddenly and unexpectedly found himself in charge of air operations.

On 16 September, Capt. Kirby led a protective patrol covering the Dakotas, which were conveying C Company of 1/Battalion DLI and 4th Light AA Battery, but its Bofors were to arrive by sea. Other units were also on their way by destroyer, motor launches and caiques. Two Dakotas were slightly damaged by Turkish AA as they returned to Ramat David. Two sections of Spitfires were scrambled on reports of a probable recce aircraft approaching, one led by including Capt. Kirby (JK466), but it was the other section that scored a success when Lt Red Taylor (JK148) and Lt Alex Cheesman (JK140) shot down Ju 88 4U+RK of 2.(F)/123 some thirty-odd miles from Rhodes. Uffz Heinz Hanke and crew were reported missing.

During the evening, an Italian observer post on Kos reported seven Ju 52s – presumably from TG4 – escorted by two Bf 109s passing close by en route to Rhodes. Two patrolling Spitfires of 7SAAF flown by Lts Ray Burl with Lt Dennis Fisher as his No.2 were ordered to investigate. The formation was soon sighted flying over Stampalia at about 300 feet and the Spitfires dived to attack, Burl opening fire on the nearest transport:

> Flames and smoke erupted from one of the Ju 52s, the stricken aircraft flipped suddenly and plunged to destruction in the sea. As the two Spitfires swept through the German formation, a fluke burst from a gunner in one of the Junkers raked the leading Spitfire piloted by Burl. Bullets smashed into the fuselage severely and put its radio out of action. Ray Burl had no alternative but to break off the engagement and Lt Fisher, flying as his number two, in turn had no option but to escort the crippled aircraft back to base.[18]

Ray Burl later added:

> If it had not been for a lucky burst by a German gunner that afternoon, I think Snoek [Fisher] and I could have shot down most of the Ju 52s in that formation.

The German counter-attack began on 17 September with heavy air bombardment. The Bf 109s and Ju 88s involved met at first with varying success for the RAF gunners and the Spitfires gave a good account of themselves. Butterfly bombs, however, made Antimachia temporarily unserviceable and damaged the transport Dakotas, but the first detachments of the DLI were landed, although one Dakota came down in the sea and its occupants were rescued but interned in Turkey. At dawn on 18 September, a single reconnaissance Ju 88 appeared over Kos, the crew checking for signs of aircraft. It carried out a bombing attack on Italian gun emplacements near the coast and then headed for Antimachia where it carried out a low level bombing and strafing attack on the airfield. An RAF Regiment gunner was killed at his station by cannon fire but the bomber had also sustained damage in return. As it veered away and headed out to sea, the standing patrol of Spitfires arrived. Lts Burl and Fisher were again the fortunate pair as the former recalled:

> He was almost certainly having a look around to see who had jumped the Ju 52 the previous day and where they had come from. Anyway, we bumped him off quite smartly. He went down in a vertical dive, trailing smoke and exploded on hitting the water.

It was reported that K5+LL of Einsatz KGr. Chef AW was 'shot down by Spitfires' and crashed into the sea about thirty miles west of Kalymos, taking Fw Paul Epp and his crew to their deaths. Three Beaufighters of 227 Squadron approached Kos at about this time, the pilots reporting a patch of burning oil and petrol on the sea with an aircraft main wheel floating nearby and a partially inflated yellow dinghy. A Spitfire was sighted patrolling in the immediate area.

At 11:00, apparently having received information from the reconnaissance aircraft before its demise, the Luftwaffe despatched a formation of seven Ju 88Cs from 11./ZG26 to attack the airfield and installations. These were engaged by the standing patrol of three Spitfires and dispersed, three being claimed shot down by Lts Gus Ground, Spud Kelly and Pik van Deventer. It would seem that all three attacked the same aircraft as only 3U+JV failed to return with the loss of Obfw Heinz Gründling and crew whose aircraft fell north-west of Rhodes.

With the Spitfire patrol thus engaged, the opportunity was there for the five escorting Bf 109s from 10 and 11./JG27 to sweep in unopposed from the south to create havoc on the airfield. Three Dakotas (FD892, FD893 and FD921) parked in the open were hit and burst into flames and a soldier of the DLI was killed with three others wounded. A second wave of Messerschmitts followed almost immediately, destroying two Spitfires on the ground and setting fire to another Dakota. Yet another Dakota, arriving during the raid, was loath to return to Cyprus with its cargo and passengers – part of A Company of the DLI – and landed safely on a strip near Lambia on the coast. However, one Dakota, FD806, failed to arrive. It transpired that it had struck the sea while low flying and ditched off the Turkish island of Kara (all crew and passengers, more soldiers of A Company, survived and were temporarily interned). Among the new arrivals was Wg Cdr R. C. Love (who was to have commanded Maritza airfield on Rhodes had Plan A been successful) who was to take command of the grandiose-named 243 (Fighter) Wing to be formed at Antimachia. Obviously the RAF had intended to stay.

One section of two Spitfires (Capt. Kirby and Lt Turner) was airborne during the afternoon when the latest Messerschmitt attack developed and a second pair was scrambled, but Lt Alex Cheesman's JK140 was promptly shot down into the sea north of Antimachia as it climbed for height. Cheesman was lost, though his leader Lt Red Taylor shot down one of the raiders flown by Uffz Gustav Dettmar (White 5). Taken prisoner, Dettmar reported that he had originally been a He 111 gunner and had been wounded on the Eastern Front in October 1941. Following eight months of treatment, he retrained as fighter pilot and posted to 10./JG27 four days earlier. This was his first operational flight in a Bf 109. Of his experience, he related:

Six of 10./JG27 took off from Tatoi about 1400 to strafe Kos airfield – each aircraft fitted with long-range tank (300 litres) under fuselage. One returned early with engine trouble. Remaining five flew at zero feet approaching the island and met by very accurate AA fire. [My] engine hit by splinter and lost power. Another hit the cockpit. Climbed to 1,000 feet and baled out. Landed in sea and into dinghy.

Another Messerschmitt was shot down by Capt. Kirby (JK466) who recalled:

Allan Turner (JK148) was my No.2. We were scrambled to act as top cover to the island on a routine patrol. We were told that 109s were attacking the airfield, but I couldn't see them at first. Allan said he had them in sight and then I saw them. We dived from about 8,000 feet, both of us forgetting our long-range tanks. There were about six 109s in a straggling formation and I took the rear one. I saw no other aircraft above or behind me – not even Allan – who I assumed had taken on another 109. I did see a splash and explosion to my right rear (and have always thought that this was Allan going in). My own opinion is that his tank came off in the dive (we greatly exceeded the max allowable speed with tank in the dive) and either broke the Spitfire's back or knocked Allan out against the hood as it came off. German self-destruct 20-mm ammo always gave the fighter away as he opened fire – it was like light flak bursting – and I saw none around us in the dive. I gave a 109 a long burst right on the water and he turned slightly right and ditched.[19]

Kirby's victim was probably Obfw Wilhelm Morgenstern (White 1) who was killed. Maj. van Vliet later reported:

Lt Turner was flying in company with Capt Kirby on an aerodrome cover patrol of Antimachia. They engaged a force of Me 109s with top cover who had just ground strafed the aerodrome. Reliable eye-witnesses report three aircraft crashing into the sea. Two reported to be Me 109s and one definitely a Spitfire (Lt Cheesman, JK140). Capt Kirby did not observe what happened to Lt Turner in the ensuing engagement and no definite circumstantial evidence could be obtained from eye-witnesses relating to the above aircraft.[20]

Three Spitfires were claimed shot down, two by Fw Heinz Keller of 11./JG27 who probably shot down Lt Cheesman at 15:08, some three to four miles north of Kos, and Lt Turner five minutes later north-north-west of Kos; this was probably the same aircraft as claimed by FhjUffz Manfred Hientzsch of 10./JG27 about five miles north-west of Kos. That night, two Beaufighters of 46 Squadron patrolled over Kos without incident.

In the early hours of 19 September, a lone He 111 came over and circled Antimachia for an hour or more in the pre-dawn darkness before dropping a flare and a single bomb. This was 6N+EP of Einsatz/KG100 that left the scene after being hit and slightly damaged by AA fire. The mission was aborted as a gunner had been wounded. A second Heinkel from the same unit had the misfortune to run into Beaufighter V8508 of 89 Squadron on a special ferry flight to Kos, Flt Lt Joe Astbury AFM sending 6N+AP down into the sea. Uffz Joachim Nowotny and crew were rescued and taken into captivity.

Soon after sunrise Bf 109s of 11 and 12./JG27 came winging in over the sea, just in time to catch an incoming Dakota as it landed. The transport was strafed and Sgt Gerard Newell (the WOp/AG) was killed; the other was ordered not to land and returned to Cyprus. The Dakota damaged the previous day was also strafed and burnt out. The Dakotas had been escorted to the island by six Spitfires led by Capt. Einar Rorvik (EE786). One of the new arrivals, Lt Derek de Jaeger, was intercepted by a Messerschmitt as Capt. Kirby recalled:

Svengali [de Jaeger] was chased around Kos hill about three times by a 109 but escaped uninjured and undamaged.

De Jaeger believed that the Messerschmitt chasing him crashed into a hill, but there was no confirmation of such a loss. One of the resident Spitfires attempted to provide cover and Lt Issy Seel was seen to hit a Bf 109, but was then seen to crash. Ltn Hans Hetzler claimed a Spitfire about half a mile off Kos, and Oblt Dietrich Bösler, acting Gruppenkommandeur, claimed another. Kirby wrote:

Issy Seel shot at a 109 which slowed considerably, and in attempting to tighten his turn to get behind the 109, Issy spun in from a few hundred feet. He was not shot down as far as I can recall.

Major van Vliet was of the same conclusion:

Lt Seel [JK677] was flying No.2 to Lt Burl on an aerodrome cover patrol and were the only aircraft airborne. An attack of Ju 88s at approximately 3,000 feet came in from the south. There was an escort of Me 109s above. During the ensuing engagement Lt Seel was observed attacking a single Me 109 and appeared to have the situation well in hand during several attacks, while the enemy continued flying straight and level. He appeared over-keen, however, and during a steep turn did an obviously unintentional flick-roll with an ensuing spin from which he did not recover, and crashed approximately 3-5 miles west on Antimachia aerodrome. He was definitely not fired at during the above engagement, which was witnessed by me, but may have been engaged in the earlier stages of the operation. The enemy aircraft is reported to have crashed into the sea. I later identified the body and necessary burial arrangements were made at the Jewish cemetery on the island.[21]

Two of the new arrivals, Lt Ken Prescott and Lt John Hynd, jointly claimed a Messerschmitt shot down. Uffz Walter Torge (Red 7) of 11 Staffel failed to return, possibly the victim of all three Spitfires. The defenders in their slit trenches barely had time to shake the dust off themselves when the airfield was hit again, this time by a low-level bombing and strafing attack by Ju 88s. One of the SAAF mechanics Bruce Stanley recalled:

> For me the most memorable of these attacks was when I took cover behind a mound covered with canvas, only to discover that my "protective wall" was a potentially lethal stash of Italian bombs!

Lt Ray Burl (JK466) attacked one of the Ju 88s but was hit by return fire and force-landed. On 23 September, Capt. Kirby was ordered to return to Cairo, via Nicosia, to provide a report on proceedings and to organise reinforcements. He flew onboard a returning Beaufighter. Having made his report, he was ordered not to return to Kos. The following evening a Beaufighter landed at Antimachia conveying Air Vice-Marshal R. E. Saul to the battlefront to see for himself the situation. 227 Squadron's Flt Lt J. W. D. Thomas recalled:

> On 24 September, Flight Sergeant [David] Warne and I were told to go to Nicosia to pick up Air Vice-Marshal Saul. When we arrived Group Captain Max Aitken summarily dismissed my pilot and told me he would pilot the aircraft to Kos, I was to navigate. After some persuasion by the Group Captain, the Air Vice-Marshal agreed to let me occupy the navigator's seat. I anticipated being jumped by Me 109s off Rhodes, but the Air Vice-Marshal reminded me that he had been an Air Gunner in World War One! We took off at 16:58 and arrived at 18:58. The flight to Kos, as it happened, proved uneventful, except for the rear hatch flying open; this I was able to close by minor acrobatics while the Group Captain slowed the aircraft down. The Air Vice-Marshal, sitting forlornly on the cannon ammunition covers, offered to help, but I was able to manage.
>
> At Kos we were ushered to a large hall adjacent to the cookhouse. Here No.7SAAF chaps were assembled. Air Vice-Marshal Saul, with myself as note-taker, asked the No.7SAAF chaps what they wanted. They requested candles, shoelaces etc. They were promised 87 AA guns by the weekend and other desirable goodies. During the night Air Vice-Marshal Saul slept in a hut with an armed guard, a corporal armed with a tommy gun. Group Captain

Aitken slept on a stretcher in some suitable corner and I in the cookhouse on a glorious Victorian brass-knobbed bed that the cook had obtained from somewhere! We returned to Nicosia incident-free the following day, taking off at 07:10 and arriving at 09:10. Events prevented the SAAF from receiving many of the promised articles.[22]

Also arriving on a fleeting visit was Wg Cdr John Kent DFC AFC, Wing Commander Training at 219 Group, who, at the last moment, had been advised of his appointment to oversee the Dakota operation. He had arrived at St Jean too late to see off the first flight of Dakotas, but later managed to hitch a ride to Kos:

> I went over with one of the Dakotas transporting two jeeps. By this time the
> enemy was well aware of our presence and had put the airfield out of action;
> we were forced to operate at night and to use a newly constructed strip just
> outside town [Lambi].

On arrival at Lambi, the Dakota crew found that the ramp for unloading jeeps had been returned to Palestine:

> Reluctantly we had to go around and rouse a number of soldiers who were
> sleeping in nearby ditches. I felt desperately sorry for them but they all came
> along, if not cheerfully, without a word of complaint, and together we managed
> to manhandle the jeeps and lift them bodily out of the aircraft and set them
> safely on the ground. We then set off on the long flight back to Palestine.[23]

There followed a relative subdued period – mainly as a result of US B-24 raids against Eleusis airfield near Athens and Maritza on Rhodes – following which the Germans rapidly built up the bomber force in the Athens area and Bf 109s from 8 and 9./JG27 arrived at Rhodes to bolster IV/JG27, which had suffered the loss of three of its pilots (plus three Ju 88s) in a short time. The two reinforcing Staffeln contained a sprinkling of experienced pilots who would soon make their mark on the Kos defenders.

The Luftwaffe attacked the destroyer HMS *Intrepid* and the Greek *Queen Olga* which were lying in harbour at Leros on 26 September. Both were lost and naval store buildings were destroyed. A pair of patrolling Spitfires from Kos was joined by another section but failed to intercept due to the hazy conditions. One who witnessed their destruction was Lt Adrian Seligman RNR:

> ...formations of Stukas and Ju 88s came over. No Italian anti-aircraft batteries
> opened up on them, fearing no doubt that they would become targets

themselves. The Italian naval barracks was flattened and *Queen Olga* was sunk straight away by a direct hit amidships. *Intrepid* was also hit, but was successfully towed into shallower water, and so did not sink immediately. Three more attacks soon followed, resulting in further direct hits and in the end *Intrepid* capsized and was a total loss ... From the seaplane base we watched, fascinated but helpless.[24]

During an attack at midday by two formations of Ju 88s, two patrolling Spitfires attempted to engage two Bf 109s, but were unable to close range. Two other Spitfires, which took-off from Antimachia, intercepted five Ju 88s of 4./KG6 and four Bf 109s north of Leros. Both aircraft attacked in the face of controlled return fire. Nonetheless, Lt Titch Inggs saw pieces flying off the aircraft he attacked resulting in a Ju 88 3E+GM crashing into the sea near Leros (Uffz Heinz Radünz and crew were lost).

On 27 September, 7SAAF noted:

The second German blitz began on Kos at 11:30. Five plus Me 109s attacked and shot down Lts Prescott and Hynd, who were on patrol, and immediately afterwards the island was bombed and ground-strafed by three successive waves of Ju 88s. They concentrated on the dispersal and take-off areas. During these raids Me 109s remained in the air giving top cover to the bombers. One Spitfire was damaged on the ground and the landing-ground was made unserviceable due to craters and delayed action bombs. Repairs were immediately affected and the standing patrol resumed at 14:00 hours.[25]

Between fifteen and twenty Ju 88s escorted by Bf 109s of 9./JG27 bombed Antimachia landing ground at 11:30. They bombed from altitude beyond the range of the Bofors guns which had been installed for the defence of the strip while the Messerschmitts strafed, damaging one Spitfire (JK671) on the ground. Three soldiers of the Durhams were killed. Two Spitfires – JG844 flown by Lt Ken Prescott and JK677 with Lt John Hynd – were rapidly scrambled to intercept, but as Lt Burl recalled:

Two of our chaps were shot down while taking off to intercept a German formation. The Germans were upon them before they even had a chance to retract their undercarriages. We saw it happen. Our chaps didn't stand a chance.

They were victims of ace pilot Obfw Fritz Gromotka (his tenth victory) and his wingman Uffz Hannes Löffler.

During another raid by Ju 88s and 9./JG27 in the afternoon, Lt Bassie Basson was shot down and baled out over the sea. Two claims were made, one by Obfw Gromotka at 15:17 north of the airfield (his second of the day), while Obfw Johannes Scheit claimed his three minutes later. On this occasion, a Messerschmitt was lost with Uffz Jakob Herweg falling to the guns of Maj. van Vliet, although Lt Basson may have also attacked the same aircraft. Herweg was rescued by a caique but an Arado arrived and alighted and forced the crew to hand him over at gunpoint to the crew of another Arado that landed nearby. Basson had also come down in the sea and an Arado also tried to pick him up, but he kept dodging under the plane's floats until the Germans flew off and left him. An Italian caique then picked him up and took him to Kalimnos, a large island north-west of Kos, from where he reached Turkey. Another source[26] implied that Herweg was picked up by the caique that '...already contained some Engländer'. When the Arado put down on the water nearby, Herweg jumped overboard and swam for it.

At 10:45 on 28 September, the bombers returned, twenty-four low-flying Ju 88s escorted by Bf 109s sweeping over the two airstrips. No fighter action could be taken as both airstrips were unserviceable. During the early afternoon, eight Spitfires of 74 Squadron led by Sqn Ldr Spud Hayter DFC arrived at 13:35 from Nicosia to reinforce the island, a ninth having crashed into the sea en route. At 12:15, Flt Lt Andy Anderson, a Malta veteran of some experience, baled out ten miles south-east of Casteloriso owing to engine trouble. The formation was flying below 500 feet and he had great difficulty in getting out of his aircraft (ES204) and his parachute opened too late. A high-speed launch from Casteloriso and Air Sea Rescue aircraft from Cyprus made several fruitless searches.

Four of the new arrivals – Flg Offs. Speed Norman, Trevor Bates and Bunny de Pass, together with Flt Sgt Willy Wilson RCAF – were airborne at 15:00 to familiarise themselves with the terrain, followed by a second patrol comprising Sqn Ldr Hayter, Flg Off. John Lewis, Sgt Brian Harris (known as 'Titch') and Flt Sgt David Maxwell at 16:15. Flg Off. Lewis (ER483/J) encountered five Ju 88s at 6,000 feet, part of a force of fifteen from II/KG6, escorted by 9 Staffel Bf 109s led by Major Ernst Düllberg, the new Gruppenkdr. Lewis climbed into the sun above them and carried out a quarter-astern attack with cannon at 300 yards. He encountered heavy return fire but made two more attacks, causing black and white smoke to issue from an engine. As he was now some twenty miles out to sea, he broke off the engagement and returned to Antimachia where a bullet strike was found in his starboard wing. The others failed to see the bombers although Sgt Harris glimpsed the Messerschmitts:

That day we patrolled from Kos and I saw Me 109s above, which was the first time I had ever seen any, but there was no engagement.

However, a section of 7SAAF Spitfires on standing patrol was intercepted by the Messerschmitts, which shot down Capt. Einer Rorvik (EE786) who was killed and Lt Red Taylor who baled out and was rescued from the sea. Three Spitfires were claimed, one each by Major Düllberg, his nineteenth victory, Obfw Gromotka (twelfth) and Obfw Johannes Scheit (fourth). A Messerschmitt was written off lost following a sortie to Kos, its pilot uninjured. It is not known if the engine failure it suffered was caused by combat damage.

On 29 September, an estimated eighteen Ju 88s escorted by about a dozen Bf 109s raided Antimachia at 10:50. Lts Gus Ground and Dennis Fisher were on standing patrol and engaged the bombers, claiming one jointly shot down and a second as damaged. Meanwhile, 74 Squadron scrambled Flg Off. Trevor Bates (another Malta veteran) with Flt Sgts Willy Wilson RCAF and David Maxwell to engage, but Bates was obliged to return with oxygen failure. The other two then became separated but Wilson took the fight to the enemy:

F/S Wilson RCAF took off to intercept a raid coming into Kos with one other pilot. They became separated before the enemy aircraft arrived so Wilson was working on his own during the whole time that he was airborne. He was flying at about 22,000 feet when he sighted a lone Ju 88 approaching Antimachia. He got behind it and gave it two good bursts from dead astern. The last one continuing until he had to break away at 50 yards. He last saw this aircraft diving away steeply with black smoke coming from it. This aircraft was seen to crash [sic] by Lance Bombardier Miller of the 2nd LAA Battery. By this time the controller had told Wilson that a formation was coming into Antimachia. Wilson saw nine Ju 88s and attacked them head-on. One was seen to break away and continue into a shallow dive. He saw something come off this machine during his attack but saw no further result. The anti-aircraft crew thought that they might have hit this one, though the aircraftmen of 7SAAF Squadron said that it was not hit by ack-ack but continued its dive until it crashed.

Another six Ju 88s came in behind these and the formation spread and got somewhat disorganised as Wilson pressed home another attack. He saw bits fly off one but could not observe any further results. Another formation of nine Ju 88s came in after these and Wilson again attacked them single-handed but observed no results. Almost immediately he was attacked by five Me 109s but managed to evade these after a short and very fast mix-up, and flew around the Kos mountains where the Me 109s left him. He then landed at the Salt Flats [which] were entirely unknown to him. Just before this engagement a parachute was seen to come down and two Me 109s crashed [sic]. No anti-aircraft battery claimed these and Wilson did not fire at any fighters so it appears that two of the Me 109s collided in endeavouring to get into position to attack Wilson.[27]

However, no Messerschmitts were lost in this action. Possibly the 'collision' witnessed were long-range tanks being jettisoned. A returning damaged 5./KG6 Ju 88, piloted by Ltn Hans Berstecher, crashed on landing at Larissa and was completely destroyed. The crew survived but the observer was injured. This was probably the victim of Lts Ground and Fisher. The latter pilot was one of three selected to fly non-operational Spitfires back to Cyprus, joining Lts Titch Inggs and Lafrase Moolman in this duty, probably much to their relief.

At 17:20, twenty-four Ju 88s with escorting Bf 109s again raided Antimachia. Forty craters were made on the landing ground and some buildings were demolished. A number of delayed action bombs were also dropped. Casualties on the ground were two killed and ten injured. The RAF signal station was damaged although the equipment was dug out and wireless communication re-established by 02:30.

A Walrus flew in from Leros on the morning of 30 September conveying a senior Army engineer officer to check on the landing strips as twenty-two ground crew personnel of 74 Squadron were to arrive that night. With Antimachia now unserviceable, it was decided to use the strip for Spitfire operations; however this was soon put out of action when a Dakota that had failed to get away during the night was spotted by Luftwaffe reconnaissance and promptly bombed. The final chance to operate the remaining Spitfires was a rough landing strip of 1,050 yards that had just been completed on the Salt Pans situated on the north coast of the island between Antimachia and Kos town, but this had flooded owing to blockage of drains. Another strip was being constructed at Marmari as part of the original plan for the invasion of Rhodes, but this was not usable before events overtook all efforts.

During the afternoon of the last day of the month, the Walrus was making a second flight from Leros to Kos, on this occasion with Flt Lt Frank Rashleigh at the controls, accompanied by Sgt Cliff Platt. Rashleigh was a communications expert from AHQ and was on his way to see if he could improve the situation. Unfortunately for him and his navigator, a marauding Bf 109 flown by Major Düllberg of Stab/JG27 spotted the lumbering flying boat and shot it down between Leros and Samos at 14:40. There were no survivors. One lucky escape from death was the DLI's Roman Catholic Chaplin, Rev. Reginald Anwyl who should have been onboard the Walrus:

> I meant to catch a plane (a seaplane) for Kos, where our DLI were. Through wrong information, I missed the plane, which was attacked on the way and,

I was later told, crashed with no survivors. I was believed to be on the plane by those concerned, and I was reported killed, though in fact I had returned to the centre of Leros.

It was estimated that some fifteen German aircraft (plus three probable and seven damaged) had fallen to the Spitfires, Beaufighters and AA defences during the defence of Kos in return for the loss of a dozen Spitfires and six pilots, plus the Walrus and its crew. But the fate of Kos was now sealed and sixty Ju 87s of StG.3 arrived at Rhodes for attacks on Kos, Leros and Samos.

CHAPTER IV

German Invasion and British Surrender of Kos

At midday on 1 October, Kos was bombed from about 18,000 feet, a dozen bombs falling near the main landing strip. There were no casualties and no interceptions. A reconnaissance Spitfire from North Africa reported a concentration of shipping in the ports of Crete, and early on the following morning, a convoy steaming in a north-north-easterly direction south-east of Melos was sighted by British aircraft. Urgent supplies were landed at Lambi by five Dakotas and during their unloading news came that a small German invasion fleet of ten vessels was at sea. This flotilla carried a task force composed of a battle group from the 22nd Infantry Division in Crete as well as Brandenburg special forces from the mainland under the command of GenLtn Friedrich-Wilhelm Müller whose triumphal entry was almost ended before it had begun as Uffz Theo Heckman of 7./JG27 recalled:

During the morning at 08:20 hours we took off from Argos, our mission to escort our own landing fleet. During this mission we noticed an Ar196, which flew in a NNE direction straight towards the vessels we were supposed to protect. We knew the Italians, after the Bodoglio uprising, had got hold of a couple of Arados and presumed this could be one of them, which in such a case would bring nothing good with it.

I closed in on the Arado and made two head on passes until it fired the signal of the day (recognition signal). It was the wrong signal, which only increased my suspicions. Therefore I made another pass, which only resulted in another faulty signal. That convinced me it was one of the Italians in front of me, so I turned in behind him and fired a couple of well-aimed bursts into his right-hand aileron and rudder which made him force land on the water. I then continued my escort mission and later returned to Tanagra.

To my surprise Oblt [Kurt] Hammel immediately caught up with me and told me that my shot down Arado was certainly not Italian. It had on board the commanding General of the invasion forces, GenLtn Müller, for the re-conquest of Kos! Luckily nothing had happened to the General and he was none the worse for wear after his spell on the water. I later spoke to him on the phone and convinced him I had strictly followed orders that nothing was to be allowed closer than a 6km radius of our object of protection, if it could not identify itself correctly. The incident had no aftermath and already the same day I flew from Tanagra to Gadurra, where I took part in the re-conquest of Kos.

At 04:30 on 3 October, the invasion of Kos began. The British numbered about 1,500 including 680 of 1/DLI, the remainder mostly RAF Regiment and RAF and SAAF pilots and ground personnel. There were also 3,500 Italians of the 10th Regiment of the 50th Regina Infantry Division under the command of Col Felice Leggio. There remained five serviceable Spitfires, four of which were parked at the Salt Pans ready for operations, the other at Antimachia. Only one belonged to 7SAAF. The Spitfires parked on the Salt Pans were captured by the paratroops immediately upon landing. The aircraft guards were killed. The single Spitfire at Antimachia was set alight by Capt. Richard Birchenough of the DLI who went alone across some 400 yards of ground under machine-gun fire to prevent it falling into enemy hands. Wg Cdr Love, in charge of the now-defunct 243 Wing, later wrote:

When dawn broke large forces of enemy bombers and fighters began to attack both Kos [Lambi] and Antimachia landing grounds. Half-an-hour later 21 Ju 52s were seen to drop approximately 250 parachutists some four miles west of Antimachia. One company of DLI allocated to Antimachia was reinforced by half of the crews of each of the Bofors and Hispano guns and took up positions on the west of the aerodrome to meet any attack enemy parachutists might make. It now became apparent that the enemy were landing a force of some 3,000 men with many mortars and heavy machine-guns and were moving both on the town of Kos and Antimachia.

Towards midday it became apparent that the enemy were making considerable ground and all unnecessary RAF personnel were divided into small parties under an officer and ordered to move off to the south-east. By four o'clock in the afternoon the Italian garrison at Antimachia had ceased firing, as had the Italian anti-aircraft guns. Enemy air activity was still on a large scale, Ju 88s, Ju 87s, Me 110s and Me 109s being used. One by one the Bofors guns were put out of action by bombing, and the destruction of secret publications and equipment was ordered.

By 17:00 hours, the position of Antimachia was critical and British troops were ordered to withdraw southwards towards the coast. The destruction of the wireless station was carried out and the remaining RAF personnel, except the RAF Regiment, withdrew just before dusk. Small parties made their way to the hills and parts of the coast, or joined units of the DLI which were putting up an organised resistance. Except for the RAF Regiment, however, who were armed with rifles, there was little they could do to help and in many cases were told by Army officers to make their own way from the island.[28]

7SAAF Squadron Adventures and Escapes

The majority of the SAAF pilots were sleeping in a valley about one mile east of Antimachia airstrip, but it was not until about 07:00 that Major van Vliet received a definite report that parachutists had been dropped on the Salt Flats:

As the site of our camp was purely a sleeping area there was no telephone communication, and I decided that I would get orders and see if we could in any way assist. Several Me 109s were flying around and when I got the report Ju 87s were bombing a point which appeared to be near the coast north of Antimachia, where the Italian heavy AA was situated. I instructed all the men to collect their firearms and we proceeded to Sector [Ops HQ], which was just south of Antimachia village. It took about half-an-hour to walk to the Sector, and two different bombing raids were seen taking place during this period. At Sector, Wg Cdr Love suggested that as a body we should contact the Army in the Bofors area and see if we could be of any use. As Stukas were by this time carrying out recces for targets we took cover in an orchard nearby.

The northern coastline was completely obscured, and I could not see what shipping there was off the coast, but from 07:00 to 11:00 hours we heard mortar fire from the Army positions being directed towards the Salt Flats. At 09:00, the Italians were starting to take up positions on the northern ridge of the aerodrome. This position was about 1,000 yards from us. I managed to contact a British Army captain. He advised that as our armament was very light and as we only had the clips for our Sten-guns and no reserve ammunition, he felt that we would be of no value and that we would give away the location of his own troops, who were in small pockets.

At about 10:00, I instructed the SAAF party to return to our sleeping area as I felt that we could do little by standing around, and I returned to see Wg Cdr Love [who] instructed us to make for the coast, suggesting Cardemena. He was not however sure whether this place was in our hands, but he thought there might be a chance of getting away by boat. As an alternative he suggested making for the hills until nightfall. I returned to contact the men in the valley and on the way saw two waves of about 40+ Ju 87s, separated by 15 minutes, dive-bombing the Italian positions.

We had a meal and equipped ourselves to attempt to escape, taking with us rations and firearms, and proceeded towards Cardemena. By this time, approximately 13:00 hours, the Italians had taken up a line on the LG. All the serviceable aircraft were on the Salt Flats with 74 Squadron pilots; we had one Spitfire there and I think 74 Squadron had about five. Numerous Ju 87s came over searching for targets, and we took cover every time the enemy aircraft were sighted, but managed to get down to Cardemena without mishap. The bulk of the party went into hiding about a mile from the beach, and with several others I proceeded to the coast. Lt Edmondson, the IO, told us that boats had been fixed up and a message was sent to the main party to come down to the village as soon as possible.

At about 16:00 we saw four Beaufighters right on the deck going from east to west. When the main party arrived we went into the village where we found at least 100 armed Italians. [We] were told that our exodus would cause a panic and for that reason it was arranged that the boats would come to a point further up the coast at dusk. So we proceeded there and one rowing boat arrived shortly afterwards, and a party of two officers [believed to have been Lts De Jaeger and Ground] and seven SAAF and about four RAF other ranks left in it.

A message was then received that the Italians [in the village] were panicking and seizing all the boats. We immediately set off for the village and found three of the four larger caiques filled with Italians already under way, whilst numerous Italians were swimming in an effort to get into the boats. I think some of them were drowned. A small 20-foot caique lying alongside the jetty was seized by us. There was no crew. Twenty-three of us and two Italians got aboard, the 23 being the whole of the British party which had assembled at the beach. At this stage firing of shots took place in the village but I think this was only the Italians, as we had been warned that a Fascist attempt to cause panic was being organised. We got under sail but were becalmed at about 21:00 hours. There were only two oars in the caique and one of these broke.

During the whole of the next day Ju 87s flew over us from the direction of Crete and Rhodes and orbited Kos looking for targets. We could see them bombing Cardemena and Antimachia village but no effort was made to attack us or intercept us, but every effort was made to keep as many people as possible under cover when they appeared.[29]

One of those onboard the caique, Lt Ray Burl, recalled:

We rowed virtually the whole night and collapsed exhausted when we thought we were clear of the island. Came the dawn and we discovered that the currant had carried us virtually the whole way back to Kos. After some frantic rowing we managed to get clear of the island again, only to receive a bad scare about mid-morning when two Me 109s showed up. We spotted them when they were still some distance off and everyone – bar two or three of us who pretended to be locals – scuttled below deck. The Messerschmitts came down to about 15 metres and circled us for two or three minutes – seemed like two or three hours – while we pretended to be mending nets or fishing. We held our breath, not daring to look up, and eventually they buzzed off.

But a few hours later we had another nasty moment when we spotted a formation of RAF Beaufighters coming towards us at low level in attacking, line abreast formation. One of the jobs of the Beaufighter in the Aegean was to shoot up caiques, which were widely used by the enemy for inter-island transport. It seemed as though we were to become the target of our own guns and the whole crowd of us leapt about madly on the deck, shouting like banshees and waving uniforms, caps and anything else that might be recognised by the crews of the Beaufighters. The formation was already almost on us when suddenly it parted. Once past us, the aircraft resumed course and station, leaving us alone and sweating profusely.[30]

Major van Vliet continued:

> As we got near the coast we threw all our firearms overboard and at about 16:00 hours we landed at Cape Iskandil, where a Turkish gendarme met us and escorted us to Cumali. We slept in a local school and next day walked to Dadya fishing village, a distance of approximately 18 miles.

Due to lack of transport, the party were forced to march from Dadya to Marmaris, eventually reaching the town at 17:00 on 8 October where they were greeted by a representative of the British Consul. The following day, Wg Cdr Love and his party arrived at Marmaris, as did other caiques with escapees. Onboard one of these was SAAF mechanic Bruce Stanley:

> About 20 of us managed to escape by hijacking a caique in which we escaped to Turkey. This was a nightmare because after casting off we discovered the sail was missing and it had no engine. Thus we were at the mercy of the tide. To add to our dilemma we knew that the allied pilots had instructions to attack any of these vessels on sight, but thankfully they recognised us as we waved our tin hats at them and they held their fire. When we reached Turkey we were spotted by two Turkish soldiers who escorted us for a further six days of hard marching to help us reach the coast. There they treated us exceptionally well and arrangements were made to transport us to another small island, where a civilian boat took us to Cyprus.

After dark, Major van Vliet's party departed Marmaris for Casteloriso from where he and Lts Red Taylor and Ray Burl were flown by a Cant seaplane to Egypt on 10 October, the remainder of the party going to Cyprus by sea. However, two SAAF pilots were missing from the group that had now assembled at Marmaris, Lts Derek de Jaeger and Gus Ground having been on duty at Antimachia when the attack started. They had been advised to make for the hills; their joint report revealed a similar adventure:

> When going up towards the hills, we were held up by an Italian officer in charge of a defensive position on the side of the hill. He disarmed both of us and became very abusive about the English, saying that the Italians were the only people fighting and that we had thrown in. Shortly afterwards he got a telephone call saying that Antimachia had fallen, and he became very friendly, giving us back our arms – and a couple of hand grenades.
>
> We left Antimachia at about 10:30 hours. All surface personnel on the LG were preparing to evacuate. The Italians said that the last free town was Cardemena, and we started off with them but got separated. We ate some melons on the way and arrived there towards dusk. A British officer had everything arranged and told us which boat to take. This was a rowing boat which held 13 passengers with five Greeks rowing. We were the fifth boat to leave, four caiques having sailed out earlier.
>
> We hit a storm three hours off the Turkish coast, and it is probable that the caiques were driven off course. Having left Kos at 18:00, we landed at Cape Krio at 05:00 the next day. For 11 hours the Greek oarsmen had pulled at the oars. We found a caique going to Kos with supplies and about 56 personnel. They had seen something was amiss and had pulled in there.[31]

On receiving confirmation that Kos was about to fall, the captain of the Kos-bound caique decided to return to Cyprus from whence they came. Lts de Jaeger and Ground plus the other seven SAAF personnel asked to be taken to Cyprus and joined the vessel when it departed at midday:

> We crept along the coast, passing Rhodes by night. On 5th, we saw four Beaufighters going towards Kos. We touched at Castel Rosso [sic] for one-and-a-half hours, and sent a signal. The conditions on the boat were appalling. There were 70 people aboard, and we had to lie with our heads on each other's chests and our feet mixed up. We naturally did not sleep. We landed at Famagusta (Cyprus) on 8th. The Greeks put up a superb show.

Lts de Jaeger and Ground were flown to Cairo the next day.

74 Squadron Adventures and Escapes

Meanwhile, sleeping underneath trees near the Salt Flats when the invasion started were the eight pilots of 74 Squadron. Flg Off. Guy de Pass later submitted a report, which read:

> On the morning of 3rd October I awoke at about 04:30 hours and heard the sound of aircraft above me but didn't take much notice. The aircraft continued to fly around and I heard in the distance the sound of a motor launch. By this time I was very apprehensive. Shots from the direction of the landing beaches strip were heard. We arose and moved off in the direction of the road. The firing became more persistent. Flares were being fired and mortar fire could be discerned. It appeared to all of us that the island was being invaded and that enemy troops were in the vicinity. We began to run towards the main road as we were unable to put up any sort of defence and considered that the best policy was to join up with the main party of British troops. It was still fairly dark with plenty of cloud.[32]

Sgt Brian Harris added:

> First we heard the thump of the landing crafts' heavy diesel engines, and paratroopers were dropped. We had no armament, nothing to protect ourselves, no ack-ack, nothing. So all we could do was think about escaping, getting off the island. We were getting away, across open ground, when I dropped a packet of cigarettes. You could see tracer bullets flying by. But would you believe it, I actually went back for those 20 fags! Three other pilots and myself made our way to Kos town.

Flg Off. de Pass continued:

> I saw Flying Officers Bates and Norman, Flt Sgt Maxwell, Sgt Harris and a South African and joined up with them. When we reached the main road we saw a jeep driven by a South African. We piled in and went straight to Kos. The people in the hotel at Kos, a Major and some RAF Regiment chaps did not believe that the invasion had started. I took the jeep and warned British HQ, the Bofors gun battery and all and sundry. I then handed the jeep over to an RAF Regiment officer who wanted to go to Kos aerodrome to collect some of his men. We pilots of 74 Squadron did not know that a party of our ground crews had landed by air on the previous night on Kos aerodrome [Lambi], and by 11:00 hours we had boarded an Italian boat [the water boat *Adda*] in Kos harbour and set sail for Leros. On the way out we ran into some German boats so we turned for Kefalcha on the Turkish coast, eventually reaching Casteloriso and Paphos by high speed launch.[33]

The report by fellow officers Flg Offs. Speed Norman and Trevor Bates added:

> At approximately 04:00 we were awakened by the incessant drone of aircraft overhead and the sound of machine-gun and rifle fire nearby. On looking over the shrubbery we saw and heard invasion barges upon the beach 300 yards away. S/Ldr Hayter immediately telephoned Sector Ops and told them of the invasion, which they knew nothing about. Two minutes after we found our communications had been cut off and we realised that we were practically surrounded. We then split into several parties.
>
> Five of us ran towards the road up the side of a brick wall. One of the 7SAAF ground crews drove their jeep across the field towards the road. S/Ldr John Morgan [Sector Ops] was in the jeep. S/L Hayter, F/O Lewis and F/Sgt Wilson, we think, ran also towards the road, but behind another fence where later we realised German soldiers were hidden. But we did not see any of these three again and so know nothing definite. As we ran across the field towards the road we were fired on by a machine-gun firing tracer bullets. The jeep was also fired on and we believe S/Ldr Morgan left the jeep when this happened and went towards where he had last seen our CO, but here again we know nothing definite.
>
> Eventually the jeep, driven by a South African, arrived at the road. Eight of us jumped on it and drove as fast as we could into Kos [town]. We informed the RAF Regiment, the Harbour Master, some DLIs and several others about the invasion. We made enquiries as to what we should do and eventually received orders from the Harbour Master to evacuate. Fortunately, L/Cdr Croxton RN in charge of the Italian water ship *Adda*, bound for Leros, was able to take us on board. But on rounding a point we saw that the German invasion fleet was between us and Leros, and so we went into Turkish waters.[34]

The escapees eventually reached Casteloriso from where Flg Offs. Norman and Bates were flown to Aboukir in a Cant Z.506B while the others proceeded to Cyprus onboard HSL 2517 (high-speed launch). Meanwhile, Sqn Ldr Hayter, Flg Off. Lewis and Flt Sgt Wilson had survived their brush with German paratroopers and went into the hills south of the Salt Flats where they were joined by Sqn Ldr Morgan and an MT driver. The CO, who had farmed in New Zealand, used his knowledge and experience to capture and kill a sheep with his bare hands, providing food for his men over the next two days or so. There were many other groups of soldiers and airmen wandering the hills including Lt Monty Banks of the DLI:

> We continued on our walk through the hills ... when we stumbled across a large cave, which was evidently occasionally used by local shepherds. From

the mouth of the cave a ravine led down to the sea. An occasional swastika-flagged motor boat would cross our field of vision, and in the air we began to see Spitfires. This excited us at first, but then we realised they were our own Spits being flown by German pilots [two of these would have been JL212/V and W, former 74 Squadron aircraft]. There had been no time to destroy or immobilise the aircraft in the suddenness of the attack.[35]

Lt Banks' party eventually bumped into Sqn Ldr Hayter's group and all returned to the cave. One of Banks' party was 74 Squadron clerk Tony Blythin who recalled:

[The CO] was wearing an old trilby hat and with several days' growth of beard almost looked the part of an islander, he and the others having ripped insignia from their uniforms and having doctored the cloth with mud and by tearing it in a few places, He had managed by some means to contact the SBS, who were operating at that time from a base in Turkey. As he explained to us, his priority was to get the pilots off the island and back to resume operations; this done, he would arrange for the rest of us to be taken off, too.[36]

Sqn Ldr Hayter's party departed that night, sailing first to the Turkish coast and over the following two days reached Casteloriso via Marmaris and Andifli. Lt Banks' party followed in their wake. The Germans captured 1,388 British and 3,145 Italians on Kos. They executed Col Felice Leggio and eighty-nine of his officers in accordance with Hitler's directive of 11 September to execute all captured Italian officers. The loss of Kos would have disastrous consequences for British operations in the Dodecanese Islands. Deprived of air cover, they were in the long run unable to hold the other islands while the Germans pressed their advantage. Leros was ripe for the taking.

German Invasion of Symi

Meanwhile, 74 Squadron's sea party en route for Kos – thirty-eight men under the command of Flt Lt Hank Ferris, the MO – had been stopped by the SBS on 3 October, advised of the state of play at Kos and diverted to Symi to await further instructions. However, events overtook them since the German invasion of Symi commenced at first light on 6 October. A Kommando party nearly a hundred strong arrived in a caique from Rhodes. They were fired upon but landed at Pedi Bay and made their way up to a ridge overlooking Symi town. Some penetrated to the upper town and sniped from the houses. These troops had only rifles, machine guns and hand grenades, so the Breda and Bren guns available to the defenders were of great value. The next day, at about 06:00, three Stukas dropped bombs and a Greek hospital was hit causing several civilian casualties who were attended to by 74 Squadron's MO Flt Lt Ferris.

The following day, 8 October, at about 08:00, two Stukas dropped bombs causing Greek casualties. However, one of the Stukas was claimed shot down by Breda fire by 74 Squadron's Flt Sgt C. L. Schofield and the other was hit and made off to sea losing height rapidly and was seen by the Greeks to hit the hills and crash (*sic*). Schofield, who wore spectacles on account of short sight, continued to use his gun even when his spectacles were broken by vibration, the flash eliminator burned off and the sights had fallen off from the overheated weapon. All the time he was exposed to ground and air attack, sustaining a wounded arm in the process. He was later awarded the Military Medal for his gallantry.

At midday, a bomb hit the HQ building. One SBS man, two soldiers and LAC Norman Gay, a 74 Squadron cook, were killed. Flt Lt Ferris and rescue parties worked for thirty hours to extricate two trapped SBS men who later died from their injuries. He received an MC for his performance, the citation stating:

> ...his HQ was subjected to severe enemy air attacks. On one occasion four men were killed and two others were buried under the debris. Flt Lt Ferris immediately set to work removing the bodies and releasing the buried men. His medical equipment had been destroyed and he was compelled to work with a pair of scissors and a small wood saw with which he succeeded in releasing one man after amputating his leg. Flt Lt Ferris accomplished this while an air attack was in progress and worked with very little light and while held upside down by his legs. During an engagement between British and enemy ground forces he worked incessantly under most rigorous conditions. His coolness and courage proved a source of inspiration to all.

Working alongside Flt Lt Ferris was Canadian/American Pvt Porter Jarrell, a medical orderly with the SBS, who received the George Medal for his part in the rescue:

> Jarrell worked for 27 hours without rest to the point almost of collapse, exposing himself to extreme personal risk. He continued to toil through two further raids, when a bomb falling anywhere in the vicinity would have brought the remnants of the building down on him. He was a source of inspiration to all other workers ... and with Sergeant Whittle shares the credit for the two men being rescued alive. He entirely disregarded his own risk, crawling along perilous tunnels through the debris to administer morphia, feed and cheer the trapped men; the next minute working feverishly to

clear the debris. Owing to the RAF doctor having an injured wrist, under the doctor's supervision in appalling conditions, by candlelight, on his back, he did most of the leg amputation necessary to release one man. His movement was restricted by the likelihood of the shored up debris falling in on himself and the trapped men.

The following night all 74 Squadron personnel were amongst those evacuated from Symi, joining their companions at Casteloriso before returning to Cyprus.

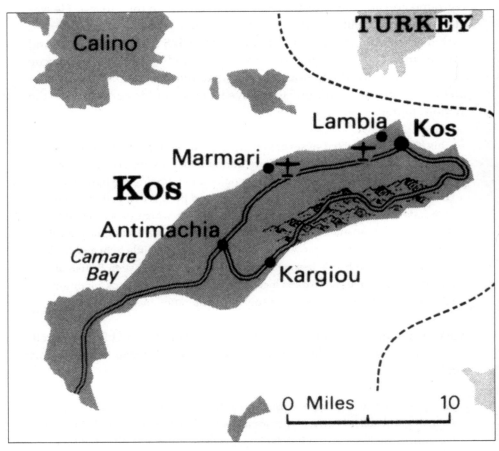

Map of Kos.

CHAPTER V

Beaufighters in Support of Kos Operations – September-October 1943

On 13 September, a section of three patrolling Beaufighters of 252 Squadron from Cyprus attacked a reconnaissance Ju 88, Flt Sgt A. B. McKeown and Flt Sgt Desmond de Villiers shooting down SM+4 of Wekusta 27 some thirty miles west of Cyprus where it ditched in the sea at 13:00. Fw Fritz Wolters, Med.Ass. Dr Christan Theussner and two crewmen survived and were rescued by a HSL and taken to Cyprus. A subsequent POW interrogation report revealed:

> Started from Tatoi at 10:00 on reconnaissance and rescue search. Whilst making a rescue search to the west of Cyprus at zero feet, their aircraft was attacked by three Beaufighters, by which it was destroyed before completing its mission. This was quite a distinguished crew. The observer, previous a Weather-Reg [Meteorological officer] with the Gold (110) War Flights Badge, while the pilot and W/T operator were both Officer Cadets. The gunner [wounded] wore the EK1.

On 17 September, eight Beaufighters of 227 and 252 Squadrons from Limassol caught a small German convoy off the south-east coast of Naxos making for Rhodes. The convoy comprised two freighters ferrying troops – the 3,830-ton *Pluto* and 3,754-ton *Paula* – and the escort vessel sub-chaser *UJ-2104* with a standing patrol of three Ar 196s of 1./126 overhead. The 252 Squadron Beaufighters went after the Arados and Sqn Ldr Keith Faulkner forced Uffz Fritz Schaar's aircraft (D1+EH) to ditch in the sea; the Arado alighted close to *UJ-2104* and Schaar and his gunner Uffz Herbert Schneider were rescued. However, north of Stampalia the convoy was again attacked, this time by destroyers. One aircraft of 252 Squadron, V8335 flown by Belgian pilot Flt Lt Charles Delcour, was repeatedly hit and navigator Flt Sgt Tom Lumsden killed.

Another Arado was attacked by Plt Off. Percy Glynn (JL766/G) of 227 Squadron, the Canadian pilot reporting that he believed its gunner had been killed before he broke off the engagement after his own aircraft had been hit. This may have been D1+MH that later crashed in the Gulf of Patras with both Uffz Kurt Dehl and Fw Benno Unsin injured. On returning to the convoy, Glynn spotted an Arado on the sea (obviously D1+EH)[37] and strafed it, in which he was joined by Plt Off. David Anderson RCAF (JL915/A). Glynn was forced to belly-land JL766 on returning to Limassol. The two cargo ships were damaged (and sunk next day by the destroyers HMS *Faulknor*, HMS *Eclipse* and the Greek *Queen Olga*) and *UJ-2104* badly damaged. Onboard the *U-jäger*, the captain and two of his officers plus a number of men had been wounded (two of whom died). About sixty survivors including the Arado crew managed to reach the coast of Stampalia where they were taken prisoner by Italian forces; they were later handed over to the British and became prisoners. Sqn Ldr Faulkner of 252 Squadron received a Bar to his DFC for his leadership and performance in this action:

> Since being awarded the Distinguished Flying Cross this officer has participated in numerous sorties and his great skill and fine fighting qualities have been amply demonstrated on many occasions. In September, 1943, he led a formation of aircraft in an attack on a heavily armed and escorted convoy near Amorgos Island. In the engagement Squadron Leader Faulkner attacked an Arado 196, which he forced down on to the sea, and afterwards attacked a merchant ship and an escorting vessel. This officer is a highly efficient flight commander, whose outstanding qualities have inspired all.

Do 24T KO+KA was called out on this date to rescue the crew of a Ju 87 from I/StG3 that had ditched in the sea. The task was successfully completed and the airmen were flown to Athens. KO+KA flew a second rescue mission after dark and on its return, at 20:00, collided with a wall on alighting due to blackout as Allied aircraft were reported in the area. The seaplane was badly damaged and some of Obfw Friedrich Becker's crew were seriously injured. This second rescue mission may have been in connection with a 15SAAF Baltimore that had crashed near the island of Stampalia.

On 18 September, Beaufighters from Cyprus were continued to harry shipping supplying the Germans on Rhodes. One 252 patrol led by Sqn Ldr George Hubbard (with Flg Off. J. C. Barrett, Flt Sgt Des de Villiers and Flt Sgt L. J. Passow) engaged a Ju 88 but could only claim it as damaged despite all four pilots having a crack at it. Two days later, a Beaufighter of 227 was shot down by flak during an attack by six aircraft on caiques and a coaster found in Vronti Bay on Scarpanto. Both Flt Sgt Wilf Webster RNZAF and Flt Sgt

Edward Taylor were lost when JL642/C failed to return. Another 227 crew was lost a few hours later when 5/227 and 6/252 attempted night attacks on the Rhodes airfield of Maritza. The Beaufighters bombed and strafed causing explosions and fires, but flak shot down 227's JL640 flown by Australian crew of Flt Sgts Bob Neighbour and Chris Hoskin. The Beaufighter crashed on the island at 04:45 (on 21 September) and both were killed.

Athens/Eleusis airfield was the target for twenty-seven B-24s from North Africa on 22 September during which sixty-four tons of bombs were dropped on runways, dispersal areas and among parked aircraft. A number of Ju 88s were believe damaged or destroyed on the ground. An Ar 196 of 1./126 was lost during the day: D1+AH on a flight from Suda Bay to Phaleron was believed to have crashed in the sea due to fog. Both Uffz Manfred Binias and Uffz Heinz Greller were posted missing. Apparently 147ªSquadriglia lost one Z.506 and two Z.501s in September. It was reported that a Z.501 engaged in combat with a He 115/Ar 196 and claimed it shot down. D1+AH may have been that aircraft.

Both 227 and 252 now began transferring from Limassol to Lakatamia airfield, south of Nicosia, where three dirt strips had been prepared. The move did not go smoothly and Beaufighter JL915 of 227 (crewed by Canadian Flg Off. David Anderson and Plt Off. Jim Timmons) swung on take-off from Limassol on 24 September. It crashed into a stationary Beaufighter (JM239) in which W/O Gerry Grennan RCAF and Sgt Stan Palmer were waiting to take-off with spare pilot Flt Sgt Bill Budd. Both aircraft burst into flames, followed by an explosion of a bomb, killing all five aircrew. On 25 September, eight Beaufighters from the two squadrons attacked the German torpedo boat *TA10* that had been beached near Cape Prasonisi on the southern tip of Rhodes following an encounter with the destroyer HMS *Eclipse*. As a result of the Beaufighter attack by four of 227 Squadron led by Flg Off. B. R. E. Amos, *TA10* was scuttled. On the next day, 227 was less successful when four aircraft carried out a shipping strike against vessels in Syros harbour as Flg Off. John Thomas, in Sgt David Warne's aircraft, remembered:

> Because Sgt Warne was an NCO, we were not to lead the strike. However, after passing Kos, the leading navigator became lost in the maze of small islands, and we were requested to take over. This we did. It was too late to enter Syros harbour from the eastern side. We were able to turn and conduct our attack in an easterly direction, flying downhill as it were! We all missed with our bombs but strafed the vessel, a minelayer.[38]

680 Squadron lost its second Spitfire PRIV on this date due to engine problems. BR644 flown by Plt Off. K. O. Bray had departed Nicosia at 08:30

to cover Leros and Kos, but ended up landing at Marmaris airfield, Turkey. Thus, the Turks gained their second PRIV and interned its pilot.

October 1943

At the start of October all hell was about to erupt in the Dodecanese. The Kos invasion force, when first sighted, was thought to be heading for Rhodes. A force of destroyers from Alexandria, already at sea and with a Beaufighter escort, was ordered to intercept but searched in the wrong area and was forced to head back when fuel ran low.

On 3 October, now armed with the knowledge that Kos was the destination of the convoy, four Beaufighters of 46 Squadron led by Sqn Ldr Tom Scade (HL475) took-off from Lakatamia at 04:00 to locate the force. They bombed and strafed the ships, one Beaufighter being hit in return and its navigator wounded in the legs. The next strike force, four Beaufighters of 227, was due off at 05:10, but one (EL476/R) crashed on take-off slightly injuring Plt Off. Cas de Bounevialle and Sgt Scott. The remaining three found the vessels at anchor from which barges were transporting troops to the beaches. Intense flak greeted the Beaufighters shooting down Flg Off. Percy Glynn's JM760/B into the sea. The Canadian pilot and his navigator thirty-three-year-old Sgt Tim Barrett were killed. The remaining two Beaufighters returned to Lakatamia, JL586/H flown by Flt Sgt Keith Thomas containing a wounded navigator, Flt Sgt R. C. Howes, who had been hit in the legs by shrapnel. Sqn Ldr Ronnie Lewis wrote to Percy Glynn's mother:

> As Percy's Flight Commander I can give you details which I feel you will want. Percy was detailed to take part in an important attack on an enemy convoy attempting to take an island in the Aegean held by us. It was a big day for us as the repulsion of the invasion force was left completely to the RAF and our particular Wing. Many of our attacks did severe damage to the enemy with losses to ourselves, but this was largely due to some pilots pressing home their attacks. Percy was one of them. He was last seen to be strafing an enemy M/V in the convoy but one of the flak ships shot him down, and he was seen to land in the sea. It was considered by his comrades that Percy had a slender chance of survival.
>
> Percy was a very popular member of the squadron and respected by his colleagues and his men. It was Percy's lot to take part in many hair-raising strikes and he was always the first to get on the job. On one occasion after attacking German ships in a fortified harbour, [he] was himself attacked by two Italian Macchi 202s. He fought them for twenty minutes and eventually

got away, though severely damaged. To be engaged by two single-engined fighters, bring a damaged twin fighter home, and land it safely is a feat in itself. Since then Percy got shot up again by flak whilst doing another attack on shipping and brought his aircraft safely home again. We all miss Percy as a friend, as a happy young boy around the mess, and as an inspiration to us all. Percy had done more than his share towards hastening the end of this war. We are doing our best also and this mishap will be avenged, you may rest assured. If Percy, but it is doubtful, has survived, I consider that the German Forces would pick him up. May God bless you in your hours of apprehension and anguish. We all trust with you that Percy will turn up.[39]

The attacks continued unabated. At 06:10, more Beaufighters departed Lakatamia, Wg Cdr Butler leading seven from 252 to strike at the invasion force disembarking troops on beaches. All aircraft attacked M/Vs with cannon fire with good effects. One Beaufighter carried two 250-lbs bombs, one of which hung up, and the result of dropping the second bomb was unobserved. A Ju 88 was seen bombing the island from 8,000 feet. All returned safely to base although four had been damaged by flak: Flt Sgt H. D. Humphries and Flt Sgt T. Burrow onboard EL388 had both suffered leg wounds, and Flg Off. J. C. Barrett (V8347) received minor shrapnel injuries. Three Beaufighters of 227 and one of 46 were next off at 10:30, Sqn Ldr Ronnie Lewis leading the strike in JM277/E that came under fire from the ground as they approached Kos. Their arrival coincided with a Stuka attack on the airstrip at Antimachia by aircraft from both I and II/StG.3. The Beaufighters waded into the dive-bombers:

As our aircraft flew up the southern tip of Kos and approached Yali, a formation of three Stukas was seen on the starboard beam about a mile away, at 1,500 feet. All Beaufighters were carrying two 250lb bombs, which were jettisoned when the formation of enemy aircraft were attacked. The e/a also believed to have jettisoned their bombs. 'E' [Sqn Ldr Lewis] attacked leading e/a, opening fire from 400 yards and closing to 300 yards, firing several bursts. Pieces were seen to fly off wings and black smoke from fuselage. This aircraft was seen to crash into the sea by the 46 Squadron pilot [Flg Off J.S. Holland]. 'G' (JL939 flown by Flg Off Tommy Deck] opened fire from 500 yards closing to 30 yards, and silenced rear gunner. Debris flew off e/a's wings and white smoke from engine. Further pieces came from e/a as attacks were made from starboard and port quarters. The e/a lost speed and appeared to be gliding to finally crash in a cloud of dust on Tilos island. 'N' (Lt A.E. Hounsom SAAF in JM648) attacked third e/a, opening fire from 800 yards to 200 yards, but no visible result and e/a lost in tight turn. All Beaufighters then attacked a lone Stuka and pieces of tail unit shot away. Air gunner shot off double red cartridge. E/a dived to sea level, rapidly losing seed, but suddenly climbed and our aircraft overshot.

46 Squadron's American pilot Flg Off. Tex Holland DFM[40] in JL910 claimed one shared and another as damaged. Three Stukas fell in this action: S7+FH in which Uffz Jordan Stifter and his gunner Gfr Arthur Achenbach were killed as were Gfr Walter Kneisel and Fw Rudolf Fischmann aboard S7+LH, which crashed near the island of Syros. The third loss was S7+?? of II Gruppe. It would seem that the crew of the latter survived their ordeal.

The next strike force comprised just three Beaufighters, one from 46 Squadron flown by the CO Wg Cdr George Reid and two from 89 Squadron departing at 07:00. Not only flak was encountered but also Ar 196s. Wg Cdr Reid's aircraft (JM238) was seen to spin into the sea killing him although his navigator, Flg Off. Wilf Peasley, managed to escape from the submerged aircraft. He was picked up by a friendly caique and taken to a hospital at Bodrum, Turkey. Flg Off. Charles Foster claimed one of the Arados probably destroyed and both Beaufighters returned safely to Lakatamia, one with a wounded navigator. Soon after midday, Sqn Ldr George Hubbard (EL528) led three of 252 to the target area where they encountered an Ar 196. This was pursued and believed damaged by their attacks but the German pilot wisely sought refuge over his own ships and the Beaufighters broke away and returned to Cyprus. This was not to be the fortune of the next strike by four Beaufighters of 46 Squadron led by Sqn Ldr Bill Cuddie. At 13:25, the Beaufighters carried out a low-level strike against the shipping now assembled in Kos harbour, as newly promoted Plt Off. Ed Ledwidge (flying JL903/N with Sgt John Rowley) recalled:

Approaching the island from the south there appeared to be no activity and there were only a couple of beached barges left stranded and deserted on the shoreline, with no sign of life. Bill Cuddie then came over the R/T, "Let's see what's on the other side", so we flew across the island and the deserted airfield south-west of the high ground. As we reached the sea on the north side of the island, away to our north-east, lying off the harbour, was the whole of the invasion fleet! Obviously the island had been recaptured and the enemy was busy either off-loading more troops or taking stores to or from the harbour. As soon as we saw them Bill Cuddie called, "There they are – let's have a go at that lot." Throttles up smartly to combat setting, friction nut screwed up tight, and we were closing in on the ships – spreading out slightly to present a more difficult target and thereby leaving room for the Beaus to weave as each of us selected individual targets. We carried two 250lb bombs (three seconds fused) on each Beau and as we closed in I remember thinking, "Mustn't forget to fuse the bombs before we drop 'em..."

We were about a mile from the ships when they started to fire at us and the puffs of black smoke, with the associated churning up of the water beneath the exploding shells, gave me the usual impression that all the shrapnel exploded downwards and that if one flew above the shell bursts one would be safer – highly wishful thinking, of course. As we approached the flak was in layers and I subconsciously weaved up and down between the layers. Suddenly Bill Cuddie's Beau veered sharply to the right in front of me and, as it did so, exploded in a great orange and black cloud immediately ahead. As I pulled sharply upwards to avoid the explosion I clearly remember the sight of that great pall of black smoke with the light shining brightly on the sea just beneath. We were now on top of the outer extremity of the ships, above the destroyers and flak ships which were in a defensive ring around the motor vessels. Having zoomed up to avoid the exploding aircraft, I found myself almost over the ring of defending vessels at about 400 to 500 feet above a destroyer. I had to pull the Beau hard into a wing-over to bring my guns to bear on this ship. Through the gunsight I could see the churning of the water caused by my cannon shells as they ran up to and finally sprayed across the stern of the destroyer. As I began to pull hard to the right towards the motor vessels, there was a brilliant flash of an explosion and the whole rear part of the destroyer blew apart (I suppose I must have hit some depth charges). The force of the blast almost hurled the aircraft over onto its back in a roll to the right.

Sqn Ldr Bill Cuddie and Flg Off. Len Coote were killed in JL907. Plt Off. Ledwidge continued:

On pulling out I found myself heading directly towards the middle one of three big ships and as my cannon shells sprayed the side of the ship I could see grey figures moving away each side of the shell strikes. I released my bombs and pulled up over the funnels of the motor vessel – and then noticed a smell of burning cellulose. We had obviously been hit but that was the last thing one thought – it must be the electrics, or the radio equipment, and anyway the aircraft was still flying all right. My nav called over the intercom that he too could smell something burning, and that an Arado floatplane was firing at us from just above. Throughout the attack it was obvious that we were receiving hits of some sort, and we could still hear thumps and bangs around the aircraft. All I could do at this time was to keep corkscrewing the Beau to make a more difficult target for the guns, and my navigator felt the same way for he repeated over and over "Keep weaving, the shell bursts are still close." During the final part of the attack as we approached the M/Vs in the centre of the melee, I noticed Sgt Holmes' aircraft on a parallel course to me and saw his bombs drop straight towards the M/V to our left and now, as we were weaving away low over the sea, there he was, still on a parallel course, streaking across the water with one of his engines pouring black smoke. I remarked to my nav, "I wonder how far he'll get with that engine trouble?" It was obvious he wouldn't make it back to base. The nav then informed me that fuel was pouring past him on the starboard side and I thought, "Let's hope our outer tank hasn't been holed" because we needed all that fuel to get back to base. However, the nav confirmed that the fuel was coming from the inner tank. I looked out over the starboard wing and saw little damage apart from a buckled panel and a couple of small holes about midway along the wing. But the smell of burning had become much stronger and seemed to be coming from somewhere inside the fuselage. By this time we were clear of the flak and flying low towards the Turkish mainland, with Sgt Holmes about half a mile to our left, still streaming smoke. Dead ahead of us at about 10 miles I could see what appeared to be a mosque with a tall white tower.

Flt Sgt Les Holmes and Flt Sgt Mark Bell in JM264 were forced to ditch but after several hours in their dinghy they were picked by a Turkish caique and taken to Bodrum. Plt Off. Ledwidge continued:

My navigator then decided to come up through the fuselage to see if he could trace the source of the burning smell, so he disconnected his intercom and left his seat. At that moment it dawned on me that when he'd mentioned the fuel leak he'd been looking aft, and that when he saw fuel going past him on *his* starboard he had probably meant the port side of the aircraft. I looked immediately out to the port wing, just in time to see the small flap that covered the main tank filler cap pop open and a burst of whitish-orange flame quickly followed, engulfing the whole upper surface of the wing centre-section. I shouted to the navigator, somewhere behind me in the fuselage, to get back to his seat as I was going to ditch. Within seconds the side of the fuselage started to glow white, then burned with an intense white flame. The heat was almost unbearable. I had moved the gunsight to one side and was endeavouring to get the speed back as quickly as possible – until that moment we'd been belting at full throttle – whilst opening the top escape hatch. As the speed decreased the Beau became increasingly port wing heavy; obviously the result of damage to the port wing and, as I noticed later, the fact that the fabric had all burnt off the port elevator. Luckily the bank angle was about right for landing on the side of the fairly heavy swell. As we hit the water the port mainplane broke away and, still burning, went over the top of the aircraft and landed in the sea to our starboard.[41] (see Appendix II).

Of the four Beaufighters of 46 Squadron on this fateful sortie, only that flown by Flt Sgt M. W. Jackson RAAF survived, albeit badly holed, to return to Lakatamia. The final strike on this traumatic day was made by three of 227 and one of 46, which departed Lakatamia at 15:10, but by now the target area was covered by a smokescreen. Three Bf 109s attempted to attack while the flak remained accurate and fierce forcing the Beaufighters to return, the pilots unable to discern the ships through the smoke. Despite the sacrifices of the Beaufighter crews – five aircraft lost, five crewmen killed, five interned and four wounded – their efforts proved inadequate for the defenders of Kos on the ground.

On 5 October, the Beaufighters returned, Lt Hounsom SAAF leading four of 227 off at 07:30 on an offensive sweep over Kos. Barges were sighted near Naxos, but not attacked. Just over an hour later four more from 227 set off, led by Flg Off. Amos, but similarly found no specific targets so strafed transport sighted along the northern coastline. Two Bf 109s then appeared at which the Beaufighters jettisoned their bombs and took evasive action. Amos' gunner Sgt A. J. Thorogood joined Sgt B. H. L. Blake, the gunner in Canadian Plt Off. A. C. Gibbard's JL648/N, in defending their aircraft and reported definite strikes on one of the Messerschmitts, but saw no apparent damage. On returning to Lakatamia, Amos' aircraft, JL735/W, which may have been damaged in the combat, crashed on landing though neither crewman was hurt. Uffz Theo Heckman of 9./JG27 claimed a Beaufighter north of Leros flying just above sea level and this may have been Amos' aircraft.

On 6 October, two Beaufighters of 227 Squadron were lost, but not to enemy action. Both suffered malfunctions while escorting a naval force sweeping west of Kos and both crews – Plt Off. Burgess 'Burgie' Beare RCAF/Sgt C. E. Humphreys of JM648/N and Sgts R. H. Carter/H. J. Harris onboard EL516/Y – were safely plucked from the sea. The following morning the naval force intercepted a German convoy off Stampalia and in the engagement that followed succeeded in sinking the ammunition-carrying transport *Olympus*, five troop-filled F-boats and an escort. All told, about 600 German troops lost their lives.

Help was on the way for the overworked Beaufighter squadrons with the belated arrival of three squadrons of P-38s of the 1stFG, which had been tasked for operations in support of the Kos evacuation. Lt Charles L. Hoffman recalled:

On 5 October I took off from Mateur for the six-hour flight to our new base. We were told to load all of our living equipment on a C-47 that was to support us in the move. For once I played it smart – I decided to put my bedroll, air mattress, some changes of clothing, food, cigarettes, and toilet articles in the gunbay and baggage compartment of my plane. As it turned out, the C-47 crashed en route and all equipment was lost. Unfortunately, this also included the kitchen, tents, rations, water containers, and spare parts for the planes.

Our desert airfield, known as Gambut 2, was located about 20 miles from the Mediterranean coast and between Tobruk and the Egyptian border. I have no idea where it got its name – there wasn't a building or settlement with miles of the place. There were four or five Australian troops stationed there to support any aircraft that might use the field. These guys were really happy to see some English-speaking people. For the first three days my crew chief and I slept under the wing of the airplane. Each morning we received a canteen of water and were told we could drink it, wash in it, or whatever, but that was all we would get for the day. Needless to say, beards starting sprouting and you manoeuvred to the up-wind side of everyone. The water shortage was so bad that we had to use fine sand for the initial cleaning of our mess kits.

When the trucks delivered our fuel, they just dumped several 55-gallon drums on the ground in front of the plane. It took about 750 gallons to fill the wing and drop tanks of a P-38. One complete revolution of the hand pump would move about one quart of fuel from the drum to the aircraft, so refuelling took a lot of time and energy. Since we were on an air-echelon, we were working with a skeleton ground crew and they needed all the help they could get. All of the pilots were quick to assist the maintenance folks. Until our replacement kitchen arrived, we used cold 'C' rations. We ate them from the can because there wasn't any water to wash out the mess kits. Later, someone located a German water trailer out in the desert. After some tire repairs, a trailer hitch modification, and a thorough cleaning, it was cleared by our doctor for use. We hitched it to a personnel carrier and transported some water from a nearby British military installation. At last we were able to wash and shave!

I flew again the next day [7 October] and got to shoot at my first enemy airplane in flight. We spotted a German ship convoy that appeared to be a landing party. There were two Ju 88s giving them top cover and also bombing a small town on Leros. Flak was pretty heavy over the convoy. When the Ju 88s made their turns at the end of the convoy, we made a gunnery pass on them. After several passes, we saw many large pieces coming off one of the Ju 88s and it ditched between the ships of the convoy. The other '88 escaped to the north. By this time we were too low on fuel to give chase. The downed Ju 88 couldn't be credited to any one pilot, so it became a squadron victory. [*sic*] [42]

We received a very nice commendation from the commander of the RAF's 201st Group, thanking us for coming to their aid. Later in the month, Prime Minister Churchill expressed his appreciation for our support of the British operations in and around the Dodecanese Islands.

On the morning of 9 October, two patrolling Ar 196s spotted a British naval force to the west of Kos. This comprised the AA cruiser HMS *Carlisle* and four destroyers engaged on another sweep with aerial escort provided by relays of Beaufighters and P-38s. An escorting Beaufighter (JM276/C) of 227 Squadron crewed by Sgts John Swift and George Austin was warned of a bogey and told to investigate. An Ar 196 was sighted and Swift dived to engage, its rear gunner opening fire. He carried out three or four attacks from port quarter, inflicting damage to its port wing and shooting off the rear end of the port float, but the Arado managed to evade and escape and was last seen heading for Kos. However, a section of five P-38s mistakenly attacked the Beaufighter (JM230) flown by Flt Sgt Alf Pierce of 252 Squadron. With his aircraft hit in both engines, Pierce was fortunate to reach Lakatamia where a forced-landing was carried out with no injuries to himself or navigator Flt Sgt J. G. Hopgood.

Before the next relief flight of P-38s arrived, the task force was subjected to an attack by Ju 87s of I and II/StG.3 from Rhodes called in by the Arados. A direct hit was scored on the destroyer HMS *Panther* that broke in two and quickly sank while HMS *Carlisle* also sustained damage:

All 26 serviceable Doras of I. Group Stuka Wing 3 lifted off at 10:00 hrs to attack the British task force near the small island of Saria north of Karpathos. After sighting the task force, the three squadrons of I/StG.3 started at 11:55 their final approach to attack the ships. The pilots in the slow-moving Stukas could not know that just in this moment the US fighters turned away from the British force, heading south-west back to their air base. Thus there was no air cover by allied fighters to protect the warships, which were proceeding south through Scarpanto Strait ... the Stukas arrived at 11:56 overhead the ships without prior warning and commenced their attacks with great accuracy. One Stuka after another dived almost vertically with the banshee wail of their sirens to the first and largest target – HMS *Carlisle*. Evasion manoeuvres were in vain and the *Carlisle* was soon in trouble. The cruiser got several direct hits and was near-missed by two other bombs and was smoking from the stern.

Now the bulk of the Stukas concentrated on HMS *Panther*. Although the ship guns put up a tremendous barrage the 1540-ton destroyer suffered two direct hits and several near misses. Her back broken, she sank at 12:05 hrs in two separate halves ... 33 sailors were killed. Not later than 12:10, the Stukas of I/StG.3 had left the target area and landed safely at Megara. During the attack they only lost one aircraft. S7+AK of 2. Squadron StG.3 were shot down by ship anti-air artillery. In the meantime, a new threat was en route. Stukas of II/StG.3 from Argos were approaching the convoy from north-west. The time over target was scheduled for 12:15.

However, arriving just in time to prevent further attacks on the warships by the Stukas of II Gruppe were the seven relieving P-38s of the 37thFS led by Major William Leverette. On the approach of the twin-engine Lightings, the vulnerable Stukas jettisoned their bombs and diverted for the lower tip of Rhodes but were too slow to evade the onslaught as Major Leverette later described:

> We peeled off into the middle of them, and I got two almost before they knew we were there. The gunner in the first started to fire, but stopped as soon as I let go. We came back behind them and I got on the tail of another. His gunner stopped firing as soon as I opened up, and the pilot baled out. My fourth was a 30-degree deflection shot from 200 yards. Then I gave a lone plane a burst of cannon and machine-gun fire from a 20-degree deflection. That finished him.
>
> I came in directly behind the sixth. His gunner opened up before I did, but I got him with my first shots. The plane nosed down a little, and I gave him a burst in the belly. I was closing fast and had started to go under him when he nosed almost straight down his propeller shot off. I tried to dive under him, but didn't quite make it. My left prop cut two feet into his fuselage as he went down. My last hit was the best. I was closing on him from the right when he turned into me. I rolled into a steep bank to the left and got him while firing from an almost-inverted position.

While all this was going on, the leader of Leverette's second element, Lt Troy Hanna, claimed five Stukas and his wingman (Lt Homer Sprinkle) three more. After disposing of a Ju 88 (by Lt Wayne Blue) that was escorting the dive-bombers, the top-cover flight came down to shoot down another Stuka (credited to Lt Robert Margison). For his combat leadership and individual performance, Major Leverette was awarded the Distinguished Service Cross. The Americans claimed sixteen Stukas shot down, but actual losses amongst the II/StG.3 crews, although serious, were seven aircraft lost. The damaged HMS *Carlisle* was towed to Alexandria by one of her destroyers. Onboard were twenty dead and seventeen wounded.

Enter the B-25G 'Gunslingers'

Despite the successes achieved by the 1stFG, the Americans would not accede to the P-38s remaining under British command and they shortly returned from whence they came. To compensate, a squadron of B-25G Mitchells, each armed with a 75-mm nose cannon for anti-shipping work, was despatched by the 321stBG to assist the Beaufighters. Because of the urgent need for hard-hitting strafer aircraft, a version of the B-25 bomber, the B-25G, had been developed, in which the transparent nose and the bombardier were replaced by a shorter solid nose containing two fixed .50 machine-guns and a 75-mm M4 cannon, one of the largest weapons fitted to an aircraft. The cannon was manually loaded and serviced by the navigator who was able to perform these operations without leaving his crew station just behind the pilot. This was possible as the breech extended into the navigator's compartment. Twenty-one rounds of 75-mm shells were carried. The machine-guns were aimed and fired by the pilot at the same time as the cannon as anti-flak weapons and for ranging purposes in the sighting of the 75-mm cannon. The aircraft was dubbed the 'Gunslinger' by some of its crews. An air-gunner gave an enlightening account of his experiences in flying the B-25G:

I flew only ten 'G' [B-25G] missions and they were the ones we had trained so long and hard for. These were the 75mm cannon-totin' B-25s and, at the time, the most heavily armed aircraft in the world. The first of our missions were sea sweeps and they were very exciting. On these missions the entire crew could participate shooting at vessels, aircraft, and machine-gun emplacements and all at minimum-level flying. Our propellers kicked up a mist of spray as we buzzed the ocean top on shipping raids. It seemed that the highest elevation we attained while on these sea sweeps was when we returned to the field and got all the way up to maybe 500 feet to circle and land.

Each time the pilot fired his forward firing .50s and the 75mm it felt like the airplane had hit a soft, but solid wall in the air. The ship would fill up with cordite smoke, which quickly blew on out, while our cannoneer slammed another shell into the cannon breech for the pilot to shoot. As he loaded the shell the up sliding breech would push his hand out of the way. He then would step to the side to miss the recoil of the cannon. Then slam another shell into the breach. Four or five shells were used on each run with the .50s, up front, hammering away too. Then we could go to work. Waist gunner, my turret and the tail gunner could shoot as targets came to bear and the range closed. I could shoot at those ground targets only when my pilot dropped a wing to give me an opening. As we pulled off the target, the cannoneer would pick up the spent shell casings from the floor and put them back into the shell holder above the guns so he wouldn't slip on them on the next run.

These 75mm cannon shells were 26-inches long and weighed 20-pounds each. Just above the cannon breech was a rack that would hold 20 [sic] rounds. We carried mostly high explosive shells with a few armour-piercing thrown in for good measure and just in case we met the dreaded German destroyers prevalent in the area. The cannon breech and ammunition rack was just behind but much lower than the pilot's seat. This cannon could fire as fast as it could be loaded and would toss shells some miles but usually in sea sweeps 2,000 yards was the maximum range. We had a wooden paddle to use in shell loading, which got tossed quickly since it just got in the way. Hand loading was easier and faster but dangerous if you missed and got your hand caught in the up-sliding breech, not the way to earn a Purple Heart!

The cannon was a standard M4 with a specially constructed spring to absorb some of the recoil shock. The barrel extended forward under the cockpit through the tunnel formerly used by the bombardier in reaching his nose position. The muzzle emerged from a concave port on the left side of the nose. We shot up a lot of coastal shipping on the sea sweeps. E-boats were different. About the size of our PT boats they were moving flak platforms mounting 88s, 40mm, 20mm cannons and light machine-guns. They were dangerous with speed and all that firepower and their crews were experts. We tangled with them on several occasions and came out about even. We hit many, but sunk none. They hit us, but downed none.[43]

A dozen B-25Gs[44] – known as G Squadron – arrived at Gambut on 15 October under the command of Capt. Donald A. Bell. Five of these aircraft carried out their first operation from Gambut the following day together with two Beaufighters from 252 Squadron and another from 227 Squadron as revealed in extracts from the mission report. Capt. Bell (42-64587) led the mission:

Mission No.1 At 12:00, four B-25Gs took-off for shipping strike Pserimos (Cappari) – Kos area. Four shot five 75-mm shells at 14:08 from 450 feet. No hits scored on E-boat. Three Beaufighters escort strafed same boat with 20-mm cannon fire. Boat seen smoking. 250x50 calibre rounds fired by B-25s at E-boat. No hits observed. Kos channel, east of Pserimos. Caique (60-ton, one-mast vessel) sighted heading SE. Flak, light, slight, inaccurate from caique. Four aircraft returned at 16:10.

Before the first flight had returned, the remaining five aircraft set out for the same general area, led by Flt Off. James L. Peplinski (42-32488):

At 14:00, four B-25Gs took-off for shipping strike of Calino – Kos area. One returned early. Three shot 13 rounds of 75-mm shells from 100 feet. B-25s made two passes at E-boat. Closed to 2,000 yards. Near misses recorded. Ship seen smoking at middle. 150 rounds of 50 caliber shot at E-boat, no hits observed. Sighted four Me 109s at target at 4,000 yards on B-25 course. No passes made. At target after second pass B-25 and two Beaufighters escort attacked simultaneously by 3 Ju 88s. No hits on bombers, one Beaufighter hit. B-25 gunners claim two Ju 88s probably damaged. B-25s fired 1,800 rounds of .50 caliber at Ju 88s from 1,000 to 750 yards when Ju 88s turned off. Ju 88s made several passes in 15 minute running battle. Attacks made at 5 and 7 o'clock. Ju 88s echeloned to right, followed each other in.

Two Beaufighters from 46 Squadron were also conducting a sweep in the area, Flg Off. Tex Holland/Sgt Henry Bruck engaging a Ju 88 that attempted to attack the other Beaufighter. Holland claimed it damaged, but Ju 88D 5M+T Wekusta 26 failed to return and was possibly his victim. Uffz Herbert Schönwälder's crew were all lost. Further to the west, about five or six miles off the island of Amorgos (in the Cyclades group), the RN submarine *Torbay* sank the German freighter 1925grt SS *Kari*. Amongst the rescue craft despatched to her aid was Do 24 VH+SK of Seenotstfl.7, but during take-off with survivors onboard the seaplane crashed due to engine failure. Survivors of *Kari* and Do 24, among them the pilot, were picked up by sub-hunter *UJ-2110*.

A new Beaufighter strike unit arrived at Gambut on 17 October for operations over the Aegean, 603 Squadron commanded by Wg Cdr Hugh Chater. G Squadron flew its third mission on this date, five B-25Gs escorted by two Beaufighters from 252 Squadron and one from 227 to carry out a shipping strike in the Pserimos-Kos area. Two beached F-lighters were sighted on the north shore of Kos, the B-25s firing a total of seventeen 75-mm shells and claiming two direct hits on one of the craft. Light, accurate and intense AA from target area succeeded in hitting 42-32488 flown by 2/Lt James T. Edwards, causing the port engine to cut. By jettisoning his two 250-lbs bombs, two waist guns, the 75-mm and .50 ammunition and radio equipment, Edwards was able to coax the crippled aircraft back to a successful landing at Gambut, protected and guided all the way by the three Beaufighters led by Sqn Ldr Hubbard.

South of Rhodes, the light cruisers HMS *Sirius* and HMS *Aurora*, plus three destroyers, were patrolling when six Ju 88s of 6./KG51 appeared. Four escorting Beaufighters of 252 Squadron chased the bombers away from the task force, Sgt Bill Davenport (EL403) claiming two damaged, seeing strikes on the port wing and tail of one before being hit by return fire from the second. The other Beaufighters chased the Ju 88s without being able to close them down. Davenport's shooting was better than he thought, one Ju 88 ditching in the sea with pilot Ltn Norbert Marawietz and gunner both wounded, while the other two crew members were lost. The other Ju 88 crashed while landing at Heraklion and was written off; there were no casualties. Signalman Peter Deacon was aboard HMS *Sirius*:

About 13:00 Action Stations sounded off and everyone went scrambling, expecting air attack. As I reached the flag deck the battle ensign was already bent-on and everyone with binoculars was scanning the clear blue sky for the first sign of incoming planes. Minutes went by and then *Aurora* hoisted 'Enemy ahead', followed by 'Landing craft ahead, open fire at will' on her 10-inch SP.

There they were, 20 or more landing craft, packed with troops and escorted by what looked like trawlers or small coastal craft. Their course was almost diagonal from ours, they were steering southwest but had already begun to scatter. We were making about 30 knots and so were closing rapidly and it seemed that we were the closest. Some of the screening destroyers on the starboard flank had probably been advised to hold their fire but just about everyone else opened up. It was all over remarkably quickly as the convoy was decimated, with virtually every craft on fire or sinking. We seemed to plough right through the remains and there were survivors' heads bobbing in the slight swell all around. [Capt P.W.B.] Brooking ordered our port side close-range weapons to open fire on what had not been blown apart and one of the escorts, only a couple of cables away was rapidly reduced to scrap metal with fire from Oerlikons and the 4-barrel pom-poms. A state of something approaching mass euphoria reigned for a while. We secured from Action Stations but got the feeling that retribution might not be all that long in coming. 'George' [German reconnaissance aircraft] had been spotted during the recent action, flying well out of range of our guns but inevitably, our presence must have been reported.

At about 16:00, making 30 knots and steering due north Action Stations sounded once more. Almost before I reached the flag deck all hell was let loose as probably every ship in company opened up. Coming head-on at us, flying low and spread out came half a dozen planes. They came in with frightening speed but I saw that they were not Stukas, but twin-engined machines, probably Ju 88s. They seemed to be almost at masthead height, flying seemingly unscathed through the barrage of flak that was being put up. One passed so low overhead that we hit the deck instinctively and the roar of the engines was heard above the thunder of our 5.25s. What I took to be flying debris turned out to be machine-gun bullets hitting parts of the ship. Seconds later another plane zoomed in and down we went one more on to the steel deck, imagining, I suppose that the thin skirting around the flag deck would protect us.

There followed a deafening explosion and a brilliant flash and I knew we'd been hit. They came back for another run but, for some reason we were not the target this time. A couple of the destroyers had been hit but if the other cruisers had, it had not been devastating. I looked aft from the flag deck and saw the port pom-pom platform had been shot-up and there were bodies slumped inside it. X-turret was motionless and had obviously been hit. Looking down at the port waist I saw a figure in white shirt and shorts that were now soaked in blood which I recognised as the on-board NAAFI manager [there were 17 killed]. Most of us were in a state of confusion but there seemed to be no further air attack forthcoming.

Two Beaufighters of the newly arrived 603 Squadron at Gambut were called into action, HMS *Sirius* directing them to an approaching raid. However, before they could make contact, a number of Bf 109s of 11./JG27 swept down through broken cloud and Oblt Alfred Burk attacked JL761/E crewed by Flt Sgts John Hey and Eric Worrall. The Beaufighter was seen to ditch but both of the crew were lost. During another escort mission later in the day, Flt Sgt Bob Reid's 227 Beaufighter (JL735/W) was forced to ditch due to engine problems. He was safely picked up by a Walrus but his navigator, Sgt Harry Seymour, lost his life.

B-25Gs and Beaufighters were out again during the early afternoon of 18 October for an attack on Antimachia airfield on Kos. The four American crews released their bombs from a height of 400 feet claiming two hits on the runway, the others falling nearby before strafing with cannon and machine gun, ten 75-mm cannon shells being fired at various targets including at least eight aircraft observed in the dispersal areas. These included a Spitfire, a Ju 87 and three Mc.202s. Two F-lighters were seen heading away from the island and these were also attacked, one by the B-25s and the other by the Beaufighters, both craft sustaining damage. Two Beaufighters of 46 Squadron from Cyprus carried out a sweep over Rhodes during the day but were attacked by two Bf 109s of 8./JG27 and Flg Off. Tex Holland (JM249) was shot down into the sea south-west of Casteloriso at wave-top height by Oblt Kurt Hammel. The American survived unhurt but his twenty-one-year-old navigator, Flt Sgt Henry Bruck, had been mortally wounded and died soon afterwards in their dinghy.

One of the main tasks for newly arrived 603 Squadron was to provide escort for the B-25Gs, its first sorties flown on 19 October when one Beaufighter (flown by Sqn Ldr Joe Watters), plus two from 227 Squadron, escorted four Mitchells on a shipping strike in the Antikythira-Kos area. Airborne at 11:08, the strike force encountered a small convoy comprising three landing craft, a caique and an armed trawler escort some twenty miles north-east of Cape Spatha (Crete). Two Ar 196s were seen near the convoy and, a mile north, a Do 24 was observed on the water apparently involved in the rescue of the occupants of a dinghy that was bobbing in the water some twenty-five yards away. The B-25Gs led by 2/Lt John Gilluly raked all three landing craft with machine-gun fire and cannon, scoring three hits on one, two hits on another and a single hit on the third. The armed trawler was then skip-bombed by one of the B-25s. The Beaufighters strafed the trawler and confirmed that it sank. Many personnel on the craft were seen to jump into the sea. Meanwhile, the Arados were pursued and one was shot down by Sqn Ldr Watters (JM407) while the seaplane – KO+KD of Seenotstfl.7 – was strafed by another. Uffz Schröder and his crew of three were rescued although two were wounded.

The small former French liner *Sinfra* (4,470 tons), now in German hands and serving as a troop transport and part of a German convoy, was attacked north of Crete during the night of 19/20 October by radar-equipped and torpedo-armed Wellingtons of 38 Squadron.[45] With 2,664 prisoners of war onboard, including 2,389 Italians, seventy-one Greek prisoners and 204 German troops, the ship was sunk. By the end of the day, 566 survivors, including 163 Germans, had been saved leaving a death toll of 2,098. Sadly, the German authorities had failed to notify the International Red Cross of the movement and occupants of the *Sinfra*.[46]

On 20 October, Rhodes reported that a Ju 52 carrying Italian POWs had been shot down by a fighter near Melos. This was probably an aircraft (047) of Transportstfl./II that was reported missing, although it seems it had force-landed without casualties, probably due to an engine malfunction. Possibly the confusion arose over the loss of the POW-carrying *Sinfra* and the shooting down by Plt Off. Gibbard RCAF of 227 Squadron (flying JL900/S) of Ju 88 F6+AH of 1.(F)/122 some eighty miles south of Rhodes. Gibbard, leading a patrol of four Beaufighters, was vectored onto the recce aircraft and chased it down to sea level, firing three short bursts from 1,000 yards down to 300 yards, but did not observe results. He then carried out an attack from dead astern and closed to 400 yards, setting its starboard engine on fire. It glided towards the sea followed by Gibbard who gave another burst following which it crashed into the sea on fire and exploded on impact. A survivor was believed to have been in the sea but Oblt Walter Panchyrz and his crew were lost. The Ju 88 had been involved in a mission to Alexandria. Rhodes was subjected to a minor raid when an intruder Beaufighter from 46 Squadron, JL909/C flown by Sqn Ldr Dudley Arundel, bombed Calato aerodrome.

Kos was the target for the B-25Gs, two flights each of four aircraft being despatched during the early afternoon. Escort was provided by 603 Squadron. Their designated targets were F-lighters beached on the north-east coast. The first section (led by 1/Lt Edgar Dorman in 42-64587) fired eleven 75-mm shells at two F-lighters and claimed two hits on one. Accurate 20-mm and 40-mm AA fire was experienced coming from the airfield at Antimachia and coastal defences, although none was hit. The second section, led by 2/Lt John Gilluly (42-324890), also attacked the F-lighters, claiming several 75-mm hits before they set upon a two-mast schooner that was also strafed, two direct cannon hits being claimed. On the airfield at least ten aircraft were seen including two Bf 109s and two Mc.202s. Intense light but fairly accurate AA fire was experienced and two B-25s were damaged but able to return safely to Gambut. S/Sgt Ed Colby was a gunner onboard 2/Lt Gordie Prior's 42-64654 and recorded in his diary:

Mission #12. Dodecanese Isles. Get 3 holes in ship, one through radio seat, transmitter and life raft. Luckily, I had moved to machine-gun runway just seconds before.

G Squadron at Gambut was now temporarily grounded due to lack of spares (and possibly 75-mm shells) and did not fly any further operational sorties until 24 October. Although naval forces were very active in the area of the Dodecanese during this period, air operations were muted. However, the Germans lost at least two aircraft due to accidents: Ju 88 F6+PH (5745) of 1.(F)/122 failing to return from a sortie south-east of Rhodes on 21 October with the loss of Uffz Kurt Backenhausen and his crew; on the next day, Arado 7R+GK of 2./125 crashed south of Stampalia, its crew being rescued by a *U-jäger*. On 23 October, a 227 Squadron Beaufighter (JM277/E) crashed near Lakatamia on returning early with engine problems from escort duty, killing Flt Sgt Tom Morfitt and Flt Sgt Joe Jackson.

Flt Off. Peplinski led four B-25Gs on a general shipping strike of the Kalinos area on 24 October. When they returned at 18:00, the crews told of how two caiques were attacked, one a two-mast vessel and a 75-mm hit scored on each. A Ju 52 had been sighted but not attacked and three s/e aircraft, presumably Bf 109s, seen heading east over the north-east tip of Kos, but these did not interfere with the strike. Meanwhile, German forces landed on Astypalea during the day including some flown onboard Ju 52 See transports. Meanwhile at Gambut, yet another new unit arrived, 47 Squadron equipped with Beaufighter Xs, capable of carrying torpedoes, under the command of Wg Cdr James Lee-Evans DFC. The B-25Gs were out again on 25 October as noted in the unit's War Diary:

At 1300 F/O Peplinski and his 'gang' of 4 more planes set out after what is generally considered a tough target, namely, seven F-boats snug in Kos harbour. It can be admitted that it was not without foreboding that we watched them take off. However our fears were groundless and the story they told was one of sighting one solitary LC about a mile south of Kos harbour and shooting it up a bit.

Three Beaufighters of 603 Squadron provided escort and one of these, flown by Sqn Ldr Barry Atkinson, was hit by flak but managed to return to base safely. Flt Sgt Wally Eacott recalled:

On one effort, over an airfield [Antimachia on 25 October], our flight commander, Squadron Leader Barry Atkinson, claimed to have aimed his aircraft and fired his guns at a large party of soldiers, headed by an officer who, Barry said, was wearing an Iron Cross, and who pointed with a revolver at the aircraft before being blown apart (that's how low we used to fly on our raids). Such was the amazing intelligence network of the Germans, that not very long afterwards, we heard that a rebuttal had been made by them, and published in English newspapers, that there was no German officer on the airfield at that date who was entitled to wear the Iron Cross!

During the same raid, my cockpit canopy was struck on the right side by a bullet, or piece of shrapnel, that tore a large hole in the perspex, and struck my right arm with great force – not enough to break the skin, but sufficient to bruise my arm and make it feel sore for some days. On landing, we found damage also to the starboard wing, probably caused by shrapnel from a bomb burst on the airfield.

These trips were very arduous. It took about two-and-a-half hours to fly across the Med to the target. Attack usually took no more than about 3 or 4 minutes, then there was the return journey to be accomplished. One of the hazards was the fact that spray from the waves created a salt coating under the wings and fuselage, and aircraft had to be regularly cleaned to get rid of this corrosive substance. Another was the fact that it was very difficult to judge one's height over the sea. Two hundred feet and 20 feet looked very much alike in the featureless seascape.

It was necessary to set the altimeter meticulously before take-off, and descending very, very carefully to the top of the waves, usually about 20 feet above the sea. At this height, flying the Beaufighter was still hard work, from the habit of the aircraft hunting, that is, behaving like a ridden horse in rising up and down continuously, necessitating constant opposing pressure by the pilot on the control column to counteract the movements. This effect was called longitudinal instability, and was partly cured by fitting dihedral tail planes to the aircraft. It was not unknown for pilots to strike the wave-tops – in fact we lost two in our Squadron from these dreadful accidents. The aircraft were gone in the blink of an eye!'

On 24 October, 680 Squadron lost another Spitfire PRIV, Plt Off. George Hay RAAF having departed Nicosia at 07:00 in BR414. He was due back at midday but failed to return. Air-Sea Rescue carried out a search but the weather was very bad. No trace of aircraft or pilot was found. It transpired that he had crashed into a hill near Bodrum, Turkey, and was killed.

Following a day of little action, 26 October witnessed a further engagement with Ju 52s and Arados. With escort provided by three Beaufighters from 47 Squadron, flying the unit's first operation from Gambut, Flt Off. Peplinski again led three B-25Gs on a shipping strike off Amorgos, where, at 15:20, three Ju 52 floatplanes and an Arado were encountered and as the unit diarist later wrote:

[We] had quite a tiff there for about 10 minutes. When the smoke and Ju 52s had cleared away the score was: one Ju 52 in the briny drink (exploded, they say) two other 52s damaged as was their Arado 196 escort. "Peps" [Peplinski] right engine knocked out by fire from the Arado. He had to limp 380 miles home on one engine. Like Edwards [on 17 October], he had to salvo half the plane to keep from settling. A neat feat in any man's language. Jerry must have been surprised at being peppered by 75mm fire from an opposing aircraft.

The shooting down of the Ju 52, 6162 of Seetrnspstfl.1, was credited to 47 Squadron's Flg Off. John Fletcher (47/J) who reported sighting three Ju 52s escorted by three Ar 196s at sea level. He attacked a Ju 52, opening fire from long range before being attacked by one of the Arados. In an exchange of fire both machines were hit, Fletcher and his navigator Flg Off. T. E. Jones both suffering slight wounds from splinters. The American crews confirmed the Ju 52 as having been shot down. The Arado (D1+DK/0382) also crashed with the loss of Uffz Heinrich Leifeld and his observer Ltn Hans Klindert of 2./126. Flg Off John Hayden flying JM225/S attacked another Ju 52 but his cannons almost immediately jammed. His victim, however, suffered damage and alighted on the sea, but the damage was minimal and there were no casualties. The German pilots identified the B-25Gs as Lockheed Venturas. For 27 October, G Squadron's diarist wrote:

The earliest take-off for a mission so far occurred today when 4 of our aircraft took off at 07:25 to low-level bomb the Antimachia aerodrome on Kos. Soon after they had left we got another extreme in the weather - a dust storm. It came up suddenly and blew with such intensity that everyone buttoned up their tents and clouds of dust completely obliterated the landing ground form the air. Wing Ops phoned to tell us that our planes had been rerouted to the Matruh landing ground. The wind and dust subsided around 18:00 and at 18:30 our aircraft came back to this base. They seemed proud of their achievements for the day and we could readily see why. All bombs hit the aerodrome squarely and one of the bombs tossed by 2/Lt [Richard W.] Johnson hit squarely into a Ju 52, destroying it and killing many of the personnel gathered around it. Other bombs scored hits on the runway and left side of the aerodrome. Lt Gilluly was the leader on this, another successful mission.

The Americans also reported seeing eight to ten well-camouflaged biplanes on the airfield, but the report did not state that these were strafed, although it did confirm that the Beaufighter escort knocked out two flak gun emplacements. Another report stated that the Beaufighters strafed some of the abandoned Spitfires on the airfield, which the Germans were apparently endeavouring to make serviceable. Meanwhile, a pair of 252 Squadron Beaufighters escorting a naval force were directed on to a snooper, Flt Sgt Alf Pierce (EL403) carrying out a left-hand diving attack before the Ju 88 entered cloud, attacking again when it emerged. Several puffs of black smoke came from its port engine but Pierce's cannons jammed at the crucial moment and was forced to break away and the recce aircraft escaped, albeit possibly damaged.

There was a lack of trade for the Beaufighter/Mitchell patrols on 28 October, eight Beaufighters of 47 Squadron returning empty handed from the Cyclades while five B-25Gs fired their cannons at a small sailing boat 'which must have scared its occupants a bit', but no hits were claimed. The American crews of G Squadron were now advised of their imminent replacement by crews from the 310thBG who were on their way and would take over the B-25Gs. A further surprise came in a more pleasurable form:

> As a surprise to many, especially those who were taking a "helmet bath" in the area, two comely British "posies" dropped in to pay us and our Day Room a visit. To the uninitiated a "posie" is a travelling British show girl and quite a sight they were too – especially to us out in the middle of the desert. They were entranced by our modern swing records and especially enjoyed those transcriptions that are in the Special Services "B" kit. A dusty floor isn't conducive to good dancing as proclaimed by Arthur Murray but those that tripped the light fantastic.

Sqn Ldr Charles Ogilvie led eight Beaufighters of 47 Squadron (four carrying torpedoes) in an attack on a small vessel sighted south of Naxos on 29 October. Three Ar 196s from 2./126 were flying a protection patrol and Obfw Stahlbohm shot down JM225/W crewed by Flg Offs. John Dixon and George Terry, both of whom were killed. Flg Off. Joe Unwin (JM403/F) reported being attacked by an Arado, which his navigator Sgt Ken Farmer believed he hit with his Vickers GO.

Do 24Ts of Seenotstfl.7 and other ASR units were called out to help in the rescue of survivors from the German transport *Ingeborg* that had been sunk by RN submarine *Unsparing* off Syros. However, CH+EX crashed near Naxos when flying from Athens, the crew being killed, but CH+EV successfully rescued new fewer than fifty-two survivors and flew them to Kos. CH+EV's crew included Uffz Karl-Heinz Lüdtke who recalled:

> Here again we were ripped from our dreams when the alarm sounded. We hurried to the building where the cook had already prepared a quick breakfast for us. Three crews were ordered in and they arrived one after the other. After the briefing we knew the details, a transport ship, the *Ingeborg*, was torpedoed

by a submarine and we had to rescue the shipwrecked from the water. When we arrived at the scene Lange first circled the site to locate people who drifted away. The sailors all wore their yellow lifejacket and were easily identified. Lange landed the Do 24 and now we started with the heavy work of getting as many people on board as possible. Meissner and I pulled the shipwrecked on the stumps [floats] and that wasn't easy with their soaked and thus heavy uniforms.

We counted 52 people on board and with the crew that came to 58 in total; we prayed that everything would go OK. As told, Lange was a superb pilot and he could do anything with the Do 24, but an overloaded aircraft, how would he handle that? If he didn't take care on take-off we could get nose under and end up as a submarine. After a very long run we were airborne to the delight of everyone on board. We later found out that the Do 24 was only able to carry 24 people, now she had 34 extra and all were putting in extra weight with the added water, and still the Do 24 flew! The shipwrecked were soldiers of the Punishment Battalion 999 who were to take over from the Italians in occupying some of the islands.

When the *Unsparing* returned to the scene it was to find three Do 24s on the sea collecting survivors. Skipper Lt Aston Piper recorded:

09:15 periscope depth; to my amazement what I had thought to be invasion craft could now be identified as three Dornier 24 flying boats with two of the vessels that had just passed us, in close attendance. There were several Arado 196 seaplanes flying around.

09:35 another Dornier 24 had landed with two Arado 196s close by. It could now be seen that this odd assortment of craft had collected to pick up survivors from the sea. There was a very large area of the sea covered with barrels, spars, debris of all kinds, a very large number of rubber dinghies of different colours with and without German soldiers on them. The temptation to torpedo one of the Dornier flying boats was very great. I could imagine the headlines – submarine torpedoes aircraft! But I resisted the temptation and sank an escort packed with troops instead.

His victim on this occasion was the former Italian Customs patrol vessel *Nioi* that Piper recorded as *N.101*. His report concluded:

12:20 weather became very calm during the afternoon. Several more Arado seaplanes returned during the afternoon and picked up more of the survivors. One was observed to taxi away in the direction of Stampalia with survivors clinging on to the wings and floats.

G Squadron carried out its last operational mission from Gambut on 30 October and suffered its first and only operational loss:

> The first flight came in and said everything went along as scheduled. They went out after two 'F' boats at Kos harbour, which they saw when they got up there and which they shot up to the best of their ability. Flak was intense and accurate coming form about six different directions so they didn't waste any time getting out of there.
>
> While the first bunch was landing we got a radio call from Flg Off [Charles] Keith who was leading the 2nd flight saying that Lt Black's plane [42-64579] was not coming back. That cryptic message made us all apprehensive and when Keith landed we got the details of this our first casualty. Both ships went in and peppered three M/Vs in Naxos harbour with 75s and 50s with no flak encountered. But after they turned off it started. It was only moderate but was accurate enough to hit Lt Black's ship, probably in the cockpit, because both engines were last seen functioning perfect when the ship hit the water. The Beaufighter eyewitness said the aircraft broke into pieces on impact and no sight of life was seen. It was a shock to all of us as Lt Black, although the newest man in the organisation was well liked by all. Our hats are off to 2/ Lts [Gordon] Black, [William] Golden, and S/Sgts [Fenton] Horton, [Edwin] Ramsburg, [Arthur] Lang, and [Richard] Wenrich. We'll miss them.
>
> This episode can't be dismissed without mention of another amazing item. When notified that Lt Black's plane went down, S/Sgt Jacob F. Leist [assigned to this crew] was digging a latrine; he was doing that extra duty because of carelessness and laxness. He wasn't around when his plane took off and a substitute had to be procured in a hurry. The sub was S/Sgt Ramsburg and the plane was 579, Lt Black's ill-fated B-25.

The Beaufighter escort was flown by 47 Squadron's Flg Off. John Fletcher (47/L) and Flg Off. J. E. Hayter RNZAF, the latter's aircraft (JM317/S) crashing off the coast of Cape Kouroupas to the west of Naxos following an attack on one of the ships.[47] Hayter and his fellow Kiwi navigator, W/O T. J. Harper (on loan from 603 Squadron), managed to bale out over Naxos and were rescued by local Greeks who treated their injuries and later smuggled them off the island. Flg Off. Fletcher reported on the loss of the B-25:

> I saw a big flash on the Mitchell as it was going in to attack, and it then started to turn violently to port and then commenced a gradual glide to the water. He flew straight in and the aircraft broke up. I circled and then I could see no sign of life in the wreckage. The other Mitchell was proceeding southwest and I caught him and told him over VHF what had happened and we came back to

the area and both planes went over the wreckage again but still could see no sign of life in the wreckage.

A costly month for the Beaufighter crews resulted in thirteen aircraft failing to return from ops with thirteen aircrew killed and five interned in Turkey, albeit briefly. The B-25G crews had completed eighteen operational missions while flying from Gambut and the unit was now temporarily disbanded and its crews returned to their parent squadrons within the 321stBG. The following week a detachment of the 379thBS, 310thBG, would arrive at Gambut to continue the role of G Squadron.

Owing to the shortage of shipping, a paratrooper operation was undertaken that involved the dropping of 200 officers and men of the Greek Sacred Squadron on the island of Samos to reinforce the garrison. This was carried out on the nights of 31 October/1 November and 1/2 November. On both nights, five Dakotas of 216 Squadron carrying 100 troops followed by a sixth carrying supplies set off from Ramat David (Palestine) at fifteen-minute intervals. The Greek soldiers, of whom many were middle-aged men with little experience of flying and none of parachute jumping, were successfully dropped in spite of the fact that the operation was carried out on moonless nights. Only one Dakota was lost on the return flight through an error in navigation. The crew were compelled to bale out over the mountains of Southern Turkey and were interned temporarily.

Operations over and around Casteloriso, September-October 1943

Casteloriso (Kastellorizo to the Greeks) is a small island laying one mile off the southern Turkish coast, opposite Kas, seventy-eight miles east of Rhodes and 170 miles south-west of Cyprus. It is the smallest of the Dodecanese islands and is just five squares miles in area.

On 10 September 1943, special British detachments of SBS and SAS were sent to Casteloriso onboard *ML.349* and *ML.357* for the liberation of the island (Operation *Gander*) with further troops landing a week later. Two days later, the island was formally liberated by the Allies with the arrival of 350 men on the Greek destroyer *Koundouriotis* and the two French ships. During the subsequent weeks, Casteloriso's garrison for strategic purposes was hurriedly increased to some 1,300 British troops. At this crucial stage, General Wilson cabled the Chief of the Imperial General Staff accordingly:

> We have occupied Castelrosso [*sic*] island, and have missions in Kos, Leros and Samos. A flight of Spitfires will be established in Kos today, and an infantry battalion tonight by parachute. An infantry detachment is also

proceeding to Leros. Thereafter, I propose to carry out piratical war on enemy communications in the Aegean.

The harbour at Casteloriso had been used pre-war by *Air France* flying boats en route to Syria and now became a useful transit venue for Italian Co-Belligerent seaplanes flying to and from the Aegean. At the beginning of October, three Z.506B of 147ª Squadriglia RM based at Leros flew to Alexandria via Casteloriso conveying seven wounded British soldiers and a 'Maggiore' pilot. Another flew to Cyprus on 6 October together with a Z.501 and later two Z.501s and a Z.506 flew to Kulluk (Turkey) before flying to Alexandria.[48]

Beaufighter crews from Cyprus were obviously at error with their recognition and intelligence updates, a 46 Squadron aircraft attacking a Co-Belligerent Z.506 near the island on 13 October while flying cover for a naval patrol. Plt Off. W. Jenkinson (with Plt Off. L. Charles in JL905) initially engaged a Ju 88 seen in the vicinity and claimed it damaged before it escaped in low cloud. A Z.506 was then spotted near the convoy and when this was challenged it fired the wrong colours of the day. Jenkinson opened fire and the damaged seaplane promptly ditched, sinking shortly afterwards. There were no reported casualties.

On 15 October, Flg Off. Dave Lewis was flying his 454 RAAF Squadron Baltimore FA590 off Casteloriso and came across an Allied convoy. Following proper procedure, he fired off the colours of the day but soon found he was being chased by a Beaufighter that opened fire, hitting the Baltimore in the port engine, mainplane and tail. Lewis managed to limp back to St Jean and landed successfully, although the crew were somewhat shaken by the experience.

The increased activity around Casteloriso had not gone unnoticed by the Luftwaffe and, on 17 October, the island was bombed for the first time by six Ju 87s from Rhodes as recalled by fifteen-year-old schoolgirl Katina Simonides:

Dimitrios [her brother] and others killed were hurriedly buried prior to our sudden evacuation from the island and Nikos [another brother] was given emergency first aid treatment for his leg and other injuries. I left Castellorizo with our ailing aunt Skouna (who died on the boat) for Cyprus but my parents and sister Vayio remained to take care of Nikos, all going to Rhodes days later. He remained there for three months.

Two other youngsters, both six years old at the time, had their own stories to tell. Nick Loucas later recalled:

I was sent by my mother to the market to buy meat when I suddenly heard high pitched whistling. This was followed by loud noise and people screaming. A British soldier who was nearby dragged me through the door of a house and protected me under his body in the open fireplace. Some time later when the noise subsided we emerged from the house. I remember he was injured somewhat by shrapnel. He urged me to run home. Our home was fortunately close by at Mesi tou Yialou [one of the harbour-side squares of Casteloriso]. After hiding overnight in our dust-filled basement (the dust was from the damage caused to the Economou home next door), we left next day in a small boat for Turkey.

While Paul Boyatzis added:

I was playing on the harbour and I remember seeing the Stukas flying over. A British soldier who was nearby manning an anti-aircraft gun saw me in my panic and took his tin helmet off his head and placed it on mine. Without me asking, he placed me on his shoulders and I then directed him to our family home as the Stukas flew overhead.

On 18 October, the Luftwaffe returned. A dozen Ju 88s of II/KG6 – in three waves of four aircraft each – arrived over Casteloriso shortly before 10:00 and began bombing. Serious damage was caused to a number of residences with loss of life and injuries to soldiers and inhabitants. Before the attack could be completed, however, six long-range Hurricanes of 213 Squadron timely arrived from Cyprus and carried out a successful interception. The second wave of bombers was engaged, three being claimed shot down and the fourth believed possibly damaged. Flt Lt Hal Rowlands RAAF, leading the Hurricanes in HL912/C, later told the press:

We had time to get up high and were able to dive and intercept them after their bombing run. Red Haslam got the first.

Flt Sgt Peter Haslam added:

My man apparently failed to drop his bombs and turned back for a second run. As he turned he saw me for the first time but I was able to turn inside him to get the first squirt. I then got close in and he went down in flames. Yes, they gave me a bit of a party for the 200th.

A second Ju 88 fell to Plt Off. Ray Jackson RAAF, the bomber last seen by his No.2 as it headed into Turkey with an engine on fire. Wt Off. T. A. Jowett also attacked one but the result was not observed. The other was the victim of Flt Lt Rowlands:

I think my bloke must have been in the clouds and have come down to join Jackson's fight or to look for his baled-out victims. There would have been 48 Huns in those twelve kites, and it's amazing that not one of them saw us until so late. But it was OK by us.

Two Ju 88s were reported lost by II/KG6, 3E+CM flown by Uffz Karl Lilienthal and 3E+AP flown by Uffz Heinz Walter.

On 27 October, Flt Sgt Keith Thomas RAAF (EL301/Y) and Sgt Guy Fowkes (LX998/N) of 227 Squadron flew an escort patrol for a RN task force, the cruiser HMS *Aurora* and her destroyer escort returning from a patrol south of Rhodes, and at 14:27, sighted a Ju 88 dodging in and out of cloud at 2,500 feet, some seven miles ahead of the naval force. Sgt Fowkes turned towards it, pulled up and gave a two-second burst at about 200 yards. Thick smoke was seen coming from its starboard engine as he broke away and allowed Flt Sgt Thomas to attack. He fired three bursts, seeing strikes on the fuselage before the aircraft disappeared in cloud, still smoking. It was not seen again and was claimed as probably destroyed.

During a dusk patrol by four Beaufighters of 46 Squadron, a formation of fifteen Ju 88s was sighted and engaged. Owing to the heavy and controlled return fire from the bombers, combined with the poor performance of the Beaufighter at low level, only three of the bombers were claimed damaged, two by Sqn Ldr Dudley Arundel (JL848/S) whose own aircraft was hit by return fire, although he safely returned to base. A second Beaufighter, JL894 flown by W/O A. Boswell RCAF, also returned to base on one engine. On inspection, a bullet was found to have passed through the Perspex an inch above the pilot's head.

30 October proved to be a successful day for the Beaufighter crews of 227 Squadron tasked with providing escort for HMS *Aurora* as she and escort headed towards Casteloriso. During the first patrol by three aircraft, an upturned Ar 196 was seen floating ahead of the convoy. No personnel were visible so Flt Lt John Tremlett (JL585/R) and Flg Off. Dick Hutchison (JL615/X) sunk it with cannon fire. At 11:20, a Ju 88 was sighted – 4U+GK of 2.(F)/123 flown by Ltn Walter Plattner – and this was attacked and shot down jointly by Flg Off. J. M. Kendall/Plt Off. R. Mackay (HL478/F) and Flg Off. Paul Mazur RCAF/Plt Off. Ken Stakes in X7819/V, as their report revealed:

Vectored onto bandit north of cruiser at sea level. Sighted Ju 88 above, six miles away and gave chase. 'F' closed from dead astern, closing from 1,000-300 yards and gave short bursts. Closed to 300 yards and gave three bursts. E/a took strong evasive action and returned fire. No hits observed. 'F' broke away and 'V' closed in from dead astern. E/a did right turn followed by 'V', who closed to 300 yards and gave short burst. E/A did right turn again and 'V' closed to 250 yards. Strikes seen midway up fuselage and put rear-gunner out of action. 'V' broke away and 'F' closed in and gave five-second burst. Hits on both engines and front of fuselage. E/a dived into the sea. No wreckage seen but possibly two heads seen bobbing in the sea of green florescence.

In the afternoon, fourteen Ju 88s of Einsatz Gr.Ju 88 Gen d.FlAus 6, escorted by three or six Bf 109s from 9./JG27 and possibly three Mc.202s approached the task force, which now had an escort of four Beaufighters from 227 Squadron and two more from 252 Squadron. The fighters engaged the Beaufighters and 252's Flt Sgt E. H. Jones RAAF (JM240) reported attacking a Bf 109 head-on with no apparent result. Sgt E. C. James' EL647/B of 227 Squadron survived a stern attack by a Macchi, which shot away his rudder fabric before being chased away by W/O H. A. Nice RCAF (JM276/C). It was last seen going down in a slow spiral. The 'Macchi' on this occasion appears to have been a Bf 109 flown by Uffz Hannes Löffler who claimed a Beaufighter south of Casteloriso.

A further four 227 Beaufighters of the relief patrol arrived on the scene and were able to shoot down two of the Ju 88s, K5+AB (Ltn Wilhelm Glaser) and K5+BL (Uffz Erich Grimmer), although four were claimed. Flg Off. Burgie Beare RCAF/Sgt Humphreys (JL900/S) attacked one from the starboard quarter at 12,000 feet, opening fire from 150 yards, closing to fifty yards. The Ju 88 was observed to jettison its bomb load prior to exploding and disintegrating in flames. He then attacked a second at 10,000 feet, again from starboard quarter, and opened fire at 200 yards and closed to fifty yards. With its starboard engine on fire it crashed into the sea in flames. Beare then attacked a third Ju 88 head-on at 4,000 feet, opening fire from 400 yards and closing. Its starboard engine caught fire and it crashed into the sea. Meanwhile, Plt Off. Bill Yurchison RCAF (with Flg Off. Percy Wroath in JL939/G) attacked another Ju 88 at 9,000 feet causing the rear fuselage to catch fire before it crashed into the sea. The flight leader, Flt Lt Bill Kemp RNZAF, attacked another but his aircraft JM268/N stalled and was attacked from astern by a Ju 88. With his Vickers GO jammed, Flg Off. C. S. Wyles was unable to return fire and the Beaufighter suffered a badly-holed fuselage resulting in a crash-landing at Lakatamia airfield on return. There were no injuries. After the engagement, the crews reported seeing four aircraft burning on the sea and four parachutes in the air about four miles west of Casteloriso. A further Ju 88 was seen with its starboard engine on fire heading for Rhodes in a shallow dive. Despite the efforts of the escort, some of the bombers got through and HMS *Aurora* suffered a direct hit on her stern, causing serious damage and heavy casualties: forty-six killed and twenty wounded. One of the escorting destroyers, HMS *Belvoir*, was also damaged.

During the month, US heavy (B-24s) and medium (B-25s) bombers carried out a number of strikes against Athens/Eleusis airfield in an effort to subdue the Bf 109s of III and IV/JG27. On 5 October, forty-eight B-24s bombed Eleusis. The Americans estimated that thirty to thirty-five German fighters contested the attack and four Bf 109s and two Fw 190s were shot down, one probably destroyed and one damaged. Three of the attacking Liberators failed to return. On 7 October, Eleusis airfield was hit by forty-eight B-25s escorted by twenty-four P-38s. On 9 October, medium bomber raids took place on Eleusis, Salonika/Sedes and Argos airfields: 'fair results' were claimed by the attacking force. Next day, B-17s bombed Crete and Rhodes. The night of 18/19 October witnessed an attack by Liberators and Halifaxes of 178 and 462RAAF Squadron on Antimachia airfield, Kos. The next US raid took place on 22 October when thirty-six escorted B-25s bombed Eleusis airfield, but clouds prevented damage assessment. The attacking force claimed one enemy fighter destroyed in air. Two more minor raids took place on Eleusis on 24 and 29 October.

On 24 October, five Do 217Es of 5./KG100 arrived at Kalamaki from Istres, France. Each was able to carry two Hs 293 radio-controlled guided bombs. More would follow under the command of Hptm. Wolfgang Vorpahl. The captain of an Hs 293-equipped aircraft gave an account of such an attack:

> Upon reaching target distance, Uffz Z launched the Hs293 and I pressed the seconds pointer of the stop clock in my control column. As the massive bomb fell through about 100m, the red flare in the rear lit up and the rocket engine gave the bomb additional thrust for about 10 seconds. Uffz Z came up a bit on his control raising the Hs293 to eye level. His eyes and the red flare had to be brought together over the ship. I could not see the flight of the bomb myself from my seat on the left side of the cockpit. I concentrated solely on my flight instruments and counted off in 10 seconds increments the duration of the flight ... at 92 seconds a loud, eager scream about the BzB [intercom] sounded at the same time from all five occupants: "Direct hit amidships!"[49]

Meanwhile on Rhodes, *Reparto Aereo Dodecanneso* was formed on 30 October equipped with all available serviceable Italian fighters on the island including Mc.202s. These would be used to escort Ju 88s of II/KG54 and II/KG6 as well as the Ju 87s of I/StG.3 in forthcoming operations.

CHAPTER VI

The Battle for Leros

At a British Cabinet meeting held on 10 October, the decision was taken to hold the islands of Leros and Samos. It was realised that maintenance would be difficult and depended largely on the Turkish attitude. Prime Minister Churchill asked '...if nothing could be done even to regain Kos. If nothing could be done then the Middle East were authorised to evacuate the garrisons from the islands.' The Foreign Secretary told the Prime Minister after a conference with the C-in-C ME that it would be impossible to retake Kos with the existing air resources and that plans were being made to maintain Leros by submarine, air forces and caiques from Samos. And so another clash in the eastern Aegean was thus assured.

Leros was subjected to daily bombing attacks, and these were intensified on the two days before the planned invasion, sixty-five sorties being logged on 10 November including twenty by Ju 87s and by thirty-nine Ju 88s from II/KG6 and II/KG54 the following day. On the night of 10/11 November, six British destroyers bombarded German transports in Kos and Calino harbours. Little damage was caused and on their withdrawal they came under attack by six Hs 293-carrying Do 217s of 5./KG100 during which HMS *Rockwood* was severely damaged. It was the glider-bomb's first use in the Aegean. Of the attack, *Rockwood*'s captain Lt Sam Lombard-Hobson RN later wrote:

At 20 minutes past midnight, at a moment when the nearest enemy aircraft was three miles distant, I heard a dull thud on-board, as though the ship had hit a baulk of timber in the water, or someone had dropped a heavy weight on deck. The First Lieutenant then came to the bridge and said that we had been hit by some large object, like a meteorite, which had penetrated the deck, causing extensive damage and plunging the ship into darkness below ... Pushing my way through men crowding the upper deck, I was confronted by an appalling scene of carnage. There was blood and flesh everywhere. There was a hole in the deck and in the side below the water-line, large enough to take two jeeps. To my enormous relief, and greater surprise, the regulating petty officer reported one casualty only. The gory mess that I had seen was, in fact, from the beef screen which had been filled to capacity before the ship left Cyprus.

The missile (whatever it was) had bounced twice on deck, entered the screen, scattered the carcasses, and penetrated the gearing room before tearing its way through the ship below the water-line. Analysis of the missile was made. It was clearly a large glider-bomb of ten-foot wingspan, the nose fuse of which must have been knocked off when it pancaked on deck. The parts, recovered intact, were carefully packed into two sacks, and transferred to *Petard* [an accompanying destroyer] for passage to Alexandria. Later, we heard that they were immediately flown to England, where the mechanism was re-assembled, and an effective counter-measure to this new weapon quickly designed. Later still, we were thanked by the Admiralty for the part we had played!

The damaged destroyer was towed into Turkish waters by HMS *Petard* for temporary repairs before being towed back to Alexandria by another destroyer. HMS *Rockwood* was truly lucky. At 20:00 that evening, the minesweeper *BYMS 72* was also struck by an Hs 293 that toppled her mast and damaged her steering and port Oerlikon. With three of her crew lost and five wounded, the minesweeper nevertheless limped in to Alinda Bay, Leros. Lt Adrian Seligman RNR, at the seaplane base, also witnessed this attack:

From Navy House we had a clear view down the bay and out to sea. One night we saw a glider-bomb, easily recognisable by its red tail-light, pouncing on the BYMS passing the entrance to the bay. "Pounce" is the best description of the way the bomb came cruising along and then suddenly tipped up and fell upon its wretched victim. The funnel and deck clutter took the full force of the explosion, thus saving the lives of the people in the great palace of the wheelhouse further forward.'[50]

Two nights later, HMS *Dulverton* was hit and disabled by another Hs 293. Struck abreast of the bridge, three officers and seventy-five ratings were lost. Six officers and 114 ratings were evacuated from the ship before she was scuttled by HMS *Belvoir*.

The British took this latest air threat seriously and sent 680 Squadron's recce Spitfires to locate the Do 217's airfield, which they did. A force of US B-25s was despatched to Kalamaki on the night on 15 November and effectively wiped out 5./KG100. Two Dorniers were totally destroyed, two seriously damaged and four rendered operationally unserviceable. The raid was repeated two nights later with further damage being inflicted.

The German operation to capture Leros (Operation *Leopard*) was initially scheduled for 9 October, but RN ships intercepted and destroyed the German convoy headed for Kos. In addition to the loss of 700 troops, the Germans also lost most of their heavy landing craft which were in short supply. They were forced to bring in new craft via rail from Germany and it was not until 5 November that they had assembled a fleet of twenty-four light landing infantry craft. To avoid destruction by the Allies, they were camouflaged and dispersed among several of the Aegean Islands until required. The move to take Leros (now codenamed Operation *Taifun*) under the command of Generalltn Friedrich-Wilhelm Müller was rescheduled for 12 November.

In the early hours of 12 November, the Leros invasion force approached from both east and west, and amphibious forces soon established a beachhead while paratroops descended around Mount Rachi in the centre of the island. The invasion force included paratrooper veterans of the 22nd Infantry Division and from the Brandenburger special operations units (similar to the British SBS). To defend the island were over 3,200 British troops drawn from 2/The Royal Irish Fusiliers, the 4/Buffs, the 1/Lancaster and 2/West Kents. There was also an Italian garrison comprising 8,500 regulars, mainly naval personnel, under the command of Admiral Luigi Mascherpa. The Buffs' war diary revealed:

> It was about 04:30 when the light was beginning to grow in the east, that the German invasion fleet was sighted. The Italian coastal guns were powerless to prevent the German troops from being put ashore in Palma Bay and near Pasta di Sopra on the north-east coast of the Buffs' sector, also in Tangeli Bay near Leros town. This last landing was staunchly resisted by the Royal Irish Fusiliers, but although they prevented the capture of the two features of Castle Hill and Mount Appetici, they were not strong enough to drive the enemy back into the sea.

The Buffs had insufficient troops to cover the whole of their area and during the morning the Germans secured a footing on Mount Clidi. Ju 87s of I/StG.3 now entered the fray, as witnessed by Marsland Gander, a war correspondent for the *Daily Telegraph*, who had just arrived on the island:

> I scoured the sky and saw four specks resolve themselves into Stukas, our first aerial visitors of the day. The Italian coastal batteries now opened up in earnest, their shells churning up the sea all round the invasion craft … Just as the Stukas approached nearer, the AA defences of the island began to join the chorus plastering the sky with expanding black and white blobs. The Stukas, in no way inconvenienced by the AA fire, cruised round and round overhead,

seemingly in no hurry. I conjectured that the Hun intended to use them as flying artillery, sending them over in constant relays and waiting for signals from the ground before bombing. It was a furious reflection that the Stuka dive-bomber was regarded in the RAF as obsolete. Yet here, because of the lack of fighter opposition, the enemy was preparing to use them again.[51]

But not everything went according to plan, at least not for the Brandenburgers' *Küstenjäger* (coastal forces):

Above the *Jäger* groups, a liaison aircraft circled slowly the air link. A succession of flares requesting dive-bomber support went up. Within minutes, the air link had directed the Stukas to the target. However, the aircrafts' pilots mistook the target, and unleashed their bombs on the men in the rocks. Red flares rose into the sky; urgent and demanding, they cancelled the next assault. Air link established the correct target and then redirected the Stukas. Bombs crashed down with deafening explosions, marching forward in a moving barrage. The *Jägers* rose up out of the rocks and advanced behind the bomb line; a small group of men marching towards a very large mountain.

That first assault was unsuccessful. The *Küstenjägers* were unable to take the objective as they were pinned down by fire from the fusiliers' machine-gun and mortar positions. The *Jägers* lay under the British fire. It was a punishing and destructive fire which raked them. All the Brandenburger officers were killed or wounded. In an effort to revitalise the attack the Stukas were recalled, but again they mistook the target and their missiles hit the German troops. Shattered by this costly error, the *Küstenjäger* detachments pulled back under fire and then regrouped.[52]

At about 14:00, Bf 110s swept over the island from the south-west. They strafed and pounded the rugged slopes with high explosive bombs. Behind them flew a stream of Ju 52s and from these some 500 parachutists descended on the neck of land between Gurna and Alinda Bays.

As the troop-carrying aircraft drew nearer to the island, they changed formation from shallow vics to files of 12 machines in line astern, and then climbed to an altitude of 400 feet. Even at this height, they were flying below the anti-aircraft guns sited on the mountain peaks and were quickly enveloped in a devastating barrage of flak. The crashing explosions of anti-aircraft shells rocked the slow-flying Ju 52s, and streams of machine-gun tracer struck their wings and fuselages. But the aircraft held their rigid formation; a straight and level course was essential to the success of the drop. Smoke poured from some aircraft but they continued on the correct heading. It was only seconds from the jump off time.

The landing zone chosen by [Hptm Martin] Kühne, the commander of the airborne assault group, was a small strip of ground between the Gurna and Alinda Bays which offered, tactically, the best chance of splitting the island's defenders. However, it was little more than half-a-mile wide, and Kühne did not know that the area was defended by the 2nd Battalion, the Royal Irish Fusiliers, one of the three battalions of British infantry forming the island's garrison. The paratroopers dropped from an altitude of 450 feet: sufficient height for the parachute canopies to open safely, but a height that kept the descent time to a minimum. The sudden billowing of hundreds of parachutes over the British positions brought the infantry into action. But, before their fire could have any effect, the Germans were on the ground and taking cover on the rocky, scrub covered lower slopes of Mount Germano. The paras did not stop to dig in; mobility and firepower were the keys to success. Along the drop line between Mount Germano and the Rachi Ridge, whistles and flares were used to gather the scattered groups. Before long, a potent fighting force had been gathered.[53]

A few German parachutists were shot by small-arms fire, but in spite of a stiff breeze, the majority dropped successfully from a low height. Marsland Gander reported:

Roaring towards me at what seemed eye-level were two twin-engined aircraft spouting fire from their machine-guns. Afterwards I also learnt that they were scattering anti-personnel bombs, but none fell near me. I flattened against the protecting earth while bullets sang overhead. Then greatly relieved to find myself unhurt, bolted back in the tunnel.

To the east the squadron of five Me 110s which the Germans had used to make the garrison duck their heads were now bound for home. Twelve or fifteen Ju 52s were flying at a height of about 500 feet in line astern across the island's narrow waist between Alinda and Gurna Bays. As I watched fascinated something white appeared under the fuselage of the leading machine. It bellied out into a great mushroom beneath which the dark figure of the parachutist looked absurdly small and helpless. Then came another and another, fifteen altogether, mostly with grey parachutes. The first man, who was probably group leader, had touched ground before the machine-gunners on the sides of Meraviglia had recovered from the paralysing shock of surprise. Then began a wild outburst of firing from the ground till the air was criss-crossed with red tracer dashes spurting from many directions.[54]

Despite the barrage of fire directed at the troop carriers only one Ju 52, G6+CH/6763 of 2./TG4, was shot down from which there was only one survivor. As in the case of Kos, the absence of air opposition made it possible for bombers and Ju 87s to operate uninterruptedly over Leros by day with only a few Bf 109s and Mc.202s required to provide cover. In this way, the bombers were able to remain over the target areas and make more than one bombing run.

The Germans quickly succeeded in dividing the island. The British sent an urgent appeal for reinforcement from Samos, but none were forthcoming due to lack of suitable craft in which to transport them. More German troops landed by sea at dawn on 13 November, but not without loss as Marsland Gander wrote:

> Again our machine-guns chattered away furiously. Bofors guns joined in, and one of the troop carriers, hit fair and square, went flaming down into Alinda Bay, a horrifying spectacle, with one solitary parachute visible dragging behind it, the doll-like figure still attached. Another Ju 52, flying lower and lower in distress dropped all its paras into the water where the silken chutes lingered for a short time like lilies.
>
> Some, whose parachutes were evidently damp or packed in a hurry, fell to their death with a roman-candle of silk streaming tautly above them… Some reached the ground alive only to be dragged over rocks and four-foot walls, unable to twist the release catch of their harness. Some fell in the sea and their drowned bodies floated for hours with the canopy of a parachute for a winding sheet. Once again, however, it seems certain that a large number of the paratroopers did land safely, and went to reinforce their comrades.[55]

The decision to send the Ju 52s over in line astern proved unwise, the guns being able to concentrate on individual aircraft and three fell to ground fire. Two aircraft of II/TG4 fell into the sea, four crew being rescued from a Ju 52 including one who was wounded. The fate of the paratroopers is unknown. However, seven paratroopers onboard G6+FP were lost though Fw Günther Voight and three of his six Staffel crew survived including the air gunner Uffz Andreas Hutter:

> Flight control told us that the intended drop-off point (past Alinda Bay) had already been taken by German soldiers. Therefore we flew over Alinda Bay. In doing so, the first plane was hit and went down burning into the sea. Our machine was shot at too and badly damaged and as a result the radio message ordering the paratroopers to go was not released so they didn't jump. Due to heavy damage, our machine had to make an emergency landing in the sea about 2km from the coast at Palma [Vagia] Bay.
>
> The twelve paratroopers were still in the plane and unfortunately had no lifejackets as they were wearing their parachutes. The plane sank very quickly. Out of the five crew, four managed to get out together with several

paratroopers. One crew member died [the flight engineer, who had been fatally wounded] while still in the plane. We lost each other due to heavy seas … I tried to inflate the rubber dinghy but couldn't as it had been completely riddled with bullets and therefore I was unable to help the paratroopers. I had to save myself by swimming for about two to three hours (although I had a life jacket I was also wearing full uniform and shoes!) and only just managed to reach the coast where Italian soldiers captured me and handed me over to the English.[56]

Fw Voight and the other two members of his crew also swam to safety and were rescued by German troops. 4V+BT/7607 of II/TG2 was also shot down and crashed on the north shore of Alinda Bay, killing two, while 4046 was hit and damaged with one crewman killed. The pilot managed to safely carry out an emergency landing back at Athens, though the aircraft was written off. A landing barge carrying ammunition nosed into Alinda Bay under the impression that British troops had been cleared from the area to be met by a fusillade of gunfire that blew the craft out of the water. Later, an Ar 196 (0224) of 4./126 alighted in the bay and met a similar fate:

One seaplane came boldly down into Alinda Bay and attempted to alight as if the island was already in German hands. It met such a torrent of fire that it sank immediately.

A second Ar 196 (D1+EH/0341) from the same unit was shot down and ditched. Both crews survived. There ensued much bitter fighting with fortunes fluctuating. On the night of 15/16 November, a constant stream of Dakotas of 216 Squadron dropped supplies over the island and were possibly aided by Halifaxes and Liberators from 178 Squadron, but it is believed many of the supplies fell amongst German troops. The defenders surrendered on 16 November, Dakotas returning with supplies that very night, the crews unaware of the surrender. One Dakota, FD790, was obliged to ditch off the Turkish coast, its crew being rescued and interned.

A few managed to escape, others including war correspondent Marsland Gander were evacuated, but some 3,200 British troops were captured together with 5,350 Italians. Admiral Luigi Mascherpa was among the Italian officers captured and was later executed by the Germans. The Germans suffered 520 fatalities, the British 187, the Italians 164, and there were twenty civilian deaths. As soon as resistance ceased on Leros, the Germans turned their attention to Samos, and on 17 November, about seventy-five sorties were made against the island, principally on the ports. Fortunately, the Greek Sacred Squadron had been evacuated during the previous night by two destroyers. However, no further attacks were made and Samos was occupied on 22 November. With the smaller islands of Patmos, Fournoi and Ikaria having fallen on 18 November, the Germans thus completed their conquest of the Dodecanese. The official British despatch covering these failed operations remarked that:

> We failed because we were unable to establish airfields in the area of operations ... The enemy's command of the air enabled him so to limit the operations and impair the efficiency of land, sea and air forces that by picking his time he could deploy his comparatively small forces with decisive results. Had more aircraft been available, especially modern long-range fighters, and given more luck, the operations might have been prolonged, but after the loss of Kos, if the enemy were prepared to divert the necessary effort, it is doubtful if Leros could have been held indefinitely without our embarking on a major operation for which no forces were available.

Churchill, in his cable to Foreign Minister Eden, commented with his usual brilliance, analysis and eloquence:

> Leros is a bitter blow to me. Should it be raised in Parliament, I recommend the following line:
>
> One may ask, should such an operation ever have been undertaken without the assurance of air superiority? Have we not failed to learn the lessons of Crete, etc? Have we not restored the Stukas to a fleeting moment of their old triumphs? The answer is that these are very proper questions to ask, but it would not be advisable to answer them in detail. All that can be said at the moment is that there is none of these arguments which was not foreseen before the occupation of these islands was attempted, and if they were disregarded it was because other reasons and other hopes were held to predominate over them. If we are never going to proceed on anything but certainties we must certainly face the prospect of a prolonged war.
>
> No attempts should be made to minimise the poignancy of the loss of the Dodecanese, which we had a chance of getting so easily and at so little cost and which we have now lost after heavy expenditure. You should also stress the tremendous effort made by the Germans, their withdrawal of almost half their air force from Italy, where they were already outmatched, and the assistance given to our troops thereby.[57]

CHAPTER VII

Beaufighters in Support of Leros Operations – November 1943

At the beginning of November, landing craft and escorts had been observed assembling in the Piraeus but it was uncertain whether Samos or Leros was to be the German's objective. Samos had been subjected to a series of heavy air raids that suggested it was to be the target for the assault. PR Spitfires revealed nine landing craft and two escort vessels moving eastwards on 4 November, and a further four landing-craft at Kos. Every effort was made to intercept the force.

On the morning of 4 November, Baltimores had located the four small landing craft in Kos harbour and four Beaufighters were despatched to attack these. All four were claimed damaged by cannon fire. 5 November proved a costly one for the Beaufighters. Six Beaufighters of 227 Squadron took-off from Lakatamia (Cyprus) at 07:30 for a sweep around Rhodes. Flg Off. Dick Hutchison RCAF/Sgt Leslie Sawle (EL301/Y) were obliged to return early. At 09:30, four Bf 109s were sighted approaching on a southerly course at 2,000 feet. The Beaufighters turned east and opened throttles, taking violent evasive action. The Bf 109s on sighting the Beaufighters jettisoned their long-range tanks and turned into attack. The result was disastrous and only JP908/P crewed by Plt Off. Gibbard RCAF/Sgt B. H. L. Blake returned. They reported:

JL900/S (Flt Lt John Tremlett/Flt Sgt Bob Jobling) attacked and its port engine caught fire. It was seen to ditch but then a cloud of black smoke arose from the position. EL478/F (Flt Sgt John Swift/Flt Sgt George Austin) was attacked several times and was last seen with its fuselage on fire. A large splash was seen as the aircraft hit the water. JL939/G (Flg Off Bill Yurchison RCAF/ Flg Off Percy Wroath) was also attacked several times and crashed into the sea; a blaze and pall of smoke observed as it hit the sea. JM276/C (Flg Off Paul Mazur RCAF/ Flg Off Ken Stakes) was last seen heading south, still being chased. There were no survivors from the four aircraft.[58]

Gibbard's aircraft was attacked twice but not hit. The victorious German pilots were Fw Alfred Stückler (an ace), Obfw Alexander Ottnad, Uffz Friedrich Ullrich and Gfr Heinrich Pothmann, all of 8./JG27. At 18:55, Flt Lt Bill Kemp RNZAF (JM268/N) took-off to search for the missing crews. Various lights were observed but no signs of downed aircraft or crews. He returned at 22:45.

During the early afternoon at 13:45, three 'Torbeaus' of 47 Squadron led by Wg Cdr Jimmy Lee-Evans, escorted by five more including two from 603 Squadron, made an attack on shipping in Lavrion Bay where one large and two small merchant vessels were found. A torpedo attack was carried out but results were unobserved, although an escorting crew reported seeing a column of black smoke rising from the direction of the attack. Two of the 'Torbeaus' were shot down by intense and accurate flak and both ditched including the leader in 47/D, but all four crewmembers were rescued and became POWs (Wg Cdr Lee-Evans/Flt Lt David Heden and 47/B Flt Lt Tom Graham/Flg Off. John Langdon). Four Beaufighters strafed caiques, two tugs and a barge in Siphnos harbour. One tug was damaged and left smoking and all other vessels were hit with cannon fire.

On 6 November, eight Beaufighters – four each of 47 and 603 Squadrons – attacked shipping in Port Noussa (Paros) which had been reported by a Baltimore on reconnaissance. They found two large barges, two naval auxiliary vessels, one E-boat and three caiques. The caiques and barges were attacked and set on fire. The Beaufighters were then attacked by at least six Ar 196s and five Bf 109s while the flak encountered was intense and accurate. As a result, 47 Squadron's new CO Sqn Ldr Charles Ogilvie was shot down by a Bf 109 in JM352/R; he and his navigator Flg Off. Mike O'Connor managed to escape captivity and returned the following month. However, Flg Off. Lewis Rossner and Sgt Henry Levy were both killed when JM403/F crashed in flames into a hillside near Naussa Bay, the two Beaufighters the victims of Uffz Karl Höchtl and Uffz Paul Martin of 7./JG27. 603's Beaufighters meanwhile tangled with the Arados, one being claimed shot down jointly by Plt Off. Keith Hopkins RAAF and Plt Off. Reuben Giles, but Hopkins' aircraft (LX998/Y) was forced to ditch. He and his navigator W/O Keith Roget RAAF were fortunate to be picked up by a submarine and taken to Malta, returning to the squadron a week later. The commander of the submarine had seen the airmen take to their dinghy and waited until dusk to rescue them. Hopkins later told the press: 'I could not have been more surprised if Hitler came down the chimney dressed as Santa Claus.' One 603 Beaufighter (LX985/M) force-landed at Gambut after its pilot, Flt Sgt T. Truesdale, had been slightly wounded. During a separate patrol by two of 227 and four of 46, a Z.506B was sighted but fired the correct colours of the day so was left alone. It was presumably a Co-Belligerent machine.

On 7 November, two Beaufighters of 227 Squadron and two of 252 Squadron on convoy protection encountered a Ju 88 that was claimed probably destroyed by Flg Off. Burgie Beare RCAF (JL619/X). The bomber was sighted about eight miles north of the convoy orbiting at sea level. It flew north-westwards on sighting the Beaufighter and turned to starboard as Beare closed in, initially overshooting. On regaining position, Beare opened fire and saw strikes on its port engine, which later caught fire, wing and fuselage, but his cannons then jammed. When last seen the Ju 88 was at 2,000 feet, steadily losing height and its port engine pouring black smoke.

8 November proved to be more successful and less costly following an attack by a dozen Beaufighters, three carrying torpedoes, against a convoy of four merchant ships, fifteen barges and some F-lighters and E-boats sighted west of Kos. 47 Squadron's Sgt Bob Milne recalled:

> Six Beaufighters of 47 Sqn and six of 603 Sqn were despatched to attack an enemy convoy west of Kos. Three of 47 Sqn carried torpedoes. The crews, of which I was one, were certainly rather fearful that they would be shot down. We were expecting to lose some, if not all, of our Torbeaus. I remember the ground staff waving us off – waving goodbye! On reaching the target area we encountered a terrible storm, at times the waves seemed higher than the plane and it was the first time I had seen St Elmo's Fire. Then suddenly as we were coming out of the storm we sighted the ships. We attacked and a hit was seen on the leading ship. An Arado was shot down. Clearly they were not expecting Beaufighters to come from out of a storm at sea. In the event all the Beaufighters returned to base.[59]

The Arado, D1+IN of 4./126 flown by Uffz Walter Napierski, fell to the single Vickers gun of Flt Sgt Len Coulstock in Plt Off. Rueben Giles' 603 Squadron aircraft (LZ148/H). The Arado pilot was wounded and his gunner Uffz Walter Kleinknecht killed. Although no Bf 109s were encountered nor Beaufighters lost, Oblt Emil Clade of 7./JG27 nevertheless claimed one shot down about seven miles south of Syphonos from 1,000 feet.

The action continued into the next day (9 November) when four Beaufighters escorted a single 'Torbeau' on a shipping strike north-east of Amorgos. Ten landing craft and two schooners, all stationary, were sighted. Numerous Bf 109s, Ju 88s and Arados were seen patrolling the area. The torpedo was jettisoned and the strike abandoned. The Beaufighters were chased for twenty-five minutes by Ju 88s but managed to return to base undamaged. On the same day, six Beaufighters, two from 252 Squadron carrying torpedoes, made an offensive sweep south-west of Kos. An attack was made on a medium-size vessel found off the south-west coast of the island, but without success although some cannon hits were made. One of the two Arados which were protecting the vessel was shot down and the other damaged by the escorting 603 Squadron Beaufighters. The German vessel fired rockets at the Beaufighters but without effect. Plt Off. Wally Eacott (with Plt Off. Bob Pritchard in LX977/Z) accounted for both Arados:

> We escorted Beaufighters from a sister squadron, 252, armed with torpedoes, into the Aegean Sea area, once more. Some long way north of Crete, we met a convoy of small armed vessels (gunboats, corvettes) escorting some supply ships and barges. Overhead were two Arado 196 seaplanes doing their escort duty. Arados were versatile armoured aircraft, suitable for fighter escort and for rescue work. We swept in from sea level, and while the 252 Squadron aircraft attacked the shipping with their torpedoes, we took care of the escort.
>
> I saw an Arado diving down on me, from above and straight ahead, guns firing, and instinctively, I rose up to meet him. With my four cannons and six machine-guns all firing, the poor chap hadn't much chance. I think it was a case of who was to be the chicken, as we flew straight towards each other. He pulled back the stick, and cleared the top of my aircraft, but then immediately dived down on to the water, where he crash-landed. Another pilot told me afterwards that he had seen the observer's body hanging over the side of the aircraft, as he was attempting to get out. The pilot was also killed.
>
> I immediately flew off after the second Arado, which turned tail and fled. I fired several times at it, and saw smoke pouring from it, with pieces flying off the wings and fuselage before I left it, heading down towards the sea. Little did I know that my scrap with the Huns would prove my Nemesis! When we arrived back at base, my beloved Z for Zombie was damaged somewhat. Among other things, an aileron wire had been severed, clean shot through, and I hadn't full wing control.

Eacott's first victim was CT+KI/0429 of 2./125 in which Obfw Adolf Santowski and Ltn Konrad Schulze were lost. The second Arado was 7R+?K/0332 that Obfw Werner Kurth managed to alight on the sea without further damage. Bf 109s of 8 and 9./JG27 were active again on 10 November, two of 8 Staffel reporting a combat with a Beaufighter during the late morning:

> At around 11:00 hours, two Bf 109s of 8./JG27 were detailed to escort a transport ship in the Aegean when they encountered a lone twin-engined aircraft, which they identified as a Beaufighter. After a prolonged chase that lasted from south-east of Kos almost up to Kassos, the aircraft was claimed shot down at 11:15 by Gfr Gerhard Albert. However, Albert's aircraft was hit

by return fire, forcing him to ditch east of Crete. Two Ar196s were sent out for search and rescue but failed to find him.[60]

In fact, the aircraft engaged was a Baltimore of 454RAAFSquadron in which Flt Sgt John Joner and his crew were lost. Four 'Torbeaus' of 47 Squadron took-off just after midday to attack shipping and barges in the Amorgos-Leros area. Escort was provided by nine Beaufighters of 603 Squadron led by Sqn Ldr Barry Atkinson. Again, Bf 109s appeared as 47 Squadron reported:

1431: Attacked by 2 Me 109s. Formation opened up stragglers on port and starboard. Messerschmitts dropped long-range fuel tanks. 15 minutes later one Beaufighter shot into sea. Second Beaufighter starboard engine on fire, heading east. Also ditched.

The Beaufighters fell to Obfw Fritz Gromotka (his fifteenth victory) of 9./JG27 and Gfr Heinrich Pothmann of 8./JG27. Sgt Bob Milne of 47 Squadron was under the impression that the Messerschmitts had taken-off from Kos:

We were briefed to attack shipping off Kalymnos and Kos but interception from fighters on Kos prevented us from locating the target as we were attacked by Me 109s for 22 minutes.

Flg Off. John Hayden and Sgt J. McMaster were the crew of the 47 Squadron Beaufighter (LZ148/H) forced to ditch, but only McMaster survived to be rescued. Plt Off. Wally Eacott and his navigator Plt Off. Bob Pritchard were the crew of 603 Squadron's LZ275 as Eacott recalled:

I was given a brand new aircraft, just delivered to the Squadron, and there hadn't been time even to paint the aircraft identification letters on the fuselage. We flew out in the same general direction of Kos, Leros and Scarpanto, looking for enemy shipping. Suddenly, a full flight of us was attacked by half-a-dozen Me 109s. Not in true British style, but obeying standing orders implicitly, we turned tail and ran.

Beaufighters were really no good against single-engined Me 109s. We were no match for that kind of aggression. Alas and alack, I discovered that the brand-new aircraft I had taken out was alarmingly slow. Whilst the rest of the flight drew rapidly ahead of me, I dropped back just as rapidly (obviously) and became a true tail-arse Charlie. I banged desperately on the throttles, hoping to get past some imaginary stoppage and put about 50 knots extra airspeed on the cow, but destiny loomed. The Me 109s took it in turn to sit on my tail, and use me for target practice. At 20 feet over the wave tops, I jinked and jinked. "Tell me when they're lining up, Bob", I called to my observer, who was cursing in the back seat, and firing vainly with his Vickers 'pop-gun' when the occasion presented itself. He dutifully told me when the time came. Meanwhile, I flew straight and level at best top speed. As soon as the next attack came, I jinked and jinked once more.

What seemed like an age passed. I think it was all of ten minutes. A couple of the enemy planes ran out of ammo. Eventually, thick smoke filled the cockpit. I saw flames licking over the whole of the starboard wing. I throttled back on that side, found the fire extinguisher button, and pressed hard. It made no difference. We flew on, and still continued burning. Eyes smarting, unable to see ahead properly, I gave the observer the emergency message, "Dinghy, dinghy, prepare for ditching." I throttled back the port engine, and pancaked on the sea, which was fortunately reasonably calm.

The Beau was reputed to float for only five seconds. We had had lots of dry runs in the hangar, and in the desert, practising that urgent exit from the cockpit, onto the port wing, pulling the toggle to release the dinghy, and hopping over the side of the wing into the yellow lifesaver. True to life's experience, this one didn't work quite the same. No sooner had we stopped our forward motion on the water, than the kite stuck down its nose, and plunged deep beneath the waves. I threw back the top of the canopy, and attempted to rise from my seat. Horror! I couldn't move. I tried again. It grew dark around me, so swift was our descent into Neptune's grave. I tried a third time. O Foolish Youth! I remembered this time to pull the pin from my seat strap. Out I popped like a cork from a champagne bottle. Quickly the light returned, and my head broke the surface of the sea. (See Appendix II)

An hour later, two more Beaufighters of 47, plus eight of 603, set off to repeat the strafe of the ships and barges in the Amorgos-Leros area. One crew reported that a ship fired two rockets simultaneously with a low trajectory to 1,000 feet and leaving a white trail. They did not explode and were considered very inaccurate. Flt Sgt Ted Daden of 47 Squadron (47/S) saw an Ar 196 on the water at which he fired and reported that when last seen it was tail down in the sea. A sweep by Beaufighters and B-25Gs during the morning of 11 November failed to locate the Leros invasion force or other shipping targets and a further Beaufighter strike force saw only two Bf 109s circling over Leros.

In the afternoon of 12 November, another strike force comprising two 'Torbeaus' of 47 Squadron and three B-25Gs escorted by six Beaufighters of 603 Squadron were sent to search for a convoy reported north-west of Crete. Here they found two merchant vessels with an escort of five E-boats and Ar 196s overhead. Although both torpedoes were launched, no tangible results were observed. However, the Americans claimed both

Clockwise from top left: W/O Sotirios Skantzikas of 336 Squadron was shot down during Operation *Thesis* on 23 July 1943. Although he survived a crash-landing and was captured, Skantzikas was executed on 30 March 1944 following 'The Great Escape'.

Trinidadian Flt Sgt Fernand 'Fanny' Farfan of 123 Squadron was luckier. He also survived a crash-landing on 23 July 1943, but was rescued by partisans and spirited back to Egypt by the SOE.

Greek pilot Wt Off. Konstantinos Kokkas of 336 Squadron returned safely from Operation *Thesis*.

Capt. Harold Kirby of 7SAAF Squadron had a lucky escape when his Hurricane clipped a high-tension cable, returning with a piece of the wire entangled around his propeller (seen in his hand).

Hurricane KZ480/Z of 336 Squadron was shot down during a raid on Crete on 14 November 1943. Flt Sgt George Mademlis was taken prisoner.

Left: Major Corrie van Vliet DFC commanded 7SAAF Spitfires at Kos.

Below: Sqn Ldr Spud Hayter DFC RNZAF (fourth from left) took 74 Squadron Spitfires to Kos as reinforcements on 28 September 1943. The others depicted are (L to R) Guy de Pass, the Squadron MO Doc Ferris, David Maxwell, Willie Wilson, Trevor Bates, Brian Harris, Andy Anderson (lost en route), John Lewis and Speed Norman (kneeling).

Above: Lt Ray Burl and Lt Pik van Deventer of 7SAAF at Kos.

Below: Spitfires being cannibalised at Kos.

YEAR 1943 Month / Date	AIRCRAFT Type	No.	PILOT, OR 1ST PILOT	2ND PILOT, PUPIL OR PASSENGER	DUTY (INCLUDING RESULTS AND REMARKS)
—	—	—	—	—	Totals Brought Forward
SEPTEMBER 1	SPITFIRE V	466	SELF	SOLO	ST. JEAN - GAMIL
" 4	"	466	SELF	SOLO	SCRAMBLE
" 5	"	859	SELF	SOLO	SEA SEARCH
" 9	"	133	SELF	SOLO	GAMIL - ABU SWIER
" 9	"	133	SELF	SOLO	ABU SWIER - LG X
" 9	"	786	SELF	SOLO	KILO 40 - GAMIL
" 10	"	654	SELF	SOLO	GAMIL - ROIR
" 10	"	654	SELF	SOLO	ROIR - GAMIL
" 11	"	466	SELF	SOLO	GAMIL - ST JEAN
" 11	"	466	SELF	SOLO	ST JEAN - NICOSIA
" 14	"	466	SELF	SOLO	NICOSIA - ANTIMACHIA (KOS)
" 16	"	466	SELF	SOLO	PROTECTIVE PATROL
" 16	"	466	SELF	SOLO	SCRAMBLE
" 19	"	466	SELF	SOLO	PROTECTIVE PATROL
" 21	"	466	SELF	SOLO	PATROL
" 22	"	466	SELF	SOLO	PATROL
" 23	BEAUFIGHTER	466	S/L LEE	SELF	KOS - NICOSIA
" 24	"	466	F/O BEASLEY	SELF	NICOSIA - HELIOPOLIS
				SUMMARY. 1-9-43 TO 30-9-43	SPITFIRE
				DATE. 2-10-43	TOTAL SPIT
				UNIT. 7 SQDN. S.A.A.F.	BEAUFIGHTE
				SIGNATURE. H Kirby, Capt.	

GRAND TOTAL [Cols. (1) to (10)]
994 Hrs. 25 Mins.

Totals Carried Forward

Pages from Capt. Harold Kirby's logbook recording his victory over a Bf 109 on 21 September 1943, probably Obfw Wilhelm Morgenstern (White 1) of 10./JG27.

Hours	SINGLE-ENGINE AIRCRAFT				MULTI-ENGINE AIRCRAFT							PASSENGER	INSTR/CLOUD FLYING [Incls in cols. (1) to (10)]	
	DAY Dual (1)	DAY Pilot (2)	NIGHT Dual (3)	NIGHT Pilot (4)	DAY Dual (5)	DAY 1st Pilot (6)	DAY 2nd Pilot (7)	NIGHT Dual (8)	NIGHT 1st Pilot (9)	NIGHT 2nd Pilot (10)		(11)	Dual (12)	Pilot (13)
	82·25	769·25	7·00	45·25	—	—	2·65	—	—	—		11·10	17·30	·50
		1·45												
		1·15	OP	44.							KOS LOST THROUGH TREACHERY.			
		1·15									KILIS (Turkey), Friday. — A refugee who has arrived in Turkey from the island of Kos said that an Italian traitor made possible the German occupation of the island. He said a fanatically Fascist officer escaped to Rhodes after the British occupation and gave the Germans details of the British approach and landing signals for aircraft. The Germans were thus able to land a considerable force at the main airport, which they conquered, and afterwards it was easy to bring in constant reinforcements and overpower other vital points. — Sapa.			
		·25												
		·15												
		·40												
		1·00												
		6·00												
		1·25												
		1·15												
		2·10	OP	45							Escorting Beaufighter to Kos. 3 last formation of Spits			
		1·15	OP	46							Covering D.C. 3's.			
		1·10	OP	47							Red Taylor & Chapman got an 88 Ju.			
		1·15	OP	48							I got a 109 E. Shot it into the sea near Salino. Alan had it.			
		·45	OP	49										
		1·00	OP	50.							Standing patrol			
		—									Posted R.T.U.	2·00		
												2·15		
		17·45												
		23·35												
	Pass 4·15													
	82·25	787·10	7·00	115·25	—	—	2·65	—	—	—		15·25	17·30	·50

Above left: Obfw Fritz Gromotka of 9./JG27 claimed three Spitfires of 7SAAF over Kos.

Above right: Major Ernst Düllberg, Gruppenkdr of IV/JG27, shot down a Spitfire and a Walrus during the fighting over Kos.

Below left: Lt Ray Burl following his escape from Kos. He was awarded a DFC.

Below right: Lt Cecil Golding of 1SAAF Squadron flew patrols from Cyprus during the evacuation of Kos.

German photographs showing Spitfires and a CR42 of 396ªSquadriglia captured at Kos.

Above: Modified Spitfire BR114/B of 103 MU.

Right: 103 MU test pilots, Flg Off. George Reynolds AFC, Plt Off. Eric Genders DFM and Plt Off. Arthur Gold AFC.

Below: Another of the modified Spitfires, stripped and polished to increase performance.

Above: The main adversary, one of the Ju 86R high-flyers of 2.(F)/123, pictured at Kastelli, Crete.

Left: Australian pilots Flg Off. Harry Freckelton (left) and Flg Off. Hal Rowlands in front of BS342 of 103 MU. They were instrumental in shooting down Ju 86R 4U+IK of 2.(F)/123 flown by Ltn Franz Stock on 2 July 1943.

Below: Hptm. Helmut Rammig's Ju 86R (865144) of 2.(F)/123 having ditched in the Mediterranean following 'engine problems' (possibly caused by Plt Off. Eric Genders of 103 MU) on 29 August 1942. The crew of two was rescued by a Do 24 of Seenotstfl.7.

A bomb-armed Seafire getting airborne from a carrier for another Aegean sortie.

800 Squadron with its Hellcats onboard HMS *Emperor* played a major role in the Aegean. Pictured taking-off is JV102.

Above: Ju 88 4U+?K of 2.(F)/123 was intercepted and shot down north of Athens by a Seafire flown by Lt(A) David Ogle of 809 Squadron from HMS *Stalker* on 14 October 1944. He photographed the bomber with his oblique camera as he closed to engage.

Left: Six Dutch naval pilots served with 800 Squadron including Sub-Lt(A) Gerardus Greve (pictured here) who shared in shooting down a Ju 52 of 13./TG1 with fellow Dutchman Sub-Lt(A) Herman 'Harm' deWit on 4 October 1944.

A German photograph depicting a Beaufighter attack against the Kos invasion force on 3 October 1943. Believed to be aircraft of 227 Squadron, the German caption stating that one had just been shot down, hence the splash to the right of the target.

Beaufighters attacking a convoy.

Caiques were encountered on the many offensive flights and were unable to withstand the Beaufighters' heavy armament.

Aircrew of 603 Squadron's B Flight at Gambut, March 1944: (L–R) F/L Matthews, S/L Joe Watters RNZAF, W/C Ronnie Lewis, F/L R. L. Oddy, S/L C. D. Pain, F/L Partridge, S/L Pat Pringle and F/O Tony Ross.

603 Squadron commanders mid-1944: CO Wg Cdr Foxley-Norris flanked by S/L C. D. Pain on his right and Flt Lt Tommy Deck DFC on his left.

merchant vessels were set on fire as were two of three E-boats as the result of their 75-mm cannon fire, but LX912/B of 47 Squadron was shot down by flak with the loss of Flg Off. Athol Greentree RNZAF (from Invercargill) and Sgt George Freeman while two Arados were claimed damaged.

Five Beaufighters of 47 Squadron, two B-25Gs and four escorting Beaufighters of 603 Squadron set out at 07:00 on 13 November on what proved to be an uneventful sweep apart from the loss of LX977/Z that reported engine problems and was seen to ditch. Its tail broke off and sank immediately. There was no sign of the Australian crew W/Os Frank Cox and Norman Ferguson. Half-an-hour after the departure of this formation, a second took-off comprising four Beaufighters of 47, two more B-25Gs and five Beaufighters of 603 Squadron to strafe targets of opportunity on Leros. An attack on a gun post was carried out before six Bf 109s of 7./ JG27 appeared. A running fight ensued south-west of Leros and LZ127/ A flown by Flg Off. Edgar Clary Jr, an American (from Wisconsin) in the RCAF, and Sgt Wally Finbow, was seen to ditch about five miles off Stampalia. Apparently it had been shot down by Oblt Emil Clade for his twentieth victory. However, one of the Messerschmitts failed to return and Ltn Schliedermann was lost. Of this intensive period, Sgt Bob Willis of 47 Squadron wrote:

> With the loss of eight crews in 14 days from all operations, the rather drastic step was taken to reinforce 47 Squadron with seven crews from the Torpedo Training School at Shallufa. These reinforcements, led by S/L Stan Muller-Rowland DFC, were a mixture of tour-expired instructors and experienced trainees. Later that same day Muller-Rowland was shot down while leading a formation of seven Beaufighters as it attacked and chased a group of four Ju 88s.

The Beaufighters departed Gambut at 13:40 for a fighter sweep around Leros. When north-west of the island, a dozen Ju 88s in groups of four were sighted. One group was bombing between Alinda and Gunia Bays, and as the Beaufighters approached, the pilots saw one of the bombers fall away with its starboard engine on fire. This had apparently been attacked by Flg Off. Bill Thwaites (with Flg Off. John Lovell in LZ125/W) who had been late in taking-off but had reached Leros before the main formation. Thwaites then witnessed Sqn Ldr Muller-Rowland's aircraft (LX928/D) being shot down by return fire as it closed in on another group of Ju 88s. With its port engine ablaze, the Beaufighter ditched in San Nicola Bay north of the island of Patmos. Muller-Rowland and his navigator Flt Sgt Paddy Anderson were seen to climb into their dinghy. Meanwhile, Flt Lt Lionel Daffurn and his section attacked another Ju 88 and Flg Off. Bill Thwaites reported shooting off a wheel and pieces of the fuselage of a second aircraft he attacked. Sqn Ldr Muller-Rowland (who was slightly wounded by splinters) and Flt Sgt Anderson were picked up by friendly fishermen and eventually reached Turkey from where they were flown back to Shallufa. It seems that the Ju 88s were from 11./ZG26 that lost two aircraft and their crews near Leros: 3U+PV Ltn Hans Murkowski and 3U+JV Uffz Gregor Merva. One if not both probably the victims of Flg Off. Thwaites.

A dozen Beaufighters, eight from 227 and four of 46 Squadron, departed Cyprus during the late morning of 14 November to continue the series of offensive patrols with Sqn Ldr Bill Kemp leading the formation. About ten miles east of Leros, a He 111 was sighted by the 46 Squadron section who gave chase. Flt Lt David Crerar (JL913/E) and his No.2 Flg Off. Bryan Wild (JL898/S) moved in for the kill. Crerar closed in to 100 yards and scored strikes before Wild applied the coup de grâce. Their victim, 6N+EP of II/ KG100 flown by Uffz Walter Pink, ditched in the sea between Leros and the Turkish coast, the crew being rescued although two had been wounded. A few minutes later, six Bf 109s from 8./JG27 were seen approaching from Leros, one pursuing the fleeing 46 Squadron Beaufighters while others orbited the ditched Heinkel. Beaufighter JL894/R was selected for attack by the Grpkmdr Maj. Ernst Düllberg. The crippled machine was seen to climb vertically, roll over and dive into the sea where it exploded on impact. Both W/O Ron Lindsey and Flt Sgt Alf Gardener were killed. The remaining aircraft headed for Turkish airspace but Flg Off. Joe Horsfall RCAF and Flt Sgt James Colley in JM248 also failed to return, the victim of Ofhr Alexander Ottnad of 8 Staffel.

Three B-25Gs attacked two small destroyers with cannon-fire about thirty miles west of Kos on 15 November. Both were hit and one exploded and caught fire. Escorting Beaufighters of 47 and 603 Squadrons meanwhile engaged four Ju 88s and two Ar 196s but failed to gain any successes, nor were there any losses. Another sweep by six Beaufighters of 227 Squadron off Leros was engaged by 'three Mc.202s in German markings' in addition to two Bf 109s, Flt Lt Tommy Deck (LZ133/G) claiming one damaged following his attack. He reported that its undercarriage dropped before it dived to sea level.

First off on the morning of 16 November were six Beaufighters of 603 Squadron but two returned early while the remaining four encountered two Ar 196s, Plt Off. Bruce Megone DFC (LZ239) shooting down one. The other escaped having been damaged by the combined attacks of Sgt Alan Rooks (LZ278), Sgt John Bowen (LZ139) and Flt Sgt Eddie Lynch RAAF (LZ138). Later the same morning, six Beaufighters of 47 Squadron and two from 603 carried out a strike against a Siebel ferry carrying reinforcements to Leros. Sgt Bob Milne wrote:

A Siebel ferry [*SF105*] carrying troops with an escort of two ships and fighter cover was located by reconnaissance west of Kalymnos. It was vital to prevent these forces reaching Leros. 47 Squadron had only five aircraft left, plus an old plane used for training. Only five crews of 47 were available to fly. Sqn Ldr Geoff Powell had left the squadron as his tour expired, but as he happened to be available he was asked to return and lead this strike. Two 603 Beaus were added to the strike force. I flew the training aircraft, E for Edward [with Sgt Larry Lowman as navigator]. On approaching the target area we could see enemy aircraft circling the ships. Four Ju 88s [in fact Bf 110s of 11./ZG26], seven Arados and six Me 109s. We managed to get to the target before the enemy saw us. We attacked with cannon and machine-guns, blowing up the ferry. The Me 109s attacked, chasing us for 23 minutes. Three 47 Squadron Beaufighters were lost … Leros fell that evening.

The only Beaufighter seen to go down by the surviving crews was LZ125/L crewed by Flg Off. Bill Thwaites and Flg Off. John Lovell, but LX923 (Flg Off. John Fletcher/Sgt Jack Dale) also failed to return as did LX883 flown by Flg Off. Tony Bond. However, his navigator Sgt Alf Cottle was the only survivor of the three aircraft lost and was subsequently awarded the MM for his performance, the citation stating:

Sgt Cottle was the navigator of a plane which was shot down near Kalimnos. When the aircraft hit the water he was dragged under the water by the sinking aircraft and had great difficulty in reaching and climbing into the dinghy which was by now some 100 yards away. His right arm was useless owing to a bullet wound. Late on the following night Sgt Cottle was picked up and taken to an Italian Convent Hospital at Kos. He refused to answer any questions put to him by the German interrogating officer. After a few days, he sold his watch, etc and was able to buy civilian clothes. He slipped out of the hospital and was taken to a safe hiding place by some friendly Greeks. Each night he went down to the shore to try and contact a caique and on the night of December 5th he was successful and was taken to the Turkish coast and then transported to a hospital. Sgt Cottle has shown great determination in escaping from the enemy territory, although wounded. It was a very fine achievement and an example to others of courage and initiative.

The three Beaufighters were claimed by Oblt Emil Clade of 7./JG27 (his twenty-first victory), shot down at sea level, Major Ernst Düllberg of StabIII a second (his twenty-third) east of Levita, also at wave-top height, while Ofhr Alexander Ottnad of 8 Staffel got the other, south of Tria Nisia, also at very low level. Two more Beaufighters were claimed by the escorting Bf 110 pilots including one by Obfw Regel of 11./ZG26; the other was credited to an unidentified pilot from the same Staffel. It seems probable that one of their victims was a Ju 88 of 5./KG51, 9K+CN that was lost near Leros with the deaths of Ltn Martin Franke and his crew.

For this attack, Sqn Ldr Powell received an immediate DSO and his navigator Plt Off. Cyril Adams the DFC, while DFMs went to Sgts Vic Borrowdale, George Craven and Bob Milne who added:

> ...and this phase of the Aegean campaign came to an end. 47 Squadron had no serviceable aircraft and not many crews. Summarising, the Aegean/Leros campaign as far as 47 Squadron was concerned lasted 18 days, during which time the 16 crews were reduced to five. All these losses occurred in the 12 days from 5 to 16 November, The squadron recovered quickly with an influx of new crews and planes, together with a new CO.

The new CO, Wg Cdr W. D. L. Filson-Young DFC, took command on 23 November. A former Coastal Command pilot who had flown both Sunderlands and Beaufighters, he soon had 47 Squadron back into fighting shape. Two new flight commanders were posted in, Sqn Ldr L. H. Skinner (affectionately known as 'Porky') and Major A. R. Pears SAAF, while new crews began arriving. Most of the crews came straight from the Torpedo Training School at Shallufa as 47 Squadron reverted to its torpedo-carrying role.

With the surrender of Leros, the remainder of the month was relatively subdued for the Beaufighter units following days of severe action and losses, but offensive patrols continued. On 18 November, three Beaufighter-escorted B-25Gs reported sinking a 140-foot caique.[61] The following day, six Beaufighters of 227 Squadron on a convoy escort intercepted thirteen Ju 88s from II/KG51 which attempted to attack the ships. Flt Lt Tommy Deck (LZ133/G) followed one of the Ju 88s down in its dive and opened fire from astern and above, but without apparent strikes. Following a second attack, he believed his fire had damaged its port engine since the propeller had slowed down. At 17:20, a further seven Ju 88s appeared, or some of the same group making a second attack, and again Flt Lt Deck engaged them, spraying a whole tight-knit formation. One Ju 88 was seen to emit thick black smoke, but intense accurate return fire forced him to break away. It would seem that his victim was Ltn Harro Krollpfiefer's 5 Staffel aircraft that crash-landed whereupon it was destroyed by fire. The pilot and his crew all suffered injuries.

One of the new 47 Squadron crews comprised Sgts Bob Willis and D. P. 'Tommy' Thompson who flew their first sortie on 26 November:

Feeling somewhat apprehensive, in the early morning we took off on our first operational mission, carrying a torpedo, in the company of three other torpedo Beaufighters from the squadron and three B-25 Mitchells of 310th Bombardment Group USAAF. Possibly due to the lack of senior officers on the squadron, the briefing was short and to the point. Any mention that we were new to the squadron together with a few words of advice was noticeable by its absence. If shot down we would soon be forgotten.

A supply ship sailing from Piraeus to Crete was the target. To our disappointment tinged with relief, no sighting was made. The bird had flown, so it was back to base with our torpedo still in place. Even on this uneventful sortie one Beaufighters was lost, having turned back early with engine problems. No sign of the crew, Flg Off Gregory and Flg Off Wood, was ever seen despite a search of the area over the ensuing days. Ultimately they were posted as missing.

The missing pilot of LX987/D was Flg Off. Forrest June Gregory, an American from Kansas, who had joined the RCAF; his navigator Flg Off. Alan Wood hailed from Glasgow. Support of Leros evacuation had cost the Beaufighter units some twenty-one aircraft with twenty-eight aircrew killed, seven POW and two interned in Turkey. Meanwhile, the German air-sea-rescue crews of Seenotstfl.7 were being kept busy. Uffz Karl-Heinz Lüdkte recalled:

Another mission, a life-endangering one, was a transport flight to one of the islands. I think it was Kos [on 25 November]. The harbour was near a small mountain range and we had to lay in the harbour for quite some time awaiting our further orders. When we received them we prepared for departure, all wearing our life vests, thank God for that, as I couldn't swim. Two enemy fighters suddenly appeared from behind the mountain range and in no time were attacking our Do 24 [KK+LC]. Faster than any of us were ever able to think possible we jumped out the back of the aircraft just in time before the bullets struck. We escaped wet but unhurt. The Do 24 wasn't damaged very much as the two pilots decided it was safer to leave after one strike as they were fired upon from the German ground troops. The pilots had to have been informed about our presence, maybe by one of the local people, who knows? After an inspection the Do 24 was found still airworthy and without any enemy contact (we kept a sharp look out) we flew back to Phaleron. It goes to show that not all missions, be it rescue work or transportation, were easy. (see Appendix III)

Another Greek Tragedy

In an attempt to relieve the pressure on the Leros operation, 219 (Fighter) Group planned further raids on Crete in the hope of diverting attention and resources, and to keep the Bf 109s of III/JG27 from concentrating on Beaufighter operations in the Aegean. The Greek 336 Squadron was again selected for the first strike on 9 November. Six Hurricanes led by Flt Lt Spyros Diamantopoulos departed Tobruk to carry out an attack on Kastelli at midday. There was an element of surprise and only one Hurricane was lost, KZ598 flown by Diamantopoulos, who was taken prisoner:

> Diamantopoulos, seriously injured, was picked up by a German patrol. The Germans didn't think he would live, so they didn't bother to give him emergency medical treatment. It would be "a waste of medicine", the German doctor told the officer who found him. The officer, a major, turned out to be a rather kinder soul, however, and that same night put Diamantopoulos on a transport for Athens. The Ju 52 had barely started its engines when a flight of Beaufighters appeared above Heraklion, plunging the aerodrome and the city into darkness.

Diamantopoulos made a recovery and spent the remainder of the war in a German prison camp. He later commented that these missions, although 'totally worthless, [and] only offered the Greek air force losses,' they 'were a kind of escape, something different, something exciting, a chance to fire our guns at the enemy ... and gave the exiled Greek air force a chance to prove itself the equal of the mighty RAF.'

Flak hit the Hurricane flown by Wt Off. Haralambos Stavropoulos and he returned to base aided by his wingman Flt Sgt Dimitrios Soufrilas – and a giant brown desert rat! The rodent had endured the whole experience, awoken from its sleep by the noise of battle, having innocently boarded the Hurricane back at Tobruk. His furry and terrified companion helped Stavropoulos take his mind off his own predicament, and on arrival at base he gently removed the rat back to his desert home. With the loss of their CO, temporary command of 336 Squadron was assumed by Flt Lt Sarandis Skatzikas, brother of POW Sotirios, now incarcerated in Stalag Luft III.

On 10 November, a flight of Hurricanes of 336 Squadron raided Crete to strafe transport along the Heraklion-Chania road. Flying low and fast, the Hurricane flown by Flt Sgt Marios Skliris clipped some trees and lost six inches from each of its propeller blades, but remained airborne and landed safely at Tobruk. Three days later, nine Hurricanes of 41SAAF raided Crete, led by Capt. Van der Merwe. All returned safely. On 14 November, sixteen Hurricanes drawn from 94 and 336 Squadrons carried out a final raid, faring badly. The eight of 94 Squadron attacked radar stations. Sqn Ldr

Russ Foskett RAAF (KZ784) led Red Section but New Zealander Flg Off. John Hay (BN403) crashed into the camp by the RDF station, either hit by flak or collided with the W/T mast, while others attacked the lighthouse at Elafos. Meanwhile, White Section – comprising Yugoslav pilots – attacked Aliakanou RDF station, led by Capt. Igor Beran (KZ144/N) with 2/Lt Radomir Matejić (BP198), Lt Zivota Boscovi (KZ127) and Wt Off. Tihomir Babić (KZ938). They strafed the station and left it burning. The Hurricanes lost touch with each other and Babić saw one disappear into clouds in a valley. Later, he saw another crash into sea and break up about six miles north-east of Gavdhos. Capt. Beran and 2/Lt Matejić failed to return.

The Greek pilots attacked a military convoy sighted on the south coast and inadvertently found themselves flying into the face of heavy flak as they entered the Ierapetra plain fortified by guns situated on the hillsides. LD130 flown by Flt Sgt Dimitrios Sarsonis was the first to be hit, catching fire and crashed into a farmhouse. Sarsonis was killed as was a fourteen-year-old girl on the ground. The next to fall was Flg Off. Constantin Psilolignos who was probably seriously wounded. He was seen to be slumped over the controls before his Hurricane KZ672 crashed into the hills. His wingman, Flt Sgt George Mademlis, reported over the radio that his aircraft KZ480/Z had also been hit and would have to force-land. Wounded in a leg, he hid in a small church but was captured the next day. The section leader, Flg Off. Evangelos Karydis, was hit and ditched KZ628 in the middle of a marine minefield but survived to be captured. Another disastrous operation for very little gain.

Meanwhile, 74 Squadron based at Nicosia (Cyprus) had been flying sorties around Rhodes and was now relieved by a detachment of Spitfires from 7SAAF, four aircraft arriving on 14 November (Capt. Connell, Lts Deakin, Cyril Golding and Frank Montarani) joined by four more the following day (Lts Ray Burl, Gus Ground, Spuds Kelly and van Heerden). Each aircraft was fitted with a ninety-gallon long-range tank and their main task was to seek enemy aircraft operating from Rhodes and around Casteloriso, while also being called upon for convoy escort duty. 74 Squadron lost one of its aircraft on 21 November during such a patrol when Flt Sgt Willie Wilson force-landed JL329 on the Turkish coast during a sweep over Rhodes and Symi. The Canadian was interned but released a few weeks later.

During this period of intense action, heavy and medium bombers continued to bomb German airfields on the Greek mainland. On 15 November, Eleusis aerodrome sustained severe damage resulting from a raid by forty-six B-24s with an escort of P-38s. Approximately sixty tons of fragmentation bombs were dropped damaging hangars and fuel stores, and six aircraft were claimed destroyed on the ground. B-25s raided Kalamaki during the night and effectively wiped out the Do 217s of 5./KG100. On 16 November, seventy-nine B-25s with a P-38 escort bombed Eleusis airfield.

The attacking force claimed that extensive damage was caused to runways, hangars and other buildings with five aircraft destroyed on the ground and ten fires started. On the next day, Eleusis and Kalamaki airfields were the targets for forty-one B-17s with damage to hangars, buildings, taxi strip and the dispersal area with five aircraft destroyed on the ground with damage to ten more. Seventy-two B-25s from 321st and 340thBGs, operating from San Pancrazio LG, Italy, covered by P-38s raided Athens/Kalamaki and one B-25 was shot down. On 18 November, Eleusis airfield was again heavily damaged by fifty B-17s who bombed the hangar and dispersal areas and claimed to have destroyed ten aircraft on the ground. Intense AA fire damaged seventeen Allied bombers.

December 1943 – A Quieter Month

Following the loss of the last of the Dodecanese Islands, apart from Casteloriso, the primary object of the RAF was now to harness the capability of the German garrisons in the Aegean by attacking their supply lines. These included well defended convoys, large single freighters, landing craft, lighters, caiques and Ju 52s. The Beaufighters would also have to attack heavily defended ground installations, airfields and radar sites. Secondary duties were to include convoy escorts and armed reconnaissance missions. Sgt Bob Willis of 47 Squadron wrote:

> Tactics changed in December as we largely discarded our torpedoes. For the next few months most operational flying by the squadron consisted of attacking small cargo boats and caiques in the ports and harbours of the Cyclades and Dodecanese Islands. When we found any caiques of cargo-carrying size, which were usually holed up during the day in well-defended harbours, the Beaufighters attacked with cannon fire, supplemented by 100lb bombs in the target area. These operations could be quite hazardous.

603 Squadron had been pulled out of front line service for conversation to rocket projectiles, undertaking a short but intensive training programme with the new Beaufighter Mk TFX fitted with rails for the RPs and was soon to be followed by 252 Squadron. Each aircraft was able to carry eight 25-lb armour-piercing RPs for anti-shipping or 60-lb RPs for operations against buildings, trains and similar targets.

Beaufighters were claimed shot down by pilots of III/JG27 during the first few days of the new month, but it seems that their recognition was at fault. Ltn Ludwig Bauer of 7 Staffel claimed one on 3 December and Obfw Fritz Gromotka of 9 Staffel another the following day. The latter was a Baltimore of 454RAAF Squadron from which the pilot was rescued from the sea by a Do 24. Beaufighters of 47 Squadron were active during the early afternoon of 4 December as Sgt Bob Willis (LX898) recalled:

> At 13:50 we sighted four Arado 196s floatplanes circling at about 500 feet over the sea near the island of Kinaros, to the west of Leros. Now for maximum concentration, safety catch off, gun sights in place, all rather exhilarating. The first Arado I attacked was stationary on the water. It had apparently landed on the sea with engine failure with its three companion Arados circling overhead. I strafed the aircraft on the water with cannon. Arthur Unwin, as leader of the formation, was concerned that we would be jumped by Me 109s. He circled above ready to give warning if the dreaded 109s appeared. Arthur explained later at the de-briefing that he thought the Arado on the sea might be a decoy designed to get us into difficulty and here was I having a go! The Arado on the sea was an easy target. Through the gun sight I could see the plane breaking up with one of the crew clambering onto a float as it sank.

This was 1015 of 2./126 in which the pilot Uffz Karl Steinbrechter was wounded. The observer, Ltn Eberhard Ahrends, presumably the airman Willis had seen clambering onto a float, survived the attack.

> After this first success I made to attack another Arado still circling overhead. Climbing at full throttle I made a quarter turn attack. I shot off the support of one of the floats, which, as it was hanging down, made the aircraft unflyable. It went down and hit the sea with a big splash. As it was going down the rear gunner was still firing at us, well wide of the mark, but we did admire his courage. The rest of the formation, concerned at our nearness to German airfields on Crete and the possibility of Me 109s making a quick appearance, did not engage the other Arados for long, but they did strafe a high speed launch which came into view.

Willis' second victim was D1+KL also from 2./126 from which neither Obfw Walter Schindler nor Obfw Otto Albrecht survived. The HSL was S-boat *S511* whose crew reported being attacked by seven Beaufighters off Makronisi. It was heavily damaged and beached. Two of its crew were killed during the attack. About two hours later, four Beaufighters on another sweep arrived in the same area as noted in 201 Group's ORB:

> Four Beaus made a second sweep in the same area. Two attacked an 80-ton caique leaving it smouldering and listing. Three minutes later an Ar196 was seen taxiing on the water towards a 120-ton caique. The Arado was attacked and burst into flames.

This was 0302, also of 2./126, piloted by Ltn Friedrich Brunswig, which had picked up Ltn Ahrends, the observer of 1015 destroyed on the water by Willis earlier. Both Brunswig and Ahrends were killed.

Beaufighters of 47 Squadron carried out a shipping sweep on 7 December, meeting two Ar 196s both of which were claimed damaged by Flt Sgt Alf Squires and Flt Sgt A. Taylor RAAF. E-boats were also seen and it was while attacking these that Flg Off. Denis Nichol and W/O Gerald Ball were shot down in LX898/W. They had only joined the squadron the previous day. They survived and were taken prisoner. A Beaufighter (JL898) of 252 Squadron was also lost some thirty miles north-west of Cape Amouti, Cyprus, in which Flt Sgt Peter Martin RCAF and Flt Sgt John Hamilton were killed. Beaufighters of 47 Squadron were again involved in air combat on 14 December, the four aircraft encountering what they thought were a He 115 and four Ar 196s south of Stampalia. The 'Heinkel' was, in fact, a Z.506 of 2./126 in German markings and was attacked and shot down jointly by Sgt Bob Willis and Sgt Ken Thomas. The Z.506 on a ferry flight to Crete was flown by an Italian pilot, Serg.Magg. Christoffer Domeniko, who was killed together with Uffz Werner Schmidt and four ground crew passengers. Sgt Willis later wrote:

Whilst two of our Beaufighters were paying attention to the escorting Arados, I attacked this large seaplane in formation with another Beaufighter, flown by Sgt Ken Thomas. I could see my cannon-fire sparkling as it hit the wings of the 'Heinkel'. About 20 feet of the port wing of the 'Heinkel' came off – it was in real trouble. Concentrating too hard in my eagerness to finish the job I came in too close to the enemy aircraft, forcing me to fly over it to avoid a mid-air collision. We were an easy target to the 'Heinkel' rear gunner, who hit us and set us on fire. Turning and looking out I saw the 'Heinkel' splash into the sea.

With our aircraft full of smoke we were swiftly concentrated on survival. The 'Heinkel' rear gunner had shot off the tip of our starboard wing and ignited the Very cartridges stored in the rear of our aircraft. The Very cartridges, which produce a bright magnesium flare, gave off a tremendous cloud of white smoke containing magnesium powder. The whole aircraft was full of choking smoke. The instrument panel was blotted out by the magnesium deposit. Through the smoke I could not even see the horizon or any of the instruments. It appeared impossible to fly the aircraft. Tommy [Thompson] had evacuated his position at the rear. His entire navigation equipment and navigation table were burnt out, but he had very courageously beaten out the flames, despite the heat, preventing any further damage to the aircraft.

My immediate reaction was to jettison the cockpit roof with a view to baling out. We would have to go through the roof as the best option to get out whilst still airborne ... but jettisoning the roof canopy brought in an immediate rush of air, completely clearing the cockpit of smoke. Instinctively I rubbed the magnesium deposit off the instrument panel and the windscreen. The aircraft was still more or less straight and level with both engines functioning normally. By hand signal I indicated we would fly south until the coast of North Africa was sighted. We were just alright for fuel. With the wheels and flaps in good order I was able to land without any real problem.

During the early morning of 15 December, eight Beaufighters of 603 Squadron including four TFXs took-off for the first rocket-armed mission in the Middle East, but failed to find suitable targets. However, their luck changed on 22 December when four Beaufighters, of which three were TFXs, attacked caiques at Amoroso and Mykonos. Flg Off. S. J. L. Smith (LZ370/N) and Sgt Jock Gown (NE607/Q) with 60-lb rockets scored hits on a 70/100-ton caiques as did Flg Off. John Jones (LZ340/P) with 25-lb RPs and it was left sinking. A larger three-master vessel was then attacked at Mykonos by Flg Off. Jones with rockets while the other three strafed with cannon. It was left badly damaged with only one mast erect. On 23 December, four Beaufighters of 603 Squadron and four B-25Gs carried out a sweep, meeting a two-mast, sixty-ton caiques approaching Naxos. This was attacked with rockets and cannons. Four Ar 196s were sighted on the water at Port Valhi, Samos, and were attacked. Another was seen at Leos. Flg Off. W. G. King, RAAF Flg Off. W. Thame's navigator, noted in his logbook:

> Sighted one Arado 196 floatplane at Leros and destroyed it with cannon fire. Heavy flak at Leros and Samos.

D1+EL of 3./126 blew up. A number of barges were then seen and attacked in the face of intense flak. The 379thBS diarist wrote:

> The attack [in which a 100-ton barge was sunk, a naval auxiliary vessel and a 200-ton barge were set on fire] proved the most eventful and costly mission. This was the second mission sent out. Our four planes sighted three boats just west of Antiparos and went into attack in spite of intense and very accurate flak, which hit and damaged all four planes, wounding four crew members and killed the co-pilot of one of the planes, 2/Lt Lindsey L. McCall. The loss of Lt McCall was felt by everyone and it dampened any Christmas spirit we might have had.

At the end of the month 379thBS's diarist noted:

> During the month of December we flew a total of 25 missions over the Aegean Sea. However, game in the way of Jerry shipping was never large nor plentiful.

Nevertheless, our crews turned in a monthly score of 9 caiques, ranging in size from 45-200 tons, sunk; one 500-ton M/V damaged, one 100-ton barge sunk, and a 100-foot naval auxiliary vessel and a 200-ton barge set on fire.

US heavy and medium bombers continued to bomb German airfields on the Greek mainland with varying results. On 6 December, forty-five B-24s attacked Eleusis airfield, claiming good results. The crews claimed that of the fifteen to twenty Axis aircraft opposing them, three were destroyed, two probably destroyed and two damaged in return for the loss of one B-24 and one escorting fighter. On 8 December, Eleusis and Kalamaki airfields were attacked by heavy bombers. Sixty-one B-17s dropped eighty-one-and-a-half tons of bombs on Eleusis with one B-17 destroyed by AA fire and one B-24 missing. On 14 December, Eleusis and Kalamaki airfields were attacked by eighty B-17s dropping 236 tons of explosive and claimed to have covered the target areas thoroughly. On 20 December, a force of 109 B-17s with escort of sixty-six P-38s dropped 297 tons of bombs on Eleusis airfield inflicting extensive damage. The Allies claimed to have been opposed by about thirty-five aircraft of which nineteen were claimed destroyed, three probably and three damaged.

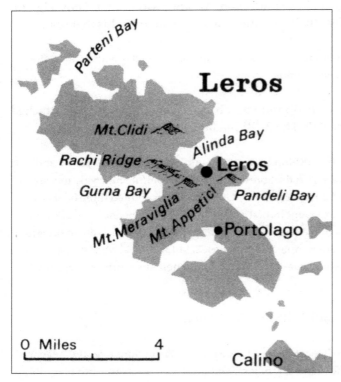

Map of Leros.

CHAPTER VIII

Beaufighters over the Aegean, Spitfires over Crete – 1944

By the beginning of 1944, four Beaufighter anti-shipping squadrons remained in the Eastern Mediterranean for operations over the Dodecanese:

47 Squadron at Gambut commanded by Wg Cdr W. D. L. Filson-Young DFC
227 Squadron at Berka commanded by Wg Cdr J. K. Buchanan DSO DFC
252 Squadron at Mersa Matruh commanded by Wg Cdr P. H. Woodruff DFC
603 Squadron at Gambut commanded by Wg Cdr J. H. R. Lewis DFC

603 Squadron had fully converted to rocket projectiles, 252 Squadron was currently converting, while 47 Squadron still had a few torpedo-armed aircraft that were rapidly becoming redundant for operations over the Aegean. New crews were arriving all the time including Flg Off. Harry Soderlund RCAF who joined 603 Squadron:

> In January 1944, I was posted to 603 Squadron flying from Gambut aerodrome in Libya. It was the job of 603 Squadron to attack enemy shipping and facilities in the Aegean Sea. The Germans were evacuating Crete at this time by sea and air. On one raid on an enemy radar station on the south coast of Crete I returned to base with a bullet hole through the fuselage just aft of my navigator's position. On returning from another night mission my Beaufighter was caught in a thunderhead and lifted into a stall position. As the plane dived and emerged below the cloud I was able to pull out in time to avoid crashing into the sea. This is called experience in flying and is not taught in class.

The B-25Gs of the 379th BS remained at Gambut to work with the strike Beaufighters. In addition to the anti-shipping units, 46 Squadron had detachments of Beaufighters operating from Abu Suier, St Jean and Tocra carrying out night intruder patrols over Rhodes, Kos and Crete. Wg Cdr T. P. K. Scade remained in command.

On 3 January, Wg Cdr Filson-Young led eight 47 Squadron Beaufighters on a sweep around the coast of Crete only to be intercepted by three Bf 109s of 8./JG27. Ltn Horst Kizina pursued Wt Off. Roger Barrett's Beaufighter (LX919) north-west of Maleme and shot it down at 15:40. Both Barrett and his navigator Sgt Bill Fairfield were killed. A Beaufighter night fighter of 46 Squadron, MM928 crewed by Flt Sgt S. M. Kent and Flt Sgt L. W. Cooper, engaged an aircraft believed to have been a Do 217 during an early morning patrol on 12 January and reported that it escaped with damage. However, Air HQ changed their claim to a Ju 88 when an intelligence report stated that a Ju 88 had returned to its base on one engine and had crash-landed. This was 4U+CK of 2.(F)/123 that crash-landed at Gadurra, Rhodes.

Wg Cdr Buck Buchanan frequently led formations of four Beaufighters of 227 Squadron in January seeking caiques among the island, sinking several, but not without loss. On 13 January, following an attack on patrol vessels *GA62*, *GA67* and *GA72*, which were sunk, JM274/T crewed by Flg Off. L. F. Morgan and Flt Sgt R. A. W. Ferguson was forced to ditch. They took to their dinghy and were rescued to become prisoners. Sqn Ldr Bill Kemp's aircraft (JM233/U) was also hit and he was wounded in the right ankle, but was able to return safely as did Wg Cdr Buchanan whose aircraft (JM235/G) suffered some damage. On 26 January, during an attack led by Wg Cdr Buchanan on another caique, Flg Off. Alex Will RAAF and Flg Off. Brian Findley were killed when JL708/E of 227 Squadron was shot down off Xili Bay. Sgt Sid Appleton's aircraft (EL509/K) was also hit but managed to return. 603 Squadron also lost a crew on this date, Flt Lt Gordon MacDonnell and Flg Off. Stan Piner (LZ138/N) being shot down by flak during an attack by four Beaufighters against Chios harbour, north of Samos. Piner was seen in a dinghy with MacDonnell swimming towards him in a calm sea. Other aircraft circled and dropped their own dinghies and other floating supplies nearby. The survivors waved but nothing more was ever heard from them.

47 Squadron suffered a loss on 22 January when Flg Off. David Hume (in LX863) was killed. His navigator Flt Sgt E. W. Peggram survived. Two more caiques were sunk by 227 Squadron on 23 January, again with the cost of a crew. Flg Off. Dick Hutchison RCAF's aircraft (JL905) was shot down, he and his navigator Flt Sgt Les Sawle losing their lives. Hutchison was an American from Ohio. A second Beaufighter (EL270/N) suffered flak damage and crashed on returning to Berka, its pilot Flg Off. Ken Judd being killed, though Sgt A. G. Thomas escaped with minor injuries. Another 227 Squadron patrol, while on convoy escort duty, encountered what they described as an 'SM79 in French markings', which was not attacked. On 24 January, Flt Lt Pat Pringle (LZ133/H) led four Beaufighters of 603

Squadron on an offensive patrol and located a 200-ton caique off Themia that was left sinking after their rocket attack. 603 Squadron continued its run of successes the following day (25 January) when Sgt Harry Yates (with Sgt John Whalley) attacked a 100-ton caique off Samos, evading coastal gunfire and fighter attack.

27 January proved to be a red-letter day for 603 Squadron, though not without cost. Flt Lt Pringle (LZ133/H) led another offensive patrol over Syros and Mykonos. Near Kythera, the four Beaufighters encountered three Ju 52/3 floatplanes escorted by three Ar 196s. Two of the Ju 52s were promptly shot down, the third ditching near the island of Delos, one each falling to Flt Lt Pringle and Flt Sgt Johnstone Edgar (LZ281/K), the third jointly being shot down by Flt Sgt Phil Spooner RAAF (603/C) and Flt Sgt Alan Rooks (LZ144/B). The three Arados followed suit, Pringle and Edgar again claiming one apiece while the third fell to Spooner and Rooks.

The Ju 52 floatplanes were from See.Fl.Stfl.1 and 3, each aircraft carrying Kriegsmarine passengers. TE+DZ of 3 Staffel flown by Uffz Kurt Werner was the first to fall. Three of the crew including the pilot were lost and two survived. The fate of the passengers is unknown. Obfw Hermann Cremer, who was flying the second aircraft of 1 Staffel to be shot down, later recalled that after the first aircraft was shot down, he took evasive action but was hit and had to ditch at 220 kph. TE+DS of 3 Staffel quickly followed suit with the loss of Obfw Heinrich Sellhorn-Timm, his crew plus eleven marines. Obfw Cremer added that with the burning wreckage of the formation scattered all round them, eleven survivors scrambled into their dinghies expecting the Beaufighters to strafe, which they did not. Filled with new hope and gratitude, they reached a neighbouring island where they lived frugally with a shepherd for some days before being rescued by a German naval cutter.

Two of the Arado crews, Gfr Horst Pfützner and his observer Ltn Wolfgang Reichel aboard D1+AH, and the crew of D1+CH, Fw Gustav Zobel and Uffz Herbert Thurner, were killed. The third 1./126 machine, D1+FH, was only slightly damaged and its crew unhurt. It was taxied onto the beach at Delos. The official German report revealed that thirteen crewmembers from the six aircraft, including two Arado crews, were lost as were at total of twenty-seven Kriegsmarine passengers. A Ju 88 and several rescue craft including *R194* and *R211* searched for survivors.

Meanwhile, return fire from the Arado attacked by Rooks had damaged one of the Beaufighter's engines. The crippled aircraft (LZ144/B with Flg Off. Morris Thom as navigator) was shepherded towards the North African coast but finally ditched forty miles south of Gados. Flt Sgt Edgar, flying his first op with 603, recalled:

On our way home, when halfway across the Mediterranean, LZ144/B experienced an engine failure. Very shortly afterwards, the second engine stopped. With both propellers feathered, the aircraft ditched and sank quite quickly. The main dinghy failed to inflate and both crewmembers were seen with only one individual dinghy between them. The remaining three aircraft circled the dinghy and transmitted to obtain an accurate fix of their position. We continued to circle until we were getting rather low on fuel, by which time a Wellington had come out to relieve us, staying overhead until nightfall.

When we returned to base we were naturally quite elated about the success of the combat. Our joy was, of course, tempered by our concern over our two colleagues who were still in the water. There was quite a party in the Officers' Mess that evening. But the celebrations were short lived, for next morning we were informed that, following a disastrous rescue operation, when all three engines of the ASR launch failed, one after the other. A second launch failed to locate them and a further air search was mounted next day. Our comrades were never rescued, and were subsequently posted missing, presumed drowned.[62]

On 28 January, four Beaufighters of 47 Squadron attacked and sank a motor lighter at Mykonos, one of the vessels involved in the rescue of survivors of the previous day's tragedy. Two days later, six 'Torbeaus' of 47 Squadron, plus two anti-flak aircraft with an escort of six Beaufighters of 603 Squadron, set out to hunt down a 2,000-ton M/V reported off Melos. When located, she was found to have an escort of a UJ-boat and two flak-ships. All torpedoes were released but none struck home with the only damaged being inflicted by rockets and cannon-fire. A Beaufighter of 47 Squadron (possibly ND203) was hit and ditched, Flt Sgts Cyril Melling and Idris Davies taking to their dinghy. They were picked by Swedish Red Cross ship *Mongabarra* and taken to Piraeus. An escorting Ar 196 was claimed damaged jointly by Flt Sgt Harry Yates (LZ272/F) and Flt Sgt Jock Gow, despite Yates having been wounded by flak during his rocket attack. His navigator Sgt John Whalley had also been wounded but managed to bind the leaking hydraulic pipes to allow Yates to nurse the crippled aircraft to a night crash-landing at El Adem. Both were off operations for two months.

Flt Lt Reg Meyer led eight rocket-armed Beaufighters of 252 Squadron on a sweep around Stampalia on 31 January, meeting three Ju 88Cs of 11./ ZG26 with a pair of Bf 109s flying cover. Meyer had time to shoot down Uffz Franz Gruber's aircraft that crashed near the coast. The crew survived and Uffz Stoll claimed a Beaufighter shot down. But then the Bf 109s attacked and shot down LZ341 and LZ377 into the sea off Stampalia. Flg Off. Darrell Hall and Sgt Alex Cowie were killed but Flt Sgt F. A. Stevenson and Sgt C. Thompson managed to reach Turkey where they were briefly interned.

252 Squadron received a new flight commander round about this time, Sqn Ldr Chris Foxley-Norris, having been posted in from the UK. He later wrote:

> Our job was to try to starve the smaller garrisons into surrender, and to render the larger ones operationally ineffective or at least eliminate their offensive capabilities. The difficulty arose, of course, that in starving the Germans we were likely also to starve the native Greeks. In attacking shipping it was usually impracticable to distinguished between those loaded with military stores and those carrying the ordinary necessities of life – with some exceptions, of course, such as fuel tankers.
>
> Luckily some of the bigger islands were more or less self-supporting for food; and the rest were maintained by small sailing or powered caiques, which we left alone unless they shot at us. On one memorable occasion we encountered, about dawn, a 16-oared boat, which might have come straight out of Homer, its crew rowing like mad to make the harbour before the light came: we wished them well but naturally they could not hear our ribald cries of "Well rowed, Leander", or "Give her ten, Argonauts."[63]

February 1944

The B-25Gs of the 379th BS had a relatively quiet January and although the Americans flew eighty-five sorties in twenty-three missions, very little trade had come their way. But no sooner had the month ended when they experienced their worst day flying from Gambut. The War Diary for 1 February reported the loss of two B-25Gs, 42-64840 flown by 2/Lt James F. Lavender and 42-64770 flown by 2/Lt Edmund N. Slater:

> This month started off in a most unfortunate manner. On the very first day in a mission of four planes, two of our planes were shot down making an attack on an enemy convoy just west of Leros. The loss was not in vain, for two direct hits were scored by Lt Slater's and Lt Lavender's planes, which were shot down, destroying a 3,000-ton merchant vessel. Damage by cannon fire was also inflicted on one of two escorting corvettes. As a result of these brave acts, both Lt Slater and Lt Lavender were recommended for the DFC.

Another entry revealed:

> ...as the formation flew broadside, over a three enemy ship convoy, it is believed that 42-64840 hit a rocket cable fired by the vessel it attacked, leaving a gap in the left wing, about a foot wide, and 9 inches deep, from which a

cable was dangling. The left engine started to throw oil, and it is believed the aircraft made a controlled belly landing in the water. It is believed that the crew survived the landing and used the dinghy, however, no trace of the six crew members was ever found.

2/Lt Slater's aircraft was last seen with its port engine and fuel tank on fire as it passed over the convoy. It crashed heavily into the sea about thirty seconds later, nose down at about twenty-five degrees. There were no survivors.

227 Squadron lost an aircraft on 3 February although the crew was saved. W/O Keith Wright's T5170/C developed engine problems while on patrol and was forced to ditch. Wright and his navigator Flt Sgt G. L. Jones were picked up by a Walrus and returned to base.

At the beginning of February, 16SAAF Squadron arrived at Berka under Lt-Col Johannes Lorentz, newly converted from Beauforts to Beaufighter Xs. Before operations commenced, however, two of the new Beaufighters collided in mid-air on 4 February killing Lt J. S. Ogilvy and his navigator Lt E. R. Scherer in LZ332, while the other aircraft flown by Capt. R. Munton-Jackson landed safely. Next day, the first operation was flown in co-operation with Marauders of 24SAAF attacking shipping at Rhodes.

Four Beaufighters of 252 Squadron attacked caiques near Lipsos on 6 February, LZ345 crewed by Flg Off. C. H. Mason and Sgt J. R. Smith being forced to ditch. They were rescued by a Turkish vessel and taken to the mainland, being returned to their unit a few weeks later. Navigator Sgt Sam 'Paddy' McAughtry on being posted to 252 Squadron at Mersa Matruh in February wrote:

The role of our squadron, and two other Beau outfits, together with two South African Baltimore light bomber squadrons and Wellington bombers for night torpedo work, was to interrupt supplies to German garrisons on the Aegean islands, particularly those on Rhodes and Crete. The Greeks were suffering terribly under the occupying forces and, as well as that, the islands and their airfields offered a distinct threat to the Allies' Mediterranean communications. The German and Italian garrisons were supplied by sea, and by Ju 52 transport aircraft, flown in by night. There were German and Italian fighters on the bigger islands. It was a strange, isolated little war that we fought. The big war had passed us by long before.

After some local flying [Plt Off Pearse] and I went off on our first operation. It was a sweep of the central Aegean, looking for shipping. Two days previously six Beaufighters had done a similar sweep. They'd run into an escorted merchant vessel and attacked it, without sinking either target or escort. One Beaufighter was lost. The thing was in Pearse's mind a great deal.

"Do we lose one every trip?" he asked the flight commander, anxiously. "How the hell would I know?" was the reply. "It's bad luck to count."[64]

On 7 February, six bomb-armed Beaufighters of 47 Squadron, led by Wg Cdr Filson-Young, struck Khios harbour, expecting to find a large merchant vessel as reported by a reconnaissance aircraft. Sgt Bob Willis recalled:

Each aircraft bombed and strafed either the merchant vessel, which was of about 1,000-tons or the many caiques moored against the north jetty. As we broke away after our first attack, much to my surprise I saw large red crosses on the side of the merchant ship. I broke RT silence and called up the leader with "Hospital Ship". Filson-Young broke off the attack and we returned to base. Apparently it was a Swedish hospital ship, rumoured to be giving some support to the Germans. The ship escaped serious damage, with the British government making suitable apologies to the Swedish authorities.[65]

On 9 February, four Beaufighters of 252 Squadron set off on an offensive shipping search over the Aegean led by Flt Lt Reg Meyer (with Flt Sgt Peter Grieve in LZ287). Bf 109s were sighted about a mile away and slightly above and these swooped on the Beaufighters. Plt Off. Frank Stanger RAAF and Flt Sgt James Reynolds in LZ141 were last seen pursued by two Bf 109s while Flt Sgt Alf Squires' LZ271 went into the sea off Cape Zulufi, taking pilot and navigator Flt Sgt Wally Boon to their deaths. Flt Lt Reg Meyer's LZ287 also failed to return. It was later learned that his Beaufighter had crashed on the island of Ikaria due west of Samos. Theohari Kioulanlis, who was then about eight or nine years old and lived on Ikaria, recalled:

A British plane was shot down by a German fighter over Cambos, a village on the north side of the island, just outside of Evdilos. Sadly, both airmen lost their lives. At the time the Germans were still occupying Ikaria. The local people managed to find the bodies and buried them in the local church. After the war the bodies were removed.

Nikos Koutoufaros added:

It seems that after the bodies were removed, the villagers went and stripped the plane. At the time life was very harsh with people dying all the time in Ikaria from hunger. Any goods coming into the island were regulated by the occupying troops and even if some things were available not many people had the money to buy them. The hull [fuselage] of the plane was turned into pots and pans.

A total of seven Beaufighters were claimed, two each by Ltn Hans-Gunnar Culemann and Uffz Franz Büsen of 7./JG27, two by Uffz Josef Kaiser of 9 Staffel and one by Gfr Walter Appel, also of 9 Staffel.

On the night of 10/11 February, a Wellington of 38 Squadron turned night fighter when a Ju 52 was sighted low down over the sea, west of Khalkis. Flt Sgt J. E. Bunyan ordered his rear gunner Sgt W. Cooksley to open fire, which he did from 150 yards. Strikes were seen but the aircraft continued on its course. A second attack was carried out at 400 yards whereupon its port engine caught fire and it hit the sea where it burst into flames. IV/TG1 reported the loss.

The first success for 16SAAF came on 11 February when Lt-Col Lorentz led four Beaufighters on a sweep between Antiparos and Dhespotiki in the Cyclades where a caique was sighted and destroyed by RPs and cannon fire. Another caique was attacked by cannon fire at Spetsai Island off the east coast of the Peloponnese, but cliffs complicated the attack and no tangible results were seen. Four Beaufighters of 227 Squadron led by the CO Wg Cdr Buck Buchanan on his fourth sortie of the month carried out an attack on shipping during which W/O Keith Wright's aircraft (JL585/A) was shot down by flak. The pilot was killed but navigator Sgt G. L. Jones was rescued and reached Turkey where he was briefly interned. The pair had survived a ditching only eight days earlier.

That night, Beaufighters of 46 Squadron carried out intruder sorties over Rhodes with some success catching Ju 52s of IV/TG1 flying in supplies to the besieged garrison. Thirty-four year-old Sqn Ldr Joe Blackburn (who had joined the RAF as Boy Entrant in 1925) with New Zealand radar officer Flg Off. M. G. Keys in LZ462/J shot down two Ju 52s and damaged another over Calato. It seems that he accounted for 1Z+LY of 14 Staffel that crashed two miles west of Rhodes in which Uffz Gerhard Kneschke and crew were all posted missing, and 1Z+LZ of 15 Staffel that crash-landed at Gadurra with observer and air gunner both wounded. Another Beaufighter crew, Flt Lt David Crerar and Plt Off. L. Charles, (LZ335/P) shot down another 15 Staffel machine, 1Z+HZ at 20:15, Obfw Emil Armborst and crew all reported missing.

47 Squadron lost an aircraft (possibly LZ240) on 13 February with Flg Off. Joe Unwin and Sgt Ken Farmer killed when attacking caiques at Hydra, shot down by Gfr Walter Appel just north of Melos at 12:07. A PR Spitfire was lost the next day. BR430 of 682 Squadron took-off from Tocra at 13:30 for a photo recce of Candia and Pireaus. Strong winds were encountered and Flt Sgt Vincent McCarthy RAAF was instructed to return at 15:45. Nothing further was heard from the aircraft and it did not return to base. At 17:20 with the aircraft overdue, air-sea rescue action was initiated but no trace of the missing aircraft or pilot was found. No distress calls from the aircraft were received.

The dazzling operational career of the legendary Wg Cdr Buck Buchanan came to an end over the Aegean when his aircraft (EL467/J) was forced to ditch on 16 February having been damaged by flak during an attack against a dredger-type vessel in the Gulf of Argolis. Buchanan and his navigator W/O Reg Howes were seen to emerge and the CO waved to circling colleagues, Flt Lt Tex Holland dropping a K-type dinghy and ditching bag close by. Unbeknown to all at the time but the crew, Buchanan had agreed to take along 'for the ride' a Bulgarian member of the ground staff, LAC Eliahou Eliav, who went down with the aircraft. The dinghy containing the two airmen drifted for some time before rescue was affected, by which time Buchanan, although seemingly unharmed, went quiet and then died. As one contemporary said of him:

> Buck, had he lived in another era, would have been a buccaneer by natural inclination and character. His dandyish outward appearance belied his courage and dash, because he had the guts of a lion when the chips were down. He was one of the very few men whom I've always felt highly privileged to have known.

On the same date, Major Johannes Bell led four Beaufighters of 16SAAF in a search for a minesweeper in harbour at Zante. On sighting the vessel, the Beaufighters attacked with RPs and cannon fire and a pall of black smoke rose from the ship. Lt W. P. Ridley's aircraft was hit in one engine during the attack and Major Bell ordered the crew to head for Taranto some 300 miles to the north-west, but the aircraft (LZ333) force-landed in southern Greece and Ridley and his navigator Lt J. A. S. Louw were taken prisoner. On 18 February, another Beaufighter was lost during an attack on a M/V between Kythera and Cape Zaurva, Lt T. J. Simpson's aircraft (LZ481) seen to plunge into the sea killing him and Capt. J. F. A. Steyn, the navigator.

Sqn Ldr Bill Kemp led the armed patrol by four Beaufighters of 227 Squadron on 21 February, attacking and seriously damaging a heavily-laden auxiliary schooner and a caique at Fiskardho. Unfortunately, a bomb overshot and destroyed a house on the quayside. That evening, a Lufthansa Ju 52 (D-AWAS *Joachim Blankenburg*) was lost near Euboea, although not apparently to 'enemy action'. Captained by Flugkapitän Jakob Leuzinger, it was en route to Athens from Salonika carrying sixteen passengers, no doubt all of some importance and including Oberst Walter Tanneberger, senior engineer officer who was on his way to take up a new appointment as Kommandant of Koflug 5./IV. There were no survivors.

Intelligence sources, probably Ultra but also air reconnaissance, revealed that a large merchant vessel, the 5,343-ton *Lisa* (formerly the Italian *Livenza*) had departed Piraeus for Herkalion, Crete, and on 22 February, the RAF decided to carry out a torpedo strike. Wg Cdr Filson-Young set out from Gambut with six torpedo-armed Beaufighters of 47 Squadron, plus two others for flak suppression with an escort provided by eight Beaufighters of 227 Squadron (led by Sqn Ldr Dennis Bennett who had assumed command following Wg Cdr Buchanan's loss) and two of 603 Squadron. Four B-25Gs were to join the party, the 379th BS's War Diary recounting:

> Our last mission before going off ops at Gambut, preparatory to moving base to Group, was an interesting mission. Four of our planes were sent out to make diversionary attack on a convoy just north of Crete. Our job was to draw off the fighters so that torpedo Beaufighters of the RAF could attack a large 4,500-ton M/V under the protection of two escort vessels. Arriving a few minutes ahead of the Beaufighters, our men engaged six Me 109s and four Ju 88s in a running fight for 20 minutes. We shot down a Me 109 and one Ju 88 and damaged another Me 109. By drawing off the fighters, the Beaufighters were able to score direct torpedo hits on the large vessel and also one of the escort vessels. For our part in this show we were commended by the RAF for a job well done.

The Beaufighter crews reported seeing five Ju 88s, four Bf 109s and six Ar 196s over the convoy. Despite the intense flak, the 'Torbeaus' carried out a successful attack on the *Liza*, which sank, and damaged one of the escorting torpedo boats. The *Liza* was carrying 1,750 tons of fuel and 660 tons of ammunition. The 'Torbeaus' surprisingly suffered no losses but 227 Squadron did lose three aircraft to flak and fighter attack.

Sqn Ldr Bennett (EL530/C) on sighting the Arados pulled ahead of the 'Torbeaus' and engaged. Flt Sgt Sid Appleton (with Flt Sgt Jack Fenton in X8103/D) was seen to turn towards an Arado that went into a steep climb in front of Bennett's aircraft who fired and saw strikes and pieces falling off as it went into a steep dive. Apparently, Appleton's aircraft had been hit by an Arado or flak since it was seen to ditch. Another Arado got on the tail of a Beaufighter that climbed away with smoke pouring from an engine. Sqn Ldr Bennett then joined Flg Off. J. W. Edwards (JL730/O) in strafing one of the destroyers and as they broke away witnessed a torpedo strike on the M/V. The rear destroyer was also in flames from another torpedo hit and the other destroyer smoking badly. As the Beaufighters struck for home, Bf 109s appeared and shot one down into the sea. Apart from the Appleton crew, 227 also lost Flt Sgt Bob Scarlett and Flg Off. Geoff Hartley in EL228/P while the third aircraft ditched killing Flg Off. John Corlett (JL731/Q), though his navigator Flg Off. Gwynfor Williams survived to be taken prisoner, the only survivor of the three Beaufighters. One of the Arado crews reported shooting down a Beaufighter, but Ltn Hans-Joachim

Hayssen of 7./JG27 claimed two. The two 603 Squadron pilots, Flt Lt Pat Pringle and W/O Phil Spooner RAAF, claimed an Arado shot down in return as did Flg Off. R. Somerville of 47 Squadron. An aircraft of 1./126 was lost and two of 4./126 damaged.

More Beaufighter losses followed as the month drew to a close, one of 47 Squadron falling to flak on 25 February when a patrol led by Sqn Ldr 'Porky' Skinner attacked a caique and a schooner off Scarpanto. On this occasion, the crew, Flg Off. Roy Euler and Flt Sgt C. A. Boffin, were rescued by a destroyer after four days in their dinghy. Sqn Ldr Skinner's navigator in 47/B, Plt Off. P. Tuhill, was wounded in the leg by shrapnel. Two days later, 227 Squadron lost another aircraft, EL509/K, shot down during a strike on Messolonghi. Flg Off. Bill Davies was killed but Flt Sgt G. A. Brown survived to be taken prisoner. Davies' DFC was Gazetted in April. It had proved another costly month for the Beaufighters with sixteen aircraft lost on operations, twenty aircrew killed, four POW and three briefly interned in Turkey.

March 1944

Ultra and other intelligence sources now revealed that the Germans were using their transport aircraft in increasing numbers to supply Crete and Rhodes, such was the devastation caused to the seaborne supply craft by Beaufighter strikes. With few suitable targets remaining in the Aegean, 47 Squadron with its torpedo-armed aircraft was soon to be withdrawn from operations and was subsequently despatched to the Far East while 16SAAF was shortly to be posted to Italy. For the remaining 227, 252 and 603 Squadrons, with daylight operations less profitable, the crews found themselves being employed more frequently on night intruder sorties over Crete and Rhodes in conjunction with 46 Squadron. Of the change of direction for the Beaufighters, Sqn Ldr Foxley-Norris of 252 Squadron later commented:

> On paper the lumbering Ju 52s should have been easy meat and indeed one of my pilots [Flg Off Taylor on 13 March] shot down two on his first operational sortie. However, they were normally used at night and made skilful use of their very low speed. If they suspected we were after them, they flew at about 60 knots at below 100 feet above sea level, which presented great difficulties to the Beaufighter. Our efforts proved discouragingly unsuccessful, partly due to the fact that being basically anti-shipping aircraft rather than specialist night fighters we were not equipped with AI radar.[66]

Flt Lt Tex Holland, now with 227 Squadron, was the first to gain a success shooting down Ju 52 1Z+FZ of 15./TG1 between Eleusis and Maleme on the night of 4/5 March. The Beaufighter (JM237/M) had been despatched on a shipping strike. Holland attacked one with bombs but intense flak forced him to break away. A Ju 52 was the seen heading for Maleme. He fired a short burst whereupon in crashed into the sea, burned briefly and then exploded. Obgfr Hugo Lübke and crew were all killed. The following day, Sgt Paddy McAughtry of 252 Squadron recorded:

A Fairchild light aircraft landed at Mersa Matruh and out of it stepped the Group Captain [Max Aitken]. At the time he was SASO at our group in Alexandria. Tanned and handsome, he called in order to brief the men on an operation to be carried out that night. Intelligence [Ultra] had advised that Ju 52 transport aircraft were expected to arrive at Heraklion airfield in Crete, carrying vital stores and troop replacements. After the briefing Max Aitken asked whether he might be given an aircraft and navigator so that he could join in the operation. Permission, naturally, was granted. Those taking part had been advised to patrol a certain strip along the coast, as it was considered to be the likely route. This they did and they had no luck at all. They came back to the desert and reported accordingly.[67]

Grp Capt. Aitken then set off with Flt Lt George Muir RCAF as navigator in LZ330/F:

18:17. Airborne for Intruder operations – Heraklion. Set course from Matruh West and flew between 500 and 1,000 feet, making landfall at Konfo at 19:50 hrs. Turned to starboard round the island and steered towards lighthouse on the south-easterly tip of Crete. When about 5 miles away this lighthouse was extinguished. Steered round eastern end of Crete to revolving beacon at Elasa Point, keeping about 3 miles to seaward. Continued north for 5 minutes and then turned west.

At 20:15 an aircraft passed across our bow from starboard to port beneath going very fast. This was identified as a Ju 88. Continued on towards Dhia, and when about 5 miles away at 20:20, saw a Ju 52 slightly beneath crossing from starboard to port. Turned left and opened fire at about 500 yards, closing rapidly and firing from the port quarter. Strikes on starboard wing, half of which immediately fell off, bits of which struck the Beaufighter's starboard engine. Ju 52 rolled over to starboard and crashed into the sea. We turned to port and saw a large white area in the sea and bits of wreckage.

Continued on towards Dhia. Flak meanwhile had started from Heraklion, and was seen to be firing indiscriminately from the end of the runway. At 20:25 we turned to starboard out to sea and met a Ju 52, which came out of the haze ahead. Opened fire, and saw one strike on aft end of Ju 52. Turned hard to port, but aircraft was lost in the haze.

At 20:30, while flying east, just north of Dhia island, overtook Ju 52 which was flying round northerly tip of island, slightly to starboard. Beaufighter at about 1,500 feet and the Ju 52 at about 1,000 feet. Dived on aircraft, quarter attack coming astern, and fired one long burst with no result. Fired two 60lb RPs [rocket projectiles] from dead astern, which also missed, but made Ju 52 dive steeply towards the sea. Further long bursts of cannon registered strikes on middle of fuselage. The dive increased and he went almost vertically into the sea. We turned to port and saw wreckage on the sea, which included a tail unit. The Beaufighter pulled out at about 50 feet.

Continued patrol north of island, with sporadic flak coming up from both the island and aerodrome, which all seemed erratic. A flashing white beacon on the island and a red beacon on the aerodrome remained on throughout the patrol. At 20:40, while flying north, overtook a Ju 52 crossing from port to starboard. Fired long burst which registered many strikes on starboard wing. The Ju 52 turned very steeply and dived to starboard. Beau could not possibly follow, and it is considered that the Ju 52 could not have recovered before striking the sea. For this operation I claim 2 Ju 52s destroyed, 1 Ju 52 probable, 1 Ju 52 damaged.[68]

Sgt Paddy McAughtry commented:

Then into the circuit, in the pale dawn light, came the Group Captain's Beau. He banked steeply and landed. At the debriefing he reported that he had tired of patrolling as suggested, and had boldly joined the circuit over the enemy airfield. It was far and away the most heavily defended point on the island. Catching the defences on the hop, Max Aitken had destroyed three Ju 52s in the circuit and had damaged two more [sic]. After recommending his navigator for a DFC, the celebrated air ace climbed back into his aeroplane and flew back to Alexandria, leaving behind a bunch of fliers with egg pouring down their faces, barring, of course, that of the guy who had been promised the medal.[69]

Although IV/TG1 reported the loss of six Ju 52s between 2-7 March, it is uncertain whether Grp Capt. Aitken scored two or three destroyed on this night. Surviving records suggest that a Ju 52 (131078) was lost on the night of 6/7 March with the death of Uffz Alois Kappseger. This, together with Holland's victory on 4 March, leaves four Ju 52s unaccounted for – so possibly Aitken's shooting was even better than he thought.

Sqn Ldr Dennis Bennett (EL530/C), acting CO of 227 Squadron, took-off at 22:45, hoping to emulate Grp Capt. Aitken's performance. He patrolled off Maleme causing chance lights to be switched on but failed to make a sighting until 01:16 when he saw an aircraft heading south-west at 400 feet. He followed and tentatively identified it as a Ju 88, closed to sixty or seventy yards and opened fire. Strikes were observed and the aircraft reared steeply and dived into the sea. The following night (6/7 March), 46 Squadron lost LZ335/P that failed to return from an intruder raid over the Kos area. Flt Lt Angus Taylor DFC (a South African) and his thirty-eight-year-old navigator Plt Off. Rhys Peace (a 252 Squadron crew on attachment) were reported missing. Three Ar 196s of 4./126 were reported to have been damaged/destroyed by strafing in Pigadia harbour and these were the victims of six Beaufighters of 47 Squadron led Sqn Ldr Porky Skinner flying 47/B. Another spectacular success came the way of Sqn Ldr Pat Pringle of 603 Squadron on the night of 8/9 March as his navigator Flg Off. Tony Ross revealed in the subsequent report:

By 8 March, the weather had improved enough for the squadron to try night intruding. The Beaufighter's ASV radar was not accurate enough for attacks in complete darkness. Some moonlight was necessary to give a good chance of success. The plan was for a single Beaufighter to fly along the north coast at Crete to Heraklion and lie in wait until a Ju 52 transport came in to land. Once the landing lights were switched on it should be an easy target.

Entry to the Aegean would be through the narrow entrance straits at the eastern end of the mountainous island. Accurate dead reckoning navigation was essential; there were no radio or long-range radar aids. At length the rocky promontory of Crete loomed up in the darkness and the Beaufighter turned along the coast flying as low as the night visibility permitted. The moon was rising and casting a long silver path across the quiet dark waters. The island of Dia could just be seen on the right when the radar showed traces of something in the water. The Beaufighter banked away in a wide arc down moon so that whatever was in the water would show up in the moon path whilst the aircraft itself would be in the darker part of the sky.

The radar relocated its target and the cautious stalking began. Suddenly there were dark shapes ahead, two large vessels in a line astern steaming towards the harbour. Once more the Beaufighter swung away, this time to make a carefully planned attack. The correct height was reached and the dive began with the navigator calling out the range as it closed. The switch was set to fire a salvo of four pairs of rockets in quick succession. Each had a 60lb high explosive head. At 800 yards the command 'fire' was given. The glowing exhaust rockets streaked ahead and a bright yellow light appeared on the leading vessel. The Beaufighter pulled sharply away to starboard to avoid silhouetting itself against the moon. As it resumed its attack position, flames were leaping high into the air from the doomed vessel. Another attack was now made on the second ship, this time with the four 20mm cannon since all the rockets were gone. Some hits were observed but the damage could not be assessed in the darkness. Reports next day from intelligence sources in the Aegean confirmed that the destroyer *Francesco Crispi*, taken over by the Germans after the Italian surrender, had been sunk.[70]

Sqn Ldr Bennett of 227 Squadron was also out this night patrolling the Kythera Straits and searching for more transport aircraft. On this occasion, however, he realised he was being shadowed by a Ju 88, so broke away and returned to base.

On 11 March, ten Beaufighters of 16SAAF were ordered to fly to Gambut for a special operation, and at 13:40 the next day, Major Johannes Bell led three Beaufighters through the Kaso Straits between Crete and Scarpanto, then past Thira and Melos. They were near Kimolos when splashes appeared in the water, indicating they were being attacked, although no enemy aircraft were visible. Major Bell called over the R/T that he had engine problems and turned towards the Turkish coast. Ten minutes later, the Beaufighter (NE248/D) hit the water where a wing broke off and burst into flames. When last seen, the Major was swimming towards the dinghy occupied by his navigator Lt N. H. 'Shorty' Stead. Capt. Clem Clements recalled:

We were attacked by an enemy aircraft and my flight commander was forced to ditch. I never even saw the enemy aircraft as there was a lot of low cloud around, but my observer managed to photograph someone in the ditched aircraft's dinghy, with the other crewmember swimming towards it. It was later reported that Major Bell did not survive.[71]

Neither Major Bell nor Lt Stead survived. Presumably they perished at sea while awaiting rescue that never came. The Beaufighter may have been the victim of Uffz Günter Striebel of 7./JG27.

Bad weather in the Mersa Matruh area had hampered 252 Squadron operations for a few days and, on 13 March, Flg Off. Ted Taylor RCAF was despatched on a weather recce to the Rhodes area and arrived just in time to meet a formation of three Ju 52s of IV/TG1. He promptly despatched two into the sea but the third escaped in damaged condition but with no casualties. Both those lost were carrying troops/passengers, 099 of 16 Staffel flown by Uffz Joachim Kleindick and his crew going down with the loss of all onboard as did 217 of 13 Staffel flown by Fw de Res Gustav Dickentmann, his crew and a total of eleven passengers.

Flg Off. Tex Holland and his navigator Flt Sgt John Templeton of 227 Squadron had a very lucky escape from death on 16 March. While pursuing what was believed to have been an enemy aircraft off Cape Spada, Holland carried out such a tight turn (in X8103/O) that the starboard wingtip hit the water. He opened the throttles and gave full opposite rudder and somehow managed to draw the wing out of the sea. The propellers and engine nacelle were badly damaged and the undercarriage doors smashed. He managed to climb to 5,000 feet and ordered his navigator to prepare to bale out, but found that he was able to control the aircraft on one engine and returned to base where a safe landing was made. On inspection it was found that a propeller blade was bent back some two inches and the other two by at least an inch.

The month ended badly for 227 Squadron. The Beaufighter (JL915/N) flown by Sgts Phil Davies and Ron Beach failed to return from a convoy escort on 30 March while Flt Sgts L. Hibbert and H. Parker's aircraft (JL626/J) was damaged during a strike led by Sqn Ldr Bennett (whose aircraft was hit in the windscreen) on Kalamata harbour. JL626 was forced to ditch five miles from Tocra on the way home and the crew was picked up next day by a RN destroyer. 603 Squadron also lost a Beaufighter when 603/C force-landed at base having been hit by light flak. Neither Flt Sgt John Bowen nor his navigator was injured.

Wg Cdr Joe Blackburn arrived to take command of 227 Squadron on 15 March. Wg Cdr Pat Woodruff, who had finished his operational tour, was replaced by Wg Cdr Bryce Meharg, an Irishman, as CO of 252 Squadron.

April 1944

Although there were no conclusive aerial encounters for the Beaufighters during April, anti-shipping, ground-strafing and intruding were the orders of the day with all the inherent dangers associated with such missions. It proved to be a costly month for the Beaufighter crews.

The first loss of the new month befell 252 Squadron when Flg Offs. Bob Densham and Don Rooke in LZ464 failed to return from an intruder raid to Rhodes on 3 April; Densham was killed but Rooke survived and was soon back with the squadron. 46 Squadron also lost a Beaufighter (LZ369) over Rhodes this same night with the loss of Flt Sgt V. Lacey and Flt Sgt R. E. Brown. Two days later (5 April), four Beaufighters of 227 Squadron carried out a strafe of a caique off the Greek coast, Flg Off. Bob Owen's aircraft (JL730/O) striking a mast whereupon it crashed into a hillside, killing him and navigator Flt Sgt Len Everett. On 5 and 6 April, eight Beaufighters of 603 Squadron led by Sqn Ldr Pringle carried out rocket and cannon attacks against a German radar station at Palaiokhora on the south-west coast of Crete, putting it out of action. Spitfires of 94 Squadron provided protection should Bf 109s attempt to interfere, but the threat did not materialise.

On 8 April, 603 Squadron lost NE282/B during an attack on Karlovassi harbour, Samos. Sgt Bert Lacey was killed but his Scottish navigator Sgt John Foster managed to reach the shore in his dinghy and evaded capture:

> Flying low level, skimming the waves at about 180mph, the Beaufighters flew around the eastern tip of Samos, over a hill and down over Vathi harbour. We were at the back of the queue so it was pretty stirred up by the time we went in, the air was full of black clouds of heavy ack-ack. We just let off our stuff and got out. After five minutes of the return journey the plane was hit. I noticed the tip of the port slicing through the water. Next thing we were in the water. Somehow, Bert had turned a cartwheeling crash into a ditching. Believe me, that was first-class flying.[72]

Although Foster was able to extricate himself from the sinking aircraft, apparently Lacey had been injured and thrown some twenty yards away. He drowned without Foster being able to reach him. Despite a deep gash below his left knee, Foster was able to climb into the dinghy and sailed more than 100 miles in three days with the aid of a strong wind, and eventually reached the coast of the small island of Sirina where a local fisherman towed him to dry land. The fisherman's son carried the weak airman to the small village where he was tended, fed and nurtured back to health. After eight days he was rescued by an SAS party.

Another 603 machine went down on 11 April, W/O Eddie Lynch RAAF and Flt Sgt Cyril Sykes (NE421/L) losing their lives during a sortie to Paros where a fighter landing strip was being built by the Germans. Hit by flak, Lynch tried to ditch but an engine burst into flames causing the Beaufighter to stall into the sea where it exploded. Four of 252 Squadron later visited the landing strip and strafed trucks and a diesel roller. 603 Squadron returned to Paros on 13 April to strafe the airstrip, Sgt Jock Gow's aircraft (NE311/V) sustaining flak damage but was able to return to base. However, 603 did lose an aircraft and crew on this date during a search for an F-lighter off the coast of Cape Matapan during an early morning offensive patrol. When about six miles south of the cape, three Bf 109s of 7./JG27 came upon the four Beaufighters and attacked one pair, shooting down LZ370/N crewed by Sgts Reg Gosling and Stan West who fell to Uffz Günter Striebel, the same pilot who probably shot down the 16SAAF Beaufighter a month earlier. The remaining Messerschmitts attacked 603/F flown by Sgt T. Cook and W/O T. J. Harper RNZAF that was badly damaged though able to reach base. Sqn Ldr Pat Pringle (NE400/H), leading the other pair of Beaufighters, made a beam to quarter attack on one of the Messerschmitts, which broke away and all three headed for home.

It was Sqn Ldr Pringle's turn to survive flak damage on 16 April following an attack on a caique off Nios. On reaching base, the Beaufighter was found to have been hit by a cannon shell in the tail section, but all fragments had been contained by armoured doors behind the pilot's seat. Spitfires of the newly equipped 41SAAF Squadron flew escort to SAAF Marauders bombing Crete on this date, Capt. C. S. Courtney-Clarke (MA508) and Lt D. McLeod (LZ894) chasing away three Bf 109s that attempted to attack a flak-damaged Marauder. Three days later, two Bf 109s of 7./JG27 were scrambled to intercept a high-flying PR Spitfire of 680 Squadron reported over Melos, but Uffz Theo Heckman and Gfr Fritz-Dieter Reckmeier collided on take-off and both were injured.

May 1944

May was another costly month for the Beaufighters with four operational losses. More shipping-protection Ar 196s were encountered than in recent times and several clashes ensued. The airstrip on Paros continued to be a target for the Beaufighters as noted by an entry in 603 Squadron's ORB:

> It is felt strongly that every effort must be made to prevent completion of this landing strip in such a strategic position.

On 14 May, three Arados of 4./126 were encountered by Beaufighters of 603 Squadron when Flt Lt David Simpson RNZAF led an offensive sweep. Flt Sgt W. G. Harrison damaged D1+KN flown by Uffz Josef Meidel that was then shot down by Simpson who then damaged another as did Flt Sgt Cook, but the Arados made their getaway. Uffz Meidel and his observer/gunner Obgfr Max Kakarutt were lost. Next day, it was 603 Squadron that suffered losses. Four Beaufighters led by Sqn Ldr Pringle set out in NE400/H to carry out another attack on the landing strip at Paros, sinking a 100-ton caique en route. Over Paros they encountered very heavy flak that immediately shot down LZ404/Q crewed by Flt Sgts Jim Paddison and John Rhodes. The doomed Beaufighter broke in two and exploded on hitting the ground. A second Beaufighter (LZ281/K) was shot down into the sea with the loss of Flt Sgt Eric Harman and Flt Sgt Les 'Taffy' Hopkin. Both remaining aircraft, 603/R flown by Sqn Ldr Pringle and NE367/C with Flt Sgt Johnstone Edgar at the controls were also hit but managed to evade three Bf 109s that appeared and reached base safely. Edgar recalled:

> We had been alerted by reconnaissance that a number of Ju 52s were on the recently-completed strip on Paros. The formation, led by Sqn Ldr Pringle,

approached the island from the north, as usual at very low level. We formed a diamond four. We pulled up to gain height for a rocket attack on the landing strip and immediately all hell broke loose. Q broke in two, the centre stern section breaking away from the rest of the aircraft. The machine behaved like a falling leaf, the engines obviously still at full power, but with the rear control surfaces gone there was nothing the pilot could do to control the machine. Meanwhile, K had been hit and crashed into the ground, blowing up on impact.

My own aircraft, NE367, suffered a considerable number of hits, one of which succeeded in striking the wire which operated the release of the main dinghy in the port wing. The dingy inflated and blew off the covering panel, adding a considerable amount of noise to the explosions of flak. As we cleared the island, Harry [Wood] reported that three Me 109s had appeared over the landing strip. Fortunately they must have been low on fuel, for the left us alone and proceeded to land.[73]

In spite of the damage, Flt Sgt Edgar was able to land safely:

The aircraft was so badly damaged that it took the ground crew over seven weeks to render her serviceable.

252 Squadron lost two crews in the second half of the month, the first occurring on 16 May. Four Beaufighters led by Flg Off. Clem Fowler strafed six barges near Kos during which Plt Off. Dennis Lendrum and Flg Off. Don Rooke (NE579/G) were hit by flak and crashed into the sea in flames. Fowler's aircraft (NE554/Q) was also hit, his navigator Flt Sgt Gillie Potter suffering wounds to the forehead and ankle. With his port engine feathered, Fowler made a successful single engine landing back at base. On 25 May, Flg Off. Ed Taylor (LZ518/C) led an attack by three Beaufighters against a barge and a caique off Kos, but he failed to pull out of his dive in time and struck rising ground before cartwheeling into the sea. The Canadian Taylor and Flt Sgt David Dick were both killed. Kos was still taking its toll. Sgt Paddy McAughtry later commented:

We swept inland and climbed up over the slopes of a gentle-looking hill, prior to arriving unexpectedly through the back door. When we sorted ourselves out after strafing the harbour, Taylor was missing. Somebody said he had hit the top of the hill, an unbelievably silly mistake.[74]

Spitfire IXs of 94 Squadron were now coming to the fore and were being made available for bomber escort duties. On 31 May, they escorted Marauders of 24SAAF to Crete from where four Bf 109s of 13./JG27 arose to challenge. White 11 flown by Uffz Josef Plachy was promptly shot down by Flt Lt Hugh McLachlan RCAF (MH698) who also claimed a second as damaged. Plachy belly-landed south of Kastelli, wounded.

June 1944

By the end of May, the Kriegsmarine could muster only sixteen merchant vessels of all sizes to supply the islands under German control, such had been the havoc caused by Allied aircraft and naval vessels including the Beaufighter strikes. On the evening of 31 May, a substantial convoy left Piraeus for Crete with Candia being the ultimate destination. The convoy comprised *Sabine* (2,252 tons), *Gertrude* (1,960 tons) and the 1,545-ton *Tanais* with an escort of four large torpedo boats (*TA14*, *TA16*, *TA17* and *TA19*), three UJ-boats (*UJ-2101*, *UJ-2105* and *UJ-2210*) and two small fast torpedo R-boats (*R34* and *R2110*). The M/Vs flew barrage balloons for additional close protection while four Bf 109s from 13./JG27, four Ju 88s and four Ar 196s of 4./126 were also patrolling overhead. That it was to be an important but dangerous task for aerial attack there was no doubt and this was emphasised in the AOC-in-C's message of encouragement:

> As the Navy has no ships available, it remains to the Air Force to put this convoy down. The German military garrison in Crete is badly in need of supplies and the destruction of one or more ships of this convoy will be an important victory. There is bound to be flak and there may be fighter opposition and the AOC-in-C wishes you good luck and good hunting in your important mission.

A total of sixty-three aircraft were assembled for the strike, which was to be carried out in two waves during late afternoon of 1 June. The first wave comprised twelve Marauders of 24SAAF, fifteen Baltimores of 15SAAF and three from 454RAAF with an escort provided by seven Spitfire IXs of 94 Squadron and six Spitfires and four Mustang IIIs of 213 Squadron. The second wave was an all-Beaufighter affair: ten of 252 Squadron led by Wg Cdr 'Willie' Meharg; eight of 603; two of 227 as fighter escort; and four of 16SAAF, the majority carrying rockets. Sgt Paddy McAughtry of 252 Squadron wrote:

> The whole effort was to be led by our squadron. Very interesting. It would, therefore, be led by our Wing Commander [Meharg]. A squadron of real live American Mitchells arrived to take part, but when their cigar-chewing colonel was told that his men would have to sleep on the ground at Gambut

after the attack was over, with three blankets to cover each, in accordance with practice, he told his crews to get back to their aircraft, and off they flew back to Algeria where, presumably, living was easier.[75]

The bomber force was led by Lt-Col Cecil Margo of 24SAAF. The convoy was sighted a few minutes before 19:00 and the Marauders and Baltimores attacked. Much of the bombing was inaccurate, although one hit was claimed on the leading M/V, the *Sabine*. Sgt Ernest Wall, WOP/AG with 24SAAF, later wrote:

> The convoy was located in the Mandri Channel about 20 miles north of its destination, Candia harbour. It consisted of four M/Vs plus an escort of one destroyer, one light cruiser, eight flak ships and several Me 109s and Arado 196s. The Beaufighters went in to attack at sea level, the medium bombers at their normal height of 10,000 feet. Unfortunately the enemy concentrated on making things difficult for the Beaufighters, of which four were lost. One Baltimore was also hit and lost.

Sgt Paddy McAughtry onboard Flg Off. Clem Fowler's Beaufighter continued:

> The scene north of Crete when we hit the convoy and its cover was something to remember. The sky was blackened and torn asunder by heavy, medium and light flak. The ships in the convoy had scattered and their wakes were twisted, tortured streaks on the boiling sea. Ahead of us an Arado 196 floatplane dived for the sea, its starboard float in flames. The float was also the petrol tank.
> When the attack proper developed, fighters appeared and Beaus jinked and turned frantically. Overhead, in almost stately procession, the light bombers tried their luck on the heeling, turning ships. The first Beaufighter wave was the anti-flak force, strafing the decks of the escorting vessels to keep the gunners' heads down as the second wave attacked the soft ships with rockets. Before the eyes of the whole force, the Wing Commander's Beau [NE293/M] burst into flames. Failing to pull out of its dive, the machine hit the sea, cartwheeled and broke up.[76]

The first two of 252 Squadron to attack were W/O John Bates RAAF and Plt Off. H. A. Stevenson RCAF in their anti-flak role, followed by Sqn Ldr Ian Butler and Plt Off. Alf Pierce with rockets. They attacked *Sabine* and apparently blew off her stern. The *Tanais* was then targeted before Plt Off. Bill Davenport successfully rocketed the *Gertrude*, scoring hits on the bridge and superstructure. The Beaufighters of 603 Squadron followed suit, losing Flt Sgts Ron Atkinson and Dennis Parsons in LZ517. The South Africans also lost Beaufighter NE641/G, but Capt. E. A.'Tiny' Barrett and Lt A. J. Haupt – who had seen their rockets strike *TA16* – were able to reach Crete where they made a successful force-landing to become prisoners. Barrett's aircraft may have been hit by one of the Arados since his No.2, Lt G. B. Cruickshank, came under attack from the floatplanes as he released his rockets. Another of the SAAFs, Lt Peppie Richards fired his salvo of eight rockets into *TA16* and saw men frantically jumping overboard. All flak from this ship was silenced following his attack. The *Sabine* and *Gertrude* were left blazing wrecks, although the latter was towed into harbour in the early hours of the morning while the badly-damaged *Tanais* was able to limp into harbour that evening. *UJ-2101* and *UJ-2105* were sunk and *TA16* badly damaged.

Meanwhile, the Arados had put up a fierce fight and claimed no fewer than four Beaufighters shot down including the 603 machine (JM235/W) flown by Flg Offs. John Jones and Ron Wilson, which came down off the north-east coast of Crete. Jones was taken prisoner but Wilson fell into friendly hands and was soon on his way back home. The crews of 4./126 who claimed were Obfw Fritz Rupp/Oblt Richter; Obfw Werner Kurth/Ltn Böckling; Obfw Hässler/Uffz Büsse; and Obfw Kurt Chalupka/Oblt Schäfer. The other 227 Squadron pilot, Flt Sgt Fred Sheldrick (with Flt Sgt J. E. Ash in JL897/V) reported shooting down an Arado in return, witnessed by a 16SAAF crew, and Flg Off. J. A. T. Macintosh RCAF with Flt Sgt R. H. Alderton in 252 Squadron's NE479/E claimed another as damaged. Two Ar196s were reported to have been slightly damaged with no crew casualties. Flt Sgt Paddy McAughtry commented:

> When we got back from the action, we went straight into the bar. Somebody had brought back a length of anti-aircraft steel wire trailing from a wing, and this was laid along the bar as a souvenir. After we got thoroughly tight, we all went ceremoniously out and dismantled the red-and-white barrier pole and peed all over the whitened stones. Then we forgot all about the wing commander.[77]

It seems that 13./JG27's Messerschmitts were kept at bay by the escorting Spitfires and Mustangs. Two of the Spitfires flown Flt Lt Claude 'Tigger' Smith (MH696) and W/O F. E. Mitchell (MA427) attacked two of the Bf 109s at extreme range, 700-800 yards, as they attempted to get at the rear vic of the Baltimores, but no hits were claimed. The Mustangs dived down to attack three Ar 196s but were mistaken for Bf 109s and fired upon by the bomber gunners.

Although it was believed that Wg Cdr Willie Meharg and his navigator Flg Off. Ernest Thompson had been killed, they somehow survived the spectacular crash, as recalled by the latter:

I was wondering vaguely in my confused mind why everything was so peaceful. Slowly I became conscious of the fact that my body was in water which was steadily coming up to my head. Suddenly I realised fully everything that had happened and I knew that I must get out quickly before the aircraft sank. Two mistakes in the next few seconds might have cost me my life there and then. I tried to throw myself out of the hatch but I had not released the seat strap harness which held me securely at the moment of the terrific impact with the water. Frantically the straps were undone and I dived through the hatch to be pulled up short with a sudden jolt which seemed almost to break my neck. The lead from my headphones to the intercom socket was still plugged in but fortunately the strain jerked the earphones from the helmet.

As I came up to the surface my eye caught sight of the yellow rubber dinghy not more than 10 yards away. I struck out for it immediately only to find that the enemy fire had accounted for this as well – it was holed and useless. However, this shattering blow was temporarily forgotten when I turned back towards what was left of the aircraft. There was the nose and the pilot's cockpit still above water and I was so relieved to see this that I found myself shouting "Willie! Willie!" and trying to swim my fastest at the same time. I was about half-way there when I saw the skipper already in the sea hanging on to a small piece of floating wood. I called out "You OK Willie?" and heard him reply "I'm all right. How about yourself?"

I thought for the first time, how am I? I glanced down at my left arm and it looked horrible, a piece of raw flesh with streamers of skin trailing in the water like the white of an egg. But there was no pain at all – yet. We were both holding on the plank when what was left of the aircraft went down, nearly taking us with it. Heaven knows how much oil came flooding to the surface, covering us with filth. No matter how much we kicked we could not make clear water and finally gave up trying but still clung to the plank.[78] (see Appendix II)

The AOC-in-C sent his congratulations to the squadrons:

As various ships cannot be found I think we may now safely claim them as resting in the arms of Neptune and I wish to congratulate everybody on their very great success in the last few days. The perfect recce of 454 Squadron, the excellent work on the part of the bombers and their escorts, especially 15 and 24SAAF and the magnificent show of the Beaufighters may result in one of the greatest defeats the enemy has suffered in the Aegean. Finally I would like to express my thanks to the ground crews and maintenance personnel whose efforts have enabled us to put so many aircraft into the air.

The AOC 212 Group, Air Commodore N. S. Allinson, sent his own congratulatory message:

It was undoubtedly a notable victory on the anniversary of a famous date in British history – The Glorious First of June.

Early next morning (2 June), two Mustangs on reconnaissance discovered the *Gertrude* in the centre of the harbour well on fire, but of the *Sabine* there was no sign. Once again, Marauders of 24SAAF took-off escorted by Spitfires. *Gertrude* was hit from 14,000 feet and the fires increased. She sank that day and a destroyer, one of her escorts, capsized at her moorings. Sgt Wall of 24SAAF wrote:

> After the attack on the convoy there were still two of the M/Vs in Candia harbour meriting attention; one was *Gertrude* which had been badly hit, and the other the *Tanias*, 24SAAF took next day under the leadership of Capt D. Liddell with an escort of nine Spitfires. A near miss was observed on the *Gertrude*, which was seen burning. Four Marauders were holed by ack ack. Candia was a difficult target, having to be approached from the sea.
>
> 12 Marauders led by Major Johnny Davis DFC and six Baltimores of 15SAAF with an escort of eight Spitfires from 94 Squadron again bombed Candia harbour on 3 June. They missed the *Tanias* but scored direct hits on the installations and a few caiques. Nine Marauders were holed by ack-ack.

Following the excitement of the convoy attacks, the Beaufighters returned to 'normal' duty, intruding and convoy escorting. On the night of 4/5 June, Flt Sgt A. M. Webster (ND273/O) of 46 Squadron was tasked to carry out an intruder sortie to Kos. There, on Antimachia airfield, he sighted four Ju 52s and carried out a strafing attack. One Ju 52 was set on fire and two others claimed as damaged. An unusual incident occurred in the early hours of 6 June when Sqn Ldr Russ Foskett RAAF (MA766/F) CO of 94 Squadron was scrambled to investigate a bogey and encountered a low-flying Ju 52 over the coast near Tmimi at 04:00. Foskett carried out an attack and the Ju 52 force-landed ten miles west of Tmimi. It transpired that IZ+GZ of 15./TG1 flown by Gfr Siegmund Swieczkowski (a German of Polish extraction) had taken-off from Maleme at 23:50, leaving the rest of his crew behind since his intention was to defect to the Allies. He flew north from Maleme, round Cape Spatharia and the south to the North African coast at a height of seventy-five feet. Sqn Ldr Foskett's intervention made him carry out an emergency landing. That night, a Beaufighter of 46 Squadron failed to return from an intruder in the Rhodes/Kos area with the loss of Flt Sgt Allan Lord RAAF and Flt Sgt Tom Dawes. Their aircraft (ND273/O) crashed on Rhodes, presumably the victim of flak.

Hunting for the few remaining German supply ships remained the order of the day for the Beaufighter units, the most important of these being *Agathe* (1,259 tons), *Anita* (1,165 tons) and *Carola* (1,348 tons), all former

Italian vessels. Apart from *UJ*-boats and smaller R-boats, there was only the former Italian destroyer/torpedo boat *TA19* available for escort duties, all others having been sunk or damaged.

Intelligence revealed that a small convoy comprising *Agathe* and *Anita* and five escorting craft was on its way from Leros to Rhodes and was expected to arrive on 14 June. A dozen SAAF Baltimores were despatched from Cyprus with an escort of four 41SAAF Spitfire IXs to attack the convoy but failed to score any hits. On 15 June, a repeat attack on the convoy that had by now docked at Rhodes also failed, bad weather providing some temporary respite. While returning to Lakatamia from this escort, Lt Mauritz Hartogh's Spitfire (MA257) was hit by the scatter guns of one of the Baltimores owing to a short circuit in its electrical system. The Spitfire was holed in the cockpit and Hartogh narrowly escaped serious injury, the bullets inflicting flesh wounds in his thigh. Despite the bad weather, two Beaufighters of 16SAAF on convoy escort duty sighted a snooping Ju 88. Lt Fred Begbie attempted an interception but was hit by return fire. With its cockpit on fire, the Beaufighter (LZ397/M) was ditched, the pilot losing his life, although the navigator 2/Lt Phipps managed to get into his dinghy from where he was rescued by a corvette some time later.

17 June was to see some spirited action between Beaufighters of 227 and 16SAAF and four Arados of 4./126 escorting another small convoy encountered during an offensive mission off Cape Malea. The three 200-ton caiques (*Aspassia, Ioannis Kutifaris* and *Maria*) were escorted by two heavily-armed lighters (including *GK91*) in addition to the floatplanes, which fell upon the SAAF Beaufighters. Major Munton-Jackson and Lt Duncan Strange found themselves in close combat, Strange observing strikes on the Arado he attacked. These two then carried out rocket attacks on the vessels together with the other two SAAF Beaufighters, one of which (NE551/Z) was seen to crash in flames. Capt. Keith Muir and Lt Johannes Strydom were both killed. Major Munton-Jackson's aircraft was also hit and, with its starboard engine on fire, ditched off Cape Malea. The crew were seen in their dinghy. They survived and were rescued.

Meanwhile, the four 227 Squadron Beaufighters – a truly Commonwealth mix led by Flg Off. George Snape (JL910/S) with W/O N. R. Davis RCAF (JL619/X), Flt Sgt K. W. Abbott RAAF (JL897/V) and Flt Sgt D. H. Robertson RNZAF (EL398/M) – also scrapped with the Arados. Snape attacked the second floatplane in a formation of three and sent it down into the sea, confirmed by his navigator Flt Sgt J. G. Parnell who saw it burst into flames. Davis chased another and closed to fifty yards, seeing pieces break away before it, too, crashed into the sea. A third Arado was engaged by Robertson, seeing strikes before the rear-gunner's fire became too accurate. As he broke away, the other Arado tried to get on his tail but was chased away by Abbott who saw his fire blow a three-foot-wide hole in its fuselage. The damaged machine was seen to drift down and alight on the sea. Following his encounter with the Arado, Snape carried out a strafing attack on a lighter that was smoking badly following the SAAF Beaufighter's attack. Two of the floatplanes were totally lost: D1+AN ditched with both Uffz Paduch and Ltn Böckling safe and unhurt; and D1+FN from which Obgfr Schramm and Uffz Büsse were rescued, the latter slightly wounded. This crew claimed one of the Beaufighters shot down.

On 19 June, the sole surviving destroyer *TA19* was located by Beaufighters of 252 Squadron south-west of Kalymnos with an escort of two R-boats and three Ar 196s. Flt Lt Charles Whyatt led his eight aircraft in a rocket and cannon attack. Although not sunk, a large explosion was seen amidships and *TA19* was able to reach Athens for repair – it was now out of action, albeit temporarily. The Beaufighter (NE546/Q) flown by Plt Off. Bill Davenport and Flt Sgt Cyril Grainger was hit by flak and forced to ditch, its crew being rescued to become prisoners of war. Davenport's DFC was announced shortly thereafter. One of the Arados was engaged almost by accident by Flg Off. Clem Fowler as noted by his navigator Flt Sgt Paddy McAughtry:

There was sudden movement to my right, at the port side of the Beau. Something large and grey swam into view, I couldn't believe it. We had been joined by an Arado 196. I'd seen its silhouette a thousand times. This one was alike in every detail. We were joined together for about five seconds in a line of constant bearing. The enemy's starboard side was no more than fifty yards from me. I swivelled my Browning, aimed ahead and hose-piped the floatplane with .303 and tracer. The tracer showed that it was pouring into the aircraft right where the observer sat, behind the pilot. I kept firing at the little floatplane. I could see both pilot and observer clearly. The pilot gave one urgent glance in our direction and banked to port, away from us.

Clem turned to port and got a burst of cannon in at the target before we had to break off over the ships. Then we had to go round again and dire our rockets. As far as I could see, the ships were undamaged. Somebody had seen an Arado go down. Clem and I shared the kill between us. I didn't feel terribly pleased about sharing it … I kept, for some daft reason, aiming at the observer. If I'd tried for the pilot I'd have shot the bastard down on my own. I was close enough.[79]

The Ar 196, D1+CL of 3./126, suffered only slight damage.

There were several changes in command among the Beaufighter units during the month as COs became tour-expired. 46 Squadron received Canadian Wg Cdr Richard Denison AFC (who had flown Blenheim fighters during the Battle of Britain), while Wg Cdr Dennis Butler returned to take over 252 Squadron. Wg Cdr John Revell arrived to take command of 603 Squadron vice Wg Cdr Ronnie Lewis, while 16SAAF said goodbye to Lt-Col Jacko Lorentz with Lt-Col Phlippie Loock taking over at a time when 227 Squadron was being disbanded, the latter reverting to its original bomber role. A new Beaufighter squadron emerged from the ashes, 19SAAF being declared operational under the command of Lt-Col Don Tilley DFC.

There were also changes for the miniscule Luftwaffe fighter presence in the Aegean with the arrival of pilots and Bf 109Gs of 5./JG51 at Kastelli to relieve 13./JG27 that was to return to Germany. 5/JG51 then moved to Maleme with half the Staffel transferring to Gadurra (Rhodes) under Ltn Götz Bergmann, who would be killed in a take-off crash on 20 July. At least two of 13 Staffel pilots, Uffz Jakobi and Uffz Franz Stadler, transferred to 5./JG51 and moved to Rhodes.

July-August 1944

July opened with an intruder sortie over Leros by Sqn Ldr H. St. G. Bond of 46 Squadron (in MM872 with Plt Off. J. Lamb) when they sighted a line of seaplanes in Lepida Cove. They promptly strafed and reported that a Do 24 had been destroyed together with an Ar 196 and that one of each type had been damaged. In fact, Do 24T J9+AA of Seenotstfl.7 was destroyed and another plus an Ar 196 being damaged.

Eight Beaufighters of 252 Squadron led by Sqn Ldr Ian Butler were off at 20:00 on 3 July hunting for prey on the shipping routes when, an hour before midnight, they came across *Agathe* and *Anita* with an escort of small craft about two miles apart, north-west of Rhodes. The two M/Vs, having unloaded at Rhodes, were endeavouring to return to Leros under cover of darkness. In a devastating attack by the rocket-armed Beaufighters, with Flt Lt Charles Whyatt leading the way, *Agathe* suffered several hits, caught fire and eventually sank during the early hours of the following morning. Her sister ship *Anita* escaped in the darkness but was sunk two weeks later by a submarine. Sgt Paddy McAughtry was on this sortie, flying with Flg Off. Clem Fowler:

We were flying at three-minute intervals. At our leisure we circled it, and when the moment was right and the little ship was fair in the centre of the moon lane, we attacked. The thing to remember at night was to stick to rockets, leave off cannon-fire. This way, the enemy knew nothing until the banshee wail came down out of the black sky. We scored strikes early on. The ship began to burn, and for a hundred yards on either side of it the cool moon's light changed to the red heat of hell. Then we flew away.

At first light a recce aircraft saw only wreckage floating where the ship had been. And weeks later we learned from the Greek partisans that the ship had been packed with Italian soldiers, loyal to the pro-Allied Italian regime, being taken back to Italy for imprisonment. It was said that 200 died that night, in the golden light of the moon.

Paddy McAughtry also recalled some of his thoughts and fears as a Beaufighter navigator:

Strapped into the back seat, home seemed a million miles away. There was hardly any thought of it. I used to listen to my pilot's panted fear-signals, and stare at the armour plating that divided his compartment from mine. I was wound up tighter that the gutty in a golf ball.

Somewhere up in the islands the Messerschmitt boys were doing the same. On board the ships that were our targets the gunners were eyeing the weaving, shadowing aircraft and watching the skies all around. The multiple pom-poms were at the ready, as the convoy glided through the green Aegean. Along the route, on the islands, the flak regiments watched their radar screens for evidence that the Beaus were on their way. Although we flew towards our targets below the radar range at only 50 feet, so low that the slipstreams left wind-lanes on the sea, the land lookouts would be watching for us from the Cretan hills, or from Rhodes. We could never affect total surprise. Our leading aircraft were picked out well before the attack could be launched.

It was the 20mm and the .50 machine-gun stuff that had by far and away the highest killing-rate. Time and again we came back riddled like colanders with bullet holes. Six times at least great chunks were torn out of my Beau by 20mm pom-pom shells. Then again, the ships had taken to firing rockets just as we went into the attack. These rockets trailed strong wire cable, moored to deck positions. The wire could slice a wing off like a grocer cutting cheese.[80]

603 Squadron scored a rare aerial victory on 4 July when W/O L. F. Sykes RCAF (NE304/W) and Flt Sgt Ernest Pennie (NE246/K) caught a Ju 52 floatplane off Syros while on a flight from Gadurra to Tatoi. G6+BN of 5./ TG4 was shot down into the sea with the loss of Ofhr Heinz Faulhaber and his crew. Both crew and passengers were reported to have jumped into the sea before the aircraft burst into flames. Intelligence suggested that it was carrying among its passengers a high ranking Italian official. While on sweep the following day, 603 Squadron lost an aircraft and crew some ten miles east of Melos. The Beaufighter (NE579/M) flown by Sgt Charles Dean and Sgt Doug Taylor was seen to hit the sea, bounce thirty feet into the air and crash, bursting into flames – one of the dangers of wave-skimming to avoid radar detection.

94 Squadron found itself ever more occupied with bomber escorts to Crete and, on 8 July, managed to persuade 5./JG51 to challenge. Two Messerschmitts were claimed shot down by the Spitfire IXs, one each by Flt Lt Hugh McLachlan RCAF (MH698) and Flt Lt Roger Howley, but only Ofhr Rudolf Sauer's White 8 (760288) was hit and the pilot baled out into the sea from where he was not rescued.

16SAAF and the new 19SAAF were now transferred to the Balkan Air Force and thus departed the Aegean theatre of operations leaving just 252 and 603 Squadrons to continue anti-shipping missions, although fewer and fewer targets presented themselves. Sweeps were carried out, primarily against caiques with success but also with losses. 603 Squadron lost an aircraft and crew on 19 July when Sgt H. E. Yorke's NE595/S was hit by flak over Fiskardhou and crashed into the sea. The pilot was later reported safe but his navigator Sgt John Shaw was killed in the crash. 603 Squadron lost another crew on 21 July, Flt Sgt Donald Joyce and his navigator Flt Sgt Ken Thomas in NE465/R falling to flak during an attack on vessels east of Mykonos. A Ju 52 floatplane, GR+OR of 7./TG4, was reported shot down south of Anti-Melos on this date with the loss of Ltn Walter Peters and his crew but probably fell to a naval craft rather than Beaufighters.

It was proving to be a costly month for 603 Squadron with four more Beaufighters being lost two days later (23 July) in the same area when they clashed with Ar 196s of 3./126 near Mykonos. The six Beaufighters led by Flt Lt Tommy Deck DFC (formerly of 227 Squadron on his second tour) came off second best, although it seems that only one was shot down by the Arados and one (LZ340) by flak. W/O Sykes RCAF and Sgt W. H. Foxley in NE340/H ditched between Mykonos and Delos. Their ditching drill went well and they rowed their dinghy to Delos where they were greeted by a British MI9 agent who had witnessed their crash. Soon a message was on its way to Çeşme on the Turkish coast where MI9 had a clandestine base and a HSL picked them up and returned them to safety.

Onboard the second Beaufighter, Flt Sgt Jeff Rogers was lost when Flg Off. K. Jenkinson was forced to ditch NE610/X following engine failure caused by flak damage. Jenkinson managed to get into his dinghy and bandage a head wound with a piece of his parachute. With not a drop of water to drink and only two packets of chewing gum, a bar of chocolate and barley sugar sweets to eat, the future looked grim. Several times he was thrown out of the dinghy into the sea but each time struggled back. On the seventh day he saw a convoy and fired off his remaining distress signals. Fortunately, the flares were seen and he was rescued by an escorting destroyer.

Sgt Ernest Pennie's aircraft (NE367/C) was also hit by flak and he was seriously wounded but was able to reach base and crash-land. Meanwhile, Flt Lt Deck (NE415/P) and Flg Off. Cas de Bounevialle DFC (also on his second tour) engaged the Arados and jointly shot down D1+?L that ditched and was lost, though the crew survived. Whether damaged during the combat or by flak, de Bounevialle's aircraft (NE494/A) suffered an engine failure and he was also obliged to ditch. He and his navigator Flt Sgt Gillie Potter managed to climb into their dinghy, were rescued by a Greek caique and taken to a location south-east of Athens from where partisans helped them reach Turkey. Meanwhile, it was a rather dejected Flt Lt Deck who returned to base on his own from this disastrous mission though Flt Sgt Blanchette (NE413/W) followed some twenty minutes later.

High winds and rising sand prevented flying for the rest of the month, time sorely needed for 603 Squadron to lick its wounds, toast its missing men (although six were missing, only one had been killed) and receive replacement aircraft and crews. The squadron also lost the services of its CO, Wg Cdr Revell, who had not been fully fit. His place was taken temporarily by Sqn Ldr C. D. Pain pending the arrival of newly promoted Wg Cdr Chris Foxley-Norris, former flight commander in 252 Squadron.

252 Squadron did manage a mission on 28 July, six Beaufighters carrying out a nocturnal sweep north of Crete where they located a convoy of small vessels. Flt Lt Whyatt led an attack on the second vessel of the convoy but was hit by flak. With his port engine on fire, he attempted to ditch but the aircraft (NE255/C) exploded on impact. Both Whyatt and his navigator Flt Sgt Ray Barrett were killed. 252 lost two more Beaufighters on 1 August when two pairs operated off Levkas. One pair attacked two small vessels, which fired cable rockets as well as light flak, the latter hitting Canadian W/O Charles Davis' aircraft. The Beaufighter (NT895/H) was forced to ditch, Davis evading capture but his navigator Sgt George Waller was taken prisoner. The other pair meanwhile attacked an F-lighter but both sustained flak damage, Plt Off. John Clark RCAF reporting over the R/T that he was going to ditch, but his aircraft (LZ530/K) sank almost immediately with the loss of Clark and his navigator Flt Lt Edwin Young. Only an inverted dinghy remained floating amongst the debris.

94 Squadron's Spitfire XIs enjoyed another profitable day during a bomber escort mission to Crete on 10 August. Bf 109Gs of 5./JG51 scrambled to engage the bombers but were thwarted by Spitfires led by the CO Sqn Ldr Russ Foskett (MJ328) who claimed a Messerschmitt damaged as did Yugoslavian pilot Lt Ratomir Manojlović while fellow Yugoslav Capt. Dusan Stanić claimed one shot down.

Much of the remainder of the month for the Beaufighter units was occupied with nocturnal intruder missions, 603 Squadron losing a crew on 30 August as recalled by Canadian Flg Off. Harry Soderlund (NV213):

My navigator, Sergeant Ian Nichol and I were assigned to patrol the Aegean Sea north of Crete. The enemy was evacuating the island of Crete at this time. At the halfway point of our patrol and at an altitude of 200 feet I set a course for the homeward journey and coincidentally this provided a brilliant full moon path ahead of our aircraft.

As if in an aircraft recognition class, the silhouette of a Junkers 52 passed across the moon path at a distance of perhaps 2,000 feet. The training and discipline that soldiers, sailors, and airmen undergo instil a sense of duty and without hesitation I turned the Beaufighter in pursuit of the enemy aircraft. Ian Nichol soon made radar contact and began to read off closing distances. As soon as I was able to discern the grey shape of the Junkers 52, I swung the gunsight into position in front of me and lowered speed since our aircraft was much faster. When the wingspan of the Junkers 52 filled the firing circle on the gunsight I pressed the 20mm cannon-firing button. Tracers streamed out ahead and I turned sharply to port to break off the attack. I doubt that the enemy aircraft was hit and events that followed precluded any further investigation.

In turning to port to break off the attack our Beaufighter almost collided with another Junkers 52 flying in the opposite direction to the first one. At this point I made the mistake of continuing in pursuit of the second Junkers. Bullets from his rear gun hit our port engine and it quickly lost power. I attempted to feather the propeller to reduce drag, at the same time straining to keep the aircraft flying straight against the pull of the still functioning starboard engine. The propeller did not feather and I could see flames at the back of the port engine. All my thoughts and energy were now concentrated on keeping the Beaufighter flying but a slight bump at the back of the aircraft meant the tail end had touched the water. Moments later the Beaufighter slid onto the water. I hit my head on the windscreen as the aircraft came to a sudden stop with the nose in the water. I quickly opened the overhead escape hatch and hit my parachute and seat belt release button and climbed out on the wing. Ian Nichol was already there.

In a matter of seconds the Beaufighter sank beneath us and I inflated my Mae West and Ian's. The water at this time of the year was not cold and we were not uncomfortable. It happened that a one-man dinghy, either mine or Ian's, had floated out of the aircraft and this was another of the fortunate circumstances that contributed to our survival. We inflated it and climbed in. My feet dangled in the water. We had survived the rather heavy odds of crashing into the sea at night. I am proud that I carried out my duty to the best of my ability and am thankful that neither I nor Ian had suffered debilitating injuries.

A fully lit hospital ship was passing some distance away and we tried attracting attention with one of the small lights aboard the dinghy, but to no avail. An enemy aircraft circled a couple of times with a landing light on, but did not see us. A couple of days later, when our dinghy had drifted towards the town of Candia, a German patrol boat came out and picked us up. (see Appendix II)

September-December 1944

With the war going very badly for the Germans on all fronts, particularly in the East, the decision was taken to withdraw as many troops as possible from their Aegean garrisons. More Ju 52s were drafted in to help the few remaining ships and, as the situation worsened, German troops were also evacuated from Southern Greece.

The Beaufighters were given the task of interfering with the evacuations both in the air and at sea. 46 Squadron, being a dedicated night fighter unit, was granted the opportunity to get to grips with the aerial evacuation since most of these flights were made during the hours of darkness (see Chapter X) while 252 and 603 Squadrons continued to harry any movement by caiques and other small craft.

One of the few remaining sizeable vessels was the 1,348-ton *Carola* that had been undergoing repairs at Leros. On 5 September, she was sighted together with two flak ships for protection heading for Piraeus. Eight Beaufighters of 252 Squadron with four of 603 as top cover were despatched to sink her. Led by Wg Cdr Dennis Butler, the rocket-armed Beaufighters finally located the small convoy nearing the Greek mainland, south-east of Athens. In the face of intense 37-mm and 20-mm flak as well as parachute rockets, the Beaufighters swept in leaving all three vessels severely damaged. *Carola* did not sink but was so badly damaged that she entered dry dock, though not repaired and sunk as a block ship a few weeks later by the Germans. Two of the attacking Beaufighters were hit but made it back to base while 603's top cover pursued an escorting Ar 196 of 2./126 that was damaged. This may have been the aircraft (D1+?K) flown by Oblt Klaus-Jürgen Rohwer who claimed a Beaufighter shot down.

On 7 September, Do 24 Q8+AB of Seenotstfl.7, took-off from Athens with Croatian-born Hptm. Marijan Gorecan at the controls with mechanic Fw Karl Mahl as companion. The aircraft never returned and was reported as missing. The next day the Germans intercepted a radio message that stated a German seaplane had landed in the harbour of Izmir in Turkey. The crew had defected.

During the morning of 9 September, Wg Cdr Butler led eight Beaufighters of 252 Squadron against a small convoy reported plying between Crete and Melos that turned out to be *UJ2142* accompanied by an armed caique. The

Beaufighters attacked with rockets and cannon, causing severe damage to both. Escorting 603 Squadron Beaufighters encountered an Ar 196, D1+HN of 4./126, south of Melos, which Sqn Ldr Tommy Deck (NV213) and Flt Lt David Simpson (LZ376) promptly despatched into the sea.

603 Squadron lost a Beaufighter on 13 September during a sweep made by eight aircraft. Plt Off. A. B. Woodier (NE367) was obliged to ditch with engine problems, but both he and Sgt H. Lee managed to evade capture and soon returned. As the result of a Baltimore report on 14 September, indicating that the 1,800-ton minelayer *Drache* might be in the harbour at Paros, sixteen Beaufighters (eight from each squadron) set out to launch an attack. The *Drache* was not present but a small minesweeper, the 260-ton *Nordstern*, was sunk as was a smaller craft. One Beaufighter was hit by flak but was able to return safely.

Sqn Ldr Tommy Deck (NV215/R) was at the head of eight Beaufighters of 603 Squadron on 16 September and engaged two Ju 52s and an Arado near Portolago Bay, but the transports sought the protection of fierce local flak. Nonetheless, Sqn Ldr Deck pursued the Arado as his Canadian navigator Flg Off. Lee Heide later wrote:

Tommy and I ran into trouble. We were near Naxos when I spotted an Arado 196 going in an easterly direction. "Tally-ho!" I shouted. "Where? What?" Tommy asked. "Do a tight turn to port and you'll come up behind an Arado 196." "Good stuff!" Tommy was excited. He threw the Beau into a gut-wrenching turn. But the Arado had seen us. The pilot opened the taps, dove for sea level and headed for Leros harbour. So did Tommy. The Beau was a lot faster and we caught the Arado near the harbour entrance. A burst from our four 20mm cannons sent it crashing into the rocks. "Good shooting!" I congratulated Tommy. "Like shooting quail!" he responded.[81]

We were now close to Leros harbour. "There's an anti-aircraft site on that point of ground south of the harbour entrance," I said, so that Tommy could take evasive action and avoid it. Stupid me! "Let's wake them up!" Tommy shouted as he headed straight for the gun emplacement. He fired all eight rockets and we could see carnage below; he followed this with all four cannon as he flew right over the site. There seemed to be nothing left intact but not all guns had been stilled. Just as we were pulling away the port side of the Beau was raked from stem to stern. The port engine began to vibrate, shrapnel careered around the inside as cordite and smoke filled the air.

"Get out of here!" I shouted. "Fly south." "I am ... I am. Are you OK?" "Yeah, I guess so." A shell had ripped through the fuselage right in front of me and ended up in the cannon magazines. "How about you?" "I'm not hit," Tommy replied, "but the port engine won't last long." "We'd better not try to fly across the Med," I said. "What say we hug the Turkish coast and try to make Cyprus?"

"All right." "We'll soon come to Rhodes, so stay low and very close to Turkey and maybe they won't see us." "Okay."

Shortly after passing Rhodes, Tommy feathered the port propeller and said: "Lee, we're losing fuel from the port gas tank ... it must have taken a hit." "Damn! How much fuel do we have now assuming that tank to be empty?" He gave me the number. I checked my fuel graphs for one-engine performance (with the good engine at nearly max) calculated our consumption, worked out our ground speed and measured the distance to Cyprus. "We're not going to make it to Cyprus," I said, sadly. "We'll have to put down in Turkey." "Where?" He was quite casual. "Give me a minute to look at my intelligence notes." This I did. "We are coming up to a large bay where there is a town called Antalya. It doesn't have an airfield as such but there is supposed to be a 2,000-foot strip of Summerfield stripping." "That's those metal pieces that looks like a giant Meccano set?" "Yes."

I thought for a minute. "Tommy, do you want me to lighten the aircraft by throwing things out?" "No need," he replied. "I'll fire the cannons to get rid of the spare ammunition." This he did. "I've got some stuff that I want to throw out ... have you?" "Just some let-down plates and recognition codes. I'll toss them out of my side window." "Well, I have quite a bit and I don't have a window so I'll have to jettison the canopy." "Go ahead." Nothing ever fazed him.

My bubble canopy had two locking catches on the port side and two hinges on the starboard. The manufacturer's recommended procedure to jettison was to unfasten the two catches and give the canopy a sharp push upwards; the slipstream would then tear the canopy away. But we, and our sister squadrons, had found two flaws. One – the rear hinge would not always break and that left the canopy flapping in the wind. Two – the canopy was in danger of striking the tail plane, giving the pilot a severe problem. So our technicians had installed explosive bolts at the two hinges. I released the port catches, lifted the red guard and pushed the button. There was a loud 'bang' and the canopy sailed away. "Eureka!" I shouted. "Worked all right, did it?" Tommy asked. "Like a charm . . . but it's sure draughty in here now."

I tore up all my logs, intelligence notes and other papers and watched them fly away. There were two pieces of equipment that I didn't want to fall into the wrong hands. One was the IFF. I crawled forward. The unit was amidships. It was a black box. I cut the wires to the antenna and then those to the front cockpit. Then I unscrewed the unit and threw it overboard. The other was the radio transceiver. Try as I might, I couldn't get it out of its rack, so I drove the fire axe into it a couple of times. I also took the film out of the gun camera.

Antalya was easy to spot. It seemed to be a fair-sized town. The field with the metal stripping was to the east. Tommy made a pass to look things over. "I don't think that anyone has ever used this strip," he said. "There's grass and weeds growing through the holes and alongside. It's hard to see where it begins and ends." "Are you going to lower the gear?" I asked. "Yes." "Then give me a minute to cross-switch the generators. The port one lowers the gear and it's not working." This I did. We could see from smoke rising from the town that there was virtually no wind. Tommy said: "I'll land going north ... I can see that end of the stripping better. It may be rough so brace yourself." I turned my seat around so that I was facing the rear and slumped down a little so that my head was resting against the seat back. "Oh, shit!" I mumbled. "Here we go again!"[82]

Sqn Ldr Deck skilfully force-landed the Beaufighter and faced internment in Turkey for the second time while Flg Off. Heide was less certain of his future, having evaded capture after having been shot down off Elba during his previous tour. They were soon rescued from their plight and were back in Cairo within a few days.

At last, during the morning of 23 September, the elusive minelayer *Drache* was finally located beside the jetty at Vathi, Samos, by a Beaufighter of 252 Squadron. By mid-afternoon, eight Beaufighters of 252 Squadron led by Wg Cdr Butler, accompanied by four of 603, were on their way to make an attack. The rocket-firing Beaufighters waded in, and despite return fire and cable rockets, carried out a devastating assault. There followed a series of explosions and she caught fire and was completely gutted. Another choice target had been located by an RAAF Baltimore, the 700-ton *Orion* that had recently arrived in the Aegean to help with the evacuation, was spotted taking shelter in Chendro Bay on the tiny island of Denusa, ten miles east of Naxos. Seven Beaufighters of 252 led by Flt Lt Clem Fowler, escorted by four of 603 headed by Flg Off. Cas de Bounevialle, were soon on the scene. Attacked with rockets and cannon, the ship was soon on fire and was later confirmed have been burnt out. Flak was heavy and accurate, 252 Squadron losing the aircraft (LZ456) crewed by Flt Sgt Stan Skippen and Jack Truscott, both of whom were killed. The final success of the month occurred on 27 September with Wg Cdr Butler leading eight Beaufighters to attack a small coaster, the 314-ton *Helly*, which was located tied up at the jetty on the island of Andros. She was rocketed and sunk as was a nearby caique.

In Preparation of the Allied Invasion of Greece

During the night of 13/14 September, a total of ninety-two Wellingtons, B-24s and Halifaxes dropped 194 tons of bombs on the three airfields near Athens (Eleusis, Kalamaki and Tatoi) claiming fair to excellent results. On 14

September, Eleusis, Tatoi and Kalamaki airfields were again targets for eighty-four B-24s and Wellingtons which dropped 202 tons with good to excellent results. On 15 September, a force of 327 heavy bombers escorted by eighty-four P-51s pounded Salamis submarine base and Eleusis, Kalamaki and Tatoi airfields with almost 687 tons of bombs. Claimed damage included fifty-one enemy planes destroyed on airfields, a destroyer, floating dock and submarine claimed sunk, another destroyer damaged, two floating cranes destroyed and another submarine missed. According to Allied intelligence reports, 200 Germans were reported killed. Fighters also strafed Eleusis airfield. On 24 September, 252 B-24s dropped 473 tons of bombs on airfields at Kalamaki (to where 5./JG51 had just withdrawn from it former base at Maleme), Eleusis and Tatoi. P-51s of 332FG escorted B-24s as they raided targets in Athens.

The bombardment of aerodromes around Athens by heavy and medium bombers continued into October with fighter-bomber attacks applying the finishing touches to the remains of the Luftwaffe. On 4 October, P-51s of 332ndFG (flying from Ramitelli airfield in Italy) strafed targets at Tatoi, Kalamaki and Eleusis claiming nine aircraft destroyed on the ground. Six P-51s failed to return. The Allied raid on Tatoi on the night of 7/8 October slightly damaged all four of 2.(F)/123's remaining Ju 88s. One was repaired in time to fly recce to Melos and Kythera the next day, but it crashed on landing due to brake trouble and was written off. On 9 October, Wellingtons attacked Tatoi, Eleusis and Kalamaki airfields throughout night dropping in excess of forty-five tons of bombs with hits on landing ground, hangars and buildings.

Four Spitfire IXs of the newly formed 10SAAFSquadron carried out an armed recce over Crete on 2 October, led by their CO Major Cecil 'Zulu' Swales DFC. One was obliged to return early but the other three destroyed a solitary MT on the Marathons to Vamps road. With few targets left at the beginning of October, Beaufighter day operations began to tail off, although 3 October provided some trade when 603's new CO Wg Cdr Foxley-Norris led a dozen Beaufighters, including two of 252 Squadron, to hunt down one of few remaining sizeable vessels, the 2,423-ton minelayer *Zeus*, known to be operating off the east coast of the mainland. The intended victim was not found, however, but a convoy of five small vessels was and duly rocketed, leaving three badly damaged. Return fire was intense, shooting down 603's Sgt Desmond Harrison and Derek Bannister in NT893; the pilot was killed but the navigator evaded capture. Flg Off. Cas de Bouneville's aircraft (NV205) was also hit and forced to ditch, he and Plt Off. Gillie Potter's second such experience in a few weeks. They again survived but were rescued by an UJ-boat and this time became prisoners. These were the last losses suffered by 603 Squadron that flew its last Aegean operation on 26 November and then disbanded.

Four Spitfire IXs of 10SAAF ventured over Crete again on 7 October, Capt. Trevor Fryer leading the hunt for MT travelling along the roads. Two vehicles and a ten-ton trailer were destroyed and several other vehicles damaged. Lt John du Toit's Spitfire was hit by flak in its long-range tank but he managed to reach base with ten minutes of fuel to spare. Capt. Fryer's aircraft was also hit but not seriously damaged.

On the night of 7/8 October, RN destroyers HMS *Termagant* and HMS *Tucson* encountered a small convoy comprising the minelayer *Zeus* with 1,125 evacuees crowded onboard escorted by *TA37*, *UJ2102* and a small patrol boat in the Gulf of Salonika. In a short, sharp exchange, *TA37* was sunk but *Zeus* escaped. Do 24 J9+DA of Seenotstfl.7 was among the rescue craft despatched to the area. The Dornier crew sighted a raft on which two oil-smeared men were seen and then many heads bobbing in the water. The seaplane alighted and recovered the two men from the raft including an officer and a further twenty-five were plucked from the sea. Recovery was difficult owing to the leather-clad survivors coated in oil. Ten of those recovered had gunshot wounds and complained that they had been machine-gunned in the water by the destroyers. They were the lucky ones as 104 of *TA37*'s crew were lost.

Athens was occupied on 14 October as were a number of Aegean islands including Syros, Naxos, Lemnos and Scarpanto. Kalymnos was encouraged to surrender following a 603 Squadron 'spectacular' ten days later. Wg Cdr Foxley-Norris wrote:

There were problems with isolated island garrisons, cut off and with no offensive capability but still reasonably armed and entrenched; they would have taken a lot of dislodging had they decided to fight it out. To discourage them from doing so we attacked their barracks and gun positions with rocket and cannon; but this was not always easy since the barracks were often in the centre of towns and villages and we wanted to avoid killing our Greek friends, whose hardships and deprivations were already extreme. This situation provided for me one of the classic signals of all time. The target of the mission was a small German force in the island town of Kalymnos. The executive signal from Higher Authority to me as leader read:

'Pilots will not, repeat not, open fire but will fly in such a manner as to leave no doubt in the minds of the enemy that his fate is sealed.'

After some debate and tooth sucking, we finally interpreted this oracle by flying over the town at low-level upside down. Oddly enough, it did the trick.[83]

About 18,500 German and 4,500 Italian Fascist troops remained on Crete, Rhodes, Leros, Kos and Melos, but these offered little threat to the Allies.

Some of the garrisons were left to stagnate, acutely short of food and harried by the RAF and Greek partisans until they decided to surrender. Maleme airfield on Crete was bombed on 13 October by six aircraft and the same target attacked again on 14, 16 and 18 October. This target was chosen to hamper obvious German attempts to evacuate key personnel by air now that the sea routes around Crete were dominated by Allied naval forces. This scale of attack could not hope to put the airfield out of commission although its irritant value was clear from the way in which the Germans packed more and more anti-aircraft guns on and around Maleme to protect the vital runways. On the 16 October raid, four Spitfire IXs of 10SAAF Squadron provided the escort for the bomber attack on Maleme, Lt Jack Brown (MA526) suffering engine failure and being obliged to force-land on the island. He was quickly recovered by a British commando unit and returned to his squadron.

CHAPTER IX

Seafires, Hellcats and Wildcats over the Aegean

Nine of the Royal Navy's CVE escort carriers (Task Group 88 comprising No. 4 and No.7 Naval Fighter Wings) had been employed in operations in support of the Allied invasion of Southern France (Operation *Dragoon*) during August, and four of these carriers moved into the Aegean (Operation *Outing I*) commencing 9 September, followed by three more during the month. All seven carriers were then involved in operations designed to isolate German garrisons in the Aegean and Dodecanese.

HMS *Hunter*   807 Squadron with fifteen Seafire LIII + five Seafire
  LRIIC   (Lt-Cdr(A) L. G. C. Reece RNZNVR)
HMS *Khedive*   899 Squadron with twenty Seafire LIII
  (Lt-Cdr(A) R. B. Howarth)
HMS *Pursuer*   881 Squadron with twenty Wildcat IV
  (Lt-Cdr(A) L. A. Hordern DSC)
HMS *Searcher*   882 Squadron with twenty Wildcat IV
  (Lt-Cdr(A) G. R. Henderson DSC)
HMS *Attacker*   879 Squadron with fifteen Seafire LIIC + five Seafire
  LRIIC   (Lt-Cdr(A) R. J. H. Grose)
HMS *Emperor*   800 Squadron with twenty Hellcat I + one Walrus + one
  Swordfish   (Lt-Cdr M. F. Fell DSC)
HMS *Stalker*   809 Squadron with fifteen Seafire LIII + five Seafire LRII
  (Lt-Cdr(A) H. D. B. Eaden)

HMS *Emperor*'s 800 Squadron included six Dutch pilots who had been flying with 1840 Squadron: Sub-Lt(A)s Herman 'Harm' deWit, Wladimir Saltykoff (of Russian ancestry), Willem Limque, Charles Poublon, Gerardus Greve and Jan Helfrich.

En route to her station, HMS *Emperor*'s Hellcats carried out a total of twenty-four armed recces off the island of Melos on 14 September, attacking shore targets and shipping while Seafires and Wildcats provided daylight protection for the cruiser HMS *Royalist* and her destroyer escort, which were involved in night attacks on local shipping north of Crete. The first strike of Operation *Outing I* was carried out on 16 September when bomb-armed Wildcats searched for road transport and caiques along the western coastline of Crete. Three returned with flak damage (including JV696 flown by Lt T. M. Brander, and JV677/P flown by Sub-Lt(A) R. P. Gibson) but were able to land safely.

On 17 September, aircraft from HMS *Khedive* and HMS *Searcher* again attacked road transport on Crete and caiques found offshore. On Rhodes' Maritza airfield, a degaussing-ring-equipped[84] Ju 52, 3K+HM (3404) of 4./ *Minensuchgruppe 1* (Mine-Detecting Staffel 4), was destroyed on the ground by low-flying aircraft, possibly FAA fighters. One patrol of 882 Squadron Wildcats came upon what they thought were Ju 88s and carried out an attack on one, only to find that their victim was Beaufighter NT912/H of 603 Squadron crewed by Sgts A. E. Arthurs and F. G. Richardson. The Beaufighter was badly damaged but managed to escape their attention and crash-landed back at base. The crew was unhurt. 252 Squadron's newly-promoted fighting Irishman Plt Off. Paddy McAughtry recalled the sequel to this incident:

One day four of our Beaus were in the central Aegean carrying out a sweep when they were jumped by Seafires [*sic*] from a nearby British carrier. Luckily all our pilots were experienced, otherwise there might have been severe damage done. The Beaus made for Turkey, this being a favourite dodge on our part when the Huns made an interception. The Turks practised benevolent neutrality towards the Allies, meaning that they left our aircraft in peace to fly anywhere they wanted around the coast whilst dodging German fighters, whereas the Germans got the full works from the anti-aircraft batteries. When our machines returned that day a complaint was made to the Naval HQ at Alexandria. With the complaint went a sniffy comment on the general ability of the fighters concerned.

A few days later I was in Alexandria on leave with John Bates. We hadn't been [in the *Le Petit Coin de France*] for five minutes when in walked a party of naval officers, nice and neat in their whites. They stood near us at the bar, talking in the fruity voices that naval officers adopted. They all wore pilot's badges. I nudged one of the newcomers: "You weren't by any chance up around Kos and Leros last week, were you?" Their mouths all fell open at the same time. They nodded. I tapped my chest, and pointed to John. "Beaufighters," I said. I slid off my stool. "Do you think we look like frigging Germans?"[85]

Fortunately, one of the FAA pilots recognised McAughtry as an old acquaintance and thereby prevented a brawl from breaking out. Over the course of many more drinks, McAughtry learned that some of his new companions were awaiting a court of enquiry into the Beaufighter incident.

On 18 September, eight Seafires from HMS *Khedive* and eight from HMS *Attacker*, each armed with a 500-lb bomb, attacked Suda Bay (Crete) where two BV 222s and two Do 24s escaped damage, these departing at dusk. A strafing run was not advised owing to the very strong flak defences. 899 Squadron's NN350 tipped on its nose on landing but Sub-Lt(A) G. C. Shelley was unhurt. HMS *Royalist*'s destroyer escort gained a notable success when they sank one of the last U-boats (*U-407*) still operating in the Mediterranean. During the forenoon of 19 September, a total of twenty-two bomb-carrying Seafires, ten Hellcats and ten Wildcats set out to attack shipping in Rhodes harbour, which included the transport *Pomezia*, three depot ships, a KT (Kreigstransport) and some auxiliary vessels. The Seafires of 899 Squadron from HMS *Khedive* were led by Lt-Cdr Howarth who managed to place his 500-lb bomb between the KT and the jetty. One of his pilots, Sub-Lt(A) Vic Lowden, scored a direct hit on a depot ship and another saw his bomb hit the jetty. Pilots of 879 Squadron from HMS *Attacker* scored two hits on the *Pomezia* and damaged two depot ships. Flak did not respond to the attack until it was almost over and all aircraft returned safely. During this strike an entire road convoy of eight vehicles was strafed and destroyed. The carriers returned to Alexandria on 21 September for replenishment, HMS *Khedive*, HMS *Pursuer* and HMS *Searcher* being withdrawn for return to UK waters while HMS *Attacker*, HMS *Hunter* and HMS *Stalker* joined HMS *Emperor* with the task force.

There followed a spate of deck-landing accidents. On 25 September, Sub-Lt(A) C. E. Wright bounced Seafire NF439 of 807 Squadron into HMS *Hunter*'s barrier. Two days later, 809's CO, Lt-Cdr Eaden, bounced NN112 into both barriers onboard HMS *Stalker*. Onboard HMS *Emperor* on 29 September, two Hellcats (JV232 and FN333) suffered barrier crashes but neither Sub-Lt(A) W. D. Vine nor Sub-Lt(A) C. A. S. Pain was hurt, while onboard HMS *Stalker*, Sub-Lt(A) G. H. Brittain of 809 Squadron experienced undercarriage collapse when landing Seafire MB136 and Sub-Lt(A) G. C. Morris (NM967) bounced into the barrier.

Further strikes were carried out from 30 September (Codename *Outing II*) including one against Maleme airfield (Crete) on 1 October. HMS *Emperor* was out again for a third foray into the Aegean and two days later, Hellcat JV263 failed to return from a strike on Leros and Sub-Lt(A) Keith Wilson was lost. The Hellcats destroyed Plimiri radar station on Rhodes on 4 October while two of its Dutch pilots, Sub-Lt(A) Harm deWit and

Sub-Lt(A) Gerrie Greve, jointly shot down a Ju 52 of 13./TG1 approaching Maleme. DeWit was later diverted to Turkey and force-landed JV126 at Gökova airfield where he was interned. Onboard HMS *Hunter*, Sub-Lt(A) G. E. Thomas bounced and skidded along the deck and into the barrier, damaging Seafire NM934 but escaping injury.

HMS *Hunter* and HMS *Stalker* joined cruisers HMS *Aurora* and HMS *Black Prince* for a foray into the Central Aegean on 6 October, Seafires strafing ground targets on Kos and Leros on 7 October. Sub-Lt(A) Anthony Perry (NF638/S-Z) of 809 Squadron was hit by flak while attacking lorries on Kos, collided with a church spire and crashed at Zinopoten where he died of his wounds. Shortly after noon, four bomb-armed Seafires together with four escorts located a small convoy including a 1,000-ton freighter that received a direct hit and three near-misses whereupon it sank within twenty seconds. The Seafires strafed other vessels and set a caique on fire, but flak shot down 807's NF439 from which Sub-Lt(A) Donald Stewart baled out but was lost. Two hours later, another 1,000-ton freighter, *Silva*, was located about forty miles west of Leros and was promptly despatched by Seafires.

On 8 October, the Seafires from the two carriers flew a total of sixty-one sorties, sinking a medium-sized transport off Khalkis and a small tanker off Cape Kassandra, also attacking an F-lighter, a caique and a Seibel ferry. Two Seafires were hit, one being forced to ditch, but the pilot was rescued by the destroyer HMS *Tuscan*. A pair of 809 Squadron Seafires from HMS *Stalker* on a sweep over northern Greece attacked a railway engine, Sub-Lt(A) Ray Rawbone (MB150) setting the wagons on fire and also damaged a water tower and a signal box between Larissa-Salonika. On the return flight, he sank a small coaster in conjunction with Sub-Lt(A) G. H. Brittain (MB136). A further fifty-two sorties were flown on 9 October, an attack by eight fighter-bombers of 809 Squadron with two flak-suppression Seafires of 807 Squadron against the destroyer/torpedo boat *TA38* meeting with success. The damaged vessel managed to reach Volos where she was later scuttled. Other sections of 807 Squadron Seafires destroyed two trains at Salonika, sunk a Siebel ferry and damaged another off the Kassandra peninsula. The carriers began to withdraw the next day, the Seafires attacking the harbours at Syra, Port Laki (Leros) and Kos en route.

HMS *Emperor* returned to the arena on 11 October, her Hellcats attacking convoys and the Larissa-Katerina railway line, but not without loss. Sub-Lt(A) Charles Spencer RNZNVR in JV149 was shot down and killed by flak over the Euripo Channel near Khalkis, while Sub-Lt(A) Jan Helfrich, one of the Dutch pilots, reportedly made an emergency or crash landing near Mount Olympus, some sixty miles from Salonika. HMS *Emperor* returned to Alexandria on 13 October where she replenished before departing immediately for Operation *Manna* (the occupation of Athens) in company with HMS *Attacker* and HMS *Stalker*, plus the cruiser HMS *Royalist* and six destroyers. The Athens landings began on 15 October covered by Seafire patrols from dawn to dusk. The only enemy aircraft to appear, however, was a snooping Ju 88 of 2.(F)/123 that was encountered by Lt(A) David Ogle (MB150) leading a pair of Seafires of 809 Squadron. Ogle pursued the Ju 88T (4U+?K) and shot it down into a field near Anavyssos at 10:30 in which Fw Erich Labus (pilot) and two others were killed, while W/Op Uffz Alfred Kondek survived to be taken prisoner; his interrogation report later revealed:

When 4U+?K took off from Mega at 09:00 its mission was to cover possible British landings in the Athens area. While their mission was primarily to cover the progress of Allied landings in Greece, the crew was also ordered to reconnoitre the waters of the Aegean and in particular to search for an aircraft carrier which had been reported in the entrance to the Gulf of Salonika. The pilot set course due south, and while flying on this leg at nought feet in bad visibility they nearly hit a destroyer which loomed up out of the fog. Although they circled in an attempt to locate this ship again, the visibility was too low.

The eastern coast of Greece was crossed at Platahon and course set for Larissa. The mountain road which leads across the pass of Thermopylae and down to Athens was then followed, and the retreating German forces photographed. When the harbour of Athens was reached a photographic reconnaissance of the approaches to the port was made, and targets are described as plentiful. While over the south-east of Athens they sighted some British warships in the Salonic Gulf. It was while they were flying a south-westerly course to investigate that the Spitfires [*sic*] came up. Keeping below cloud whose base was about 2,800m, the aircraft was attacked over Piraeus by a number of fighters. [Kondek] says he saw four Spitfires [*sic*], the A/G [Michna] ten plus [*sic*].

First the rudder was hit, making the aircraft unsteerable. Then the starboard petrol tank was set ablaze. The pilot then indicated over the inter-com his intention to try and ditch near the warships. When he dived to quell the flames the starboard engine caught fire and the aircraft became unmanageable. [Kondek] decided this was the time to bale out, and before jumping himself, he remembers seeing the observer reach down for his breast parachute. He thinks, nevertheless, that the three other members of the crew perished in the aircraft. During his descent by parachute he saw the plane crash among the mountains south-east of Athens, and a mushroom of smoke go up indicating that the aircraft had exploded. He himself landed near Anavyssos. He was captured by Greek partisans and received rough treatment at their hands prior to his arrival at a POW camp on 1 November.

Seafires of 809 Squadron caught a Do 24 just after it had taken off from Volos harbour on 17 October, but sadly Ltn Johann Zwarte's CM+IQ of Seenotstfl.7 was carrying wounded to Salonika. All onboard were killed. The initial attack was made by Sub-Lts(A) A. C. S. Morrison (NF607/S-G), A. B. Foley (NN134/S-U) and G. C. Morris MB269/S-A), so that by the time Sub-Lts(A) G. S. Macartney (MB133/S-S) and D. D. James (NN390/S-L) opened fire it was already blazing on the water.

Meanwhile (on the same date), HMS *Emperor*, HMS *Black Prince* and their destroyer escort were patrolling off the Sporades when four 800 Squadron Hellcats spotted four seacraft, which they took to be Siebel ferries in a bay in Skopelos. They dived to attack, too late to realise they were in fact Coastal Forces MTBs. Two of the craft, *MTB307* and *MTB397*, had just arrived from Khios with fuel supplies for *MTB398* and *399* which had recently been transferred to Skopelos. Although a two-star Very flare was fired, it was too late to prevent the attack. *MTB307* was immediately hit and the petrol drums stored on her deck were punctured. Fortunately there was no fire, but both *MTB398* and *399* were strafed before the Hellcat pilots realised their mistake. Sadly, there were nine casualties among the crews, two of which proved fatal: Able/Sea. John Hinkins onboard *MTB397* and Ord/Sea. Roy Young who died from wounds sustained onboard *MTB399*. Following the attack, a signal was sent to the task force calling for medical aid and shortly thereafter HMS *Emperor*'s Walrus (L2238) arrived with a Surgeon Lieutenant to tend to the wounded, followed by the cruiser. A service was held onboard *MTB398* and the two bodies were committed to the deep.

On 18 October, 809 Squadron Seafires attacked railway engines near Salonika. Sub-Lt(A) G. J. T. Moore RNZNVR (MA975) was hit by flak and baled out, though later reported safe. Sub-Lt(A) L. J. B. Baker was also shot down (NN134) while strafing MT – he also baled out south of Mt Olympus and was similarly reported safe. HMS *Emperor* anchored off the island of Khios on 19 October to embark 113 German and Italian prisoners of war while eight of her Hellcats dive-bombed and destroyed a radar station on Melos.

By the end of October, 800 Squadron was the only naval air unit left in the Eastern Mediterranean, all other carriers having left for the other destinations. HMS *Emperor* had been retained for one more operation – *Contempt* – that involved her Hellcats supporting an assault on the island of Melos. The squadron flew on eleven consecutive days from 26 October to 5 November, a total of 238 sorties being flown for the loss of six Hellcats to flak and twenty-three others damaged. The losses included Sub-Lt(A) W. D. Vine who was shot down on 27 October in JV227 while strafing a shore battery. He baled out and was rescued by the carrier's Walrus L2238. The final loss occurred on 3 November when Lt(A) J. G. Pettigrew crash-landed

JV179 and damaged two other Hellcats; the crash swept AB Seaman Wyton into the sea though he was rescued safely by an attendant destroyer HMS *Tyrian*. The assault on Melos failed. A naval party had been landed on the island on 30 October to support existing forces, but German resistance was too stiff and on 5 November, the party was evacuated (see Chapter XIII). HMS *Emperor* revisited Melos on 14 November on her way home to the UK flying four sorties for the protection of a Swordfish and Walrus L2238 that were spotting for HMS *King George V*. Overall, the Hellcats had flown 476 sorties during which they had delivered seventy-two tons of bombs for the loss of ten aircraft and thirty-one damaged.

CHAPTER X

'Night-Hunters' over the Aegean

The evacuation of Crete and the Aegean islands was ordered on 24 August as the Germans became more and more engrossed with the onslaught from the East. With some air transports units withdrawing, some being reinforced and others arriving, a substantial force of Ju 52s were available for the task. However, heavy Allied bombing of the Athens and Phareron airfields reduced these numbers considerably so that additional transports had to be flown in from disbanded units, workshops and training schools. Eventually, a mixed force of Ju 52s of II/TG4 and IV/TG1 supplemented by Ju 52 floatplanes of LTStaffel (See) 1 and (See) 3, a few Ju 90s and Ju 290s and at least one Piaggio P.108 of LTStaffel 5 was assembled as 14./TG4 while twenty He 111 transports from 4, 7 and 8./KG27 and 2. and 6./KG4 arrived from the Eastern Front, the latter operating between 28 September and 4 October. The remaining Do 24s were also incorporated into the evacuation task force.

To counter the aerial evacuation, 46 Squadron – a specialist night fighter unit – was called upon to provide a detachment of AI-equipped Beaufighters to operate from Gambut. Another night fighter unit that had been operating further west, 108 Squadron, also provided a detachment. While preparing for the task ahead, the unit had lost one of its experienced crews in an unfortunate accident at Mersa Matruh on 15 September. The Beaufighter crewed by Flg Off. J. Langford and Flg Off. J. R. Hall was hit by an Egyptian Hurricane flown by Flg Off. Kasdy of 2 REAF while in the circuit waiting to land. There were no survivors. To act as Master of Ceremonies and to provide invaluable assistance to the Beaufighter crews, the former Irish packet steam *Ulster Queen* had been fitted out as a Fighter Direction vessel and was stationed north of Crete supported by a destroyer escort. One of the pilots of 46 Squadron detached to Gambut was W/O Roy Butler, who has provided the excellent following account of operations between

26 September and 5 October, during which period 46 Squadron's Beaus claimed sixteen kills, one probable and four damaged:

I was a Warrant Officer pilot and my radar/navigator was W/O Ray Graham. We were just starting our second tour of operations in the Middle East, having first been members of 108 Squadron at Castel Benito in Libya. When our squadron was united with 46 we moved to Idku. We had been in the Middle East eighteen months and were due to return to England, but decided to volunteer for a second tour. We were in A Flight commanded by Flt Lt Joe Irwin.

On 24 September, the pilots and radar/navigators of A Flight attended a briefing by Sqn Ldr [G.E.] Robertson, the Commanding Officer of 46 Squadron. He told us that during the approaching full moon period, our base for intruder raids on the occupied Aegean Islands would be a desert airfield called Gambut. For the first time we would not be alone in our efforts to locate the enemy. An Irish packet steamer, the *Ulster Queen*, positioned north of Crete, had been fitted with GCI radar and would be protected by Royal Navy destroyers. The ship would act as our ground control. This was excellent news because we knew the Germans were supplying their island garrisons by air, mainly during the night and this new strategy may give us the edge we needed.

The ground staff to man the detachment left on 23 September, with F/O Kirk in charge. There were three senior NCOs and twenty-nine aircraft mechanics. They went by road and took all the tents and equipment required for the forthcoming operation. If all went well they would stop overnight at Mersa Matruh which was on the coast about 100 miles west of Idku. There were 16 aircrews going and they would fly in on 26 September. We all left the briefing excited and with high hopes. Flt Lt Irwin held another briefing. We were told that one of our aircraft had carried out tests with the *Ulster Queen* and the radar reception and the R/T was working perfectly. Another important piece of equipment, the homing beacon, had a range of 50 miles. Without this we would have a hard time finding the ship.

The following day we loaded our gear into our aircraft and took off for Gambut located about 200 miles west of Alexandria and situated on an escarpment a few miles south of the coast. There were three Beaufighters, each carrying two extra aircrew members. A Baltimore came along to transport the remaining crews. I was flying Beaufighter ND243. Once airborne we performed the Night Flying Test that was standard procedure on all night fighter squadrons. Having completed our tests, we assembled in loose formation, led by Joe Irwin and flew very low across our airfield, setting a course for Gambut. One other plane was still being worked on and would follow us later, making four available for the impending operation.

Gambut was a typical desert airfield with sandbagged dispersal areas. The maintenance and flight offices were housed in tents. There were no runways and fine sand drifted constantly across the airfield. Except for a squadron of Beaufighters of 603 Squadron, it had a deserted look. Gambut had changed hands many times during the desert war and I wondered how many lives had been sacrificed to keep possession of such a deserted, lonely place. Our ground crews that had arrived the previous day had erected the tents and everything was well organised. They were happy to see their planes arrive. We were going to Mess with 603 Squadron during our stay. We loaded our personal gear onto a pickup truck and were driven to the tents that would be our home for the next few days.

After unpacking, we returned to the dispersal area where instructions for the night operations were posted. We would be scrambled at 1½-hour intervals. Allowing for a flight time of 3 hours to reach the target and return, and spending 1½ hours over the target would mean we would be airborne approximately 4½ hours. Graham and I would scramble second and were scheduled for take-off at 8:00pm, following P/O Steele and W/O Clay. Following us would be W/O Phelan and Flt Sgt Baldwin, and W/O Hammond and Flt Sgt Harrison would man the last plane.

A small tent had been taken over by the IO and we went in to get briefed about the night's operation. Our route would be almost due north from Gambut. After flying across the Mediterranean we were to enter the Aegean Sea through the Straits of Kythera at the western end of Crete. This route avoided flying over Crete and if we kept our height to a minimum, we might be able to slip under enemy radar and arrive undetected to the target area. We were given the 'colours of the day', so in the event a ship of the Royal Navy challenged us, we could identify ourselves by firing the correct Very cartridge. We were always meticulously aware of the colours of the day, but through experience we never felt comfortable in approaching a naval vessel even after showing the colours. The Royal Navy was notorious for firing first and asking questions later... we always approached with extreme caution after allowing them to have a good look at us as the Beau looked very much liked the Ju 88. We were given the call sign of the *Ulster Queen*, which was 'Trademark', and as usual were reminded to destroy our radar equipment if we had to abandon our aircraft and to keep strict radio silence once we were airborne so as not to advertise our mission to the enemy.

We would be flying ND243, the same one we had flown from Idku. Our parachutes and helmets were still inside and we went to the plane making sure everything was in place for our take-off a few hours later. Flt Lt Irwin was at the dispersal area making sure that preparations for the coming night were proceeding smoothly and he recommended that we go to our tent and try and get some rest before dinner. I did not envy the A Flight commander. He would not be flying tonight in order to make sure everything was organised throughout the next twelve hours. He would see us off and would wait at the dispersal area until the last plane returned. We were all quite young and he was not much older, yet it was comforting to know he would be there.

We went back to our tent, but it was impossible to rest. As soon as we knew dinner was being served we went to the Mess tent to eat. It was the usual RAF Middle East fare, the main ingredients being canned Spam and hard tack biscuits ... the appeal being very much dependent on the imagination of the cook. After our meal we went back to our tent to get dressed ready for night flying.

It got dark quickly in the desert, so we lit a hurricane lamp hanging from the tent pole. We put on khaki slacks underneath a cotton flying-suit, which we tucked into calf length, suede desert boots, commonly known as brothel creepers. I had a small knife scabbard in my right boot. This wasn't for anything more lethal than to stab and deflate my Mae West if it inadvertently inflated on take-off. Most of us followed this precaution after hearing a horror story (never confirmed) about some poor soul having his Mae West inflate on take-off and crushing his chest under the safety straps! I also wore a silk scarf and put a pair of lightweight leather gloves in my pocket. There was a standing order to wear gloves while flying for protection against fire. Also, in case of fire, we had aviators goggles attached to our helmets in order to protect our eyes. I carried a tube of Gentian Violet in the pocket of my flying suit to use as first aid against burns (I believe I read later that the worst thing to do with a burn was to put this greasy stuff on!)

Operations

About 6:15 pm we made our way to the dispersal area. When we arrived, [P/O Sonny Steele] and Clay were walking out to their aircraft and we wished them luck and jokingly asked them to save some for us. Sonny Steele [a Jamaican in the RAF] and I had been friends for a long time. We had been together at Initial Flying Training School Canada and 54 OTU in Scotland. His usual navigator had been posted home just before we left for Gambut and this was his first time being crewed with W/O Clay.

Now that it was dark, the dispersal area took on a different appearance. The moon was starting to rise and our all-black aircraft looked very menacing in the dim light. Shadowy figures were gathered around Steele's plane getting ready to strap him and his navigator in and start the engines. A truck was running across the airfield placing and lighting flares ready for take-off. The flares were made from used gasoline cans that had been cut in half and filled with sand. Gasoline was poured on the sand and ignited. About a half a dozen were used for the take-off run and their main purpose was to give the pilot a straight line to follow. At best, it was a very crude type of flarepath, but it was sufficient and typical of desert practice.

By now there was a few crews gathered at the dispersal area and we watched Steele taxi to the end of the flarepath, turn into the wind and begin his take-off run. We were all silently praying that Steele and Clay would return unharmed and at the same time wishing that we were the ones taking off. Waiting was the worst part of an operation and it was at a time like this when everyone felt the close camaraderie of a combat squadron. We felt comfort by being part of this tightly knit group and any nervousness was covered up by a lot of horseplay. It wasn't too bad for Graham and I because we were next off, but some of the crews would wait for two or three hours. Steele's plane left the ground and he immediately extinguished his navigation lights. We stood in a group until the sound of the engines died. He was gone, hopefully to return in about five hours.

Graham and I went into the IO tent for last minute information. A signal had been received confirming that the *Ulster Queen* was on station and waiting for us. The latest meteorological information was good. The forecast was for a clear, starlit night with almost a full moon. We got the latest wind speed and direction and worked out a course to the western tip of Crete and I wrote it down on a scrap of paper. This was the extent of our formal navigation, as Graham had not been trained as a navigator in the truest sense of the word. Nevertheless, once we neared land, he was able to map read by using his radar. Also, I could call on the R/T when returning to our base and be given a course to fly to get us home. This worked well providing all of our equipment kept working properly! Tonight we'd fly at our economical altitude of 6,000 feet until we were about 75 miles from the enemy coast. We would then descend to 50 feet in order to try and stay under enemy radar. The IO and Joe Irwin wished us good luck and said they would be waiting for our return. We told the IO to have the brandy ready, for it was his custom to have a glass ready for returning crews during the debriefing.

I signed the Form 700 and we made our way out to the dispersal area. There was a group of ground crew waiting for us at our plane and we started our preparations for take-off. Graham climbed up a hatch located halfway down the fuselage into the radar compartment and started checking the equipment. I walked around the plane with a flashlight and made sure all the locks on the moveable control surfaces and the pitot head cover had been removed. I looked at the tyres to see if they had moved on the wheel rims (there was a yellow mark painted across the tyre and the rim. If they did not line up, it indicated, 'tyre creep', which could cause a blow-out). Next, I checked the engine nacelles for traces of oil leakage. The last check on the outside was to ensure that the gun ports in the nose and along the wings were sealed over with aircraft fabric to avoid sand getting into the gun mechanism on take-off. The first round on the cartridge belt was always non-explosive because it would break through the cover without causing damage to the plane when the guns were fired. On night fighter squadrons our main firepower was explosive shells. We did not use tracer ammunition because it destroyed the pilot's night vision.

One of the senior NCOs, Flt Sgt Clark, who was in charge of the ground crew, was there to see that everything was in order. He was his usual boisterous self and we knew that he would love to come on this intruder raid … he flew as a passenger at every opportunity. Clark was very efficient and popular with the aircrew. He had recently managed to return to the squadron from one of our planes that had crash-landed in the desert, many miles from our base. As was customary in the RAF for finding his way back to base on foot, he was presented with the Flying Boot (a silver badge in the shape of a flying boot with wings). Both the aircrew had been killed in this incident.

Satisfied, I climbed up the hatch under the nose, gripped the bars positioned on either side above the seat and swung myself over the seat back onto the parachute that was already in place on the seat pan. Flt Sgt Clark followed me up the hatch and as I pulled the lever to elevate the seat back, he handed the safety belt straps over my shoulders. I pulled the remaining straps up between my legs and pushed all four into the retaining ring and inserted the locking pin. I then strained forward as far as I could to be sure that my head would not hit the gun sight that was located immediately behind the windshield. I turned on the instrument panel lights, put on my helmet, switched on the radio and spoke to Graham on the intercom to make sure it was working. Satisfied, I gave the thumbs-up sign to Nobby Clark who stepped down and slammed the hatch shut. Before starting the engines, I asked Graham if the radar equipment appeared to be working OK. He said it was, which was a relief as it could be quite temperamental. I started the engines and let them idle at 1,200 rpm. While waiting for them to warm up, I called the control tower and checked the local channel of my radio. I also made sure that the gun sight light rheostat was in working order, ran the engines and checked the magneto drop. Everything looked good, so I flashed the navigation lights to signal the ground crew we were ready to go. The ground crew removed the wheel chocks and signalled that all was clear to start taxiing. I pulled away from the dispersal area and headed toward the first flare of the runway. I stopped perpendicular to the row of flares, put the propellers into fine pitch, rechecked the fore and aft trim and called the tower and asked for permission to take-off.

I turned onto the runway, opened the throttles and concentrated on keeping a straight run with the flares on my left-hand side. This was the time to pray that a truck had not been inadvertently parked on the runway! We became airborne and I called the tower, turned off the navigation lights, set course almost due north and started climbing. The time was 8:10pm. After a few minutes we crossed the coast and headed out over the Mediterranean. As we reached 6,000 feet I levelled off, trimmed the aircraft to fly straight and level at 230mph and settled down for the 200-mile flight across the water. This would take us to within about 75 miles from the coast of Crete. At that point, we would have to lose height and prepare to go into enemy territory.

It was a beautiful night. The moon was almost full, there were no clouds and the stars were extremely bright. From this height the Mediterranean looked like a vast mirror. I mentally began figuring what would be the best approach to make an attack on another plane, assuming we were lucky enough to find one. We were trained to keep on the dark side and never get in a position where we were silhouetted against clouds. The classic night fighter attack was to approach from behind and below. Then identify the target from directly underneath, throttle back and climb ... at the same time raking the enemy aircraft with gunfire as it moved through the gun sight. On a night like this the best approach would be to keep the target silhouetted by the moon if possible.

In slightly less than an hour I throttled back and started to lose height. As we got to about five hundred feet it was possible to see the whitecaps on the waves and now that we were a long way from our base, the sea looked a lot more menacing. I carefully lost altitude until I judged we were about fifty feet above the water and set the altimeter to read zero. At the same time, I trimmed the plane to be slightly tail-heavy. Every pilot at that time had his own method of low flying over water at night ... this was my approach to do it as safely as possible. When the altimeter registered zero, I knew we were still about fifty feet above the water, while at the same time the plane had a tendency to climb away from danger. Maintaining the height at fifty feet we approached Crete.

As we neared the coast we started to hear a low humming noise on the intercom system. It was enemy radar sweeping the shoreline. This did not unduly concern us because we had experienced it before. However, it had been rather disconcerting the first time we had heard it, when we realised that this meant the enemy was searching for us. Tonight our plane was low enough not to send back a signal. We were still holding height at 50 feet and airspeed steady at 230mph. All the instruments appeared normal. The gunbutton was on the right hand side of the control column and I operated the switch to arm the guns. Then I turned on the gunsight and rotated the rheostat to adjust the brilliance until I could clearly see the ring with a cross in the middle, but without it being too bright to blind me. The theory was, that a wingspan of 50 feet would fit into the ring at a range of 250 yards. All the firepower of the cannons and machine-guns was synchronised to fill a ten feet square at a range of 250 yards, making this range the most devastating.

If you encountered a plane with a wingspan of 100 feet, then only half of the span would be required to fit into the ring to be at a range of 250 yards, and so on. Graham switched on our radar and I concentrated on flying by instruments, even though it appeared bright enough outside to fly visually.

Approaching the Straits of Kythera, we sighted Cape Gramvonsa at the western end of Crete. The time was 9:45pm and we had been in the air 1 hour 35 minutes. Graham announced that he was picking up another aircraft on his radar at a range of just over 10 miles. The other plane was showing the IFF. We deduced it could only be Steele and Clay and I decided to find out. I pushed the transmit key and quickly asked if they had seen anything. Steele replied that there was bags of trade. He sounded excited and I would like to have talked some more, but it was not the time to be holding a conversation. Graham said that the homing beacon on the *Ulster Queen* was showing very clearly on the radar at a range of ten miles. I called 'Trademark' and gave my call sign, which was Pistol Five Zero. Immediately the reply came back that they were receiving us loud and clear and we were to patrol on an east/west course at 500 feet. The QFE was 1010.6. I reset the altimeter to the QFE. The time was 9:50pm and we were now under the control of the *Ulster Queen*.

We climbed to 500 feet and started the patrol. 'Trademark' was giving instructions to Steele, who appeared to be having difficulty locking on to a bogey. A few minutes later we heard 'Trademark' tell Steele to go to Angels 10 and head for base. We faintly heard Steele acknowledge and suddenly we felt quite lonely as we thought of them going back to base. We had no idea of what success they had experienced on their patrol and wouldn't know until we also returned. We now had the patrol and 'Trademark' turned his attention to us.

Communication between the Controller and us now became very relaxed. There were no verbal formalities during an interception and all that was required was quick, concise directions. This was also the case between Graham and me. During the two years we had crewed together, we had developed and practiced a certain patter to use during an interception. Typically, after the Controller had given directions to get us to within 10 miles of the target, Graham would expect to see the target on his radar. At this point he would follow the target until he was comfortable that he had it firmly established. Then he would tell me to inform the Controller we wished to take over the interception. I would do this by using the code word 'Tally-ho'. The Controller would then follow the interception and be ready to help us if needed, but he would not talk to us. Graham would continue giving me directions every few seconds until he had talked me into a position where I should be able to see the target. He would relay such information as slight changes of course to follow, the approximate speed of the target, the range as it diminished, and changes in height as required. I had become so familiar with the way he presented all this data during an interception that I could usually tell by the inflection in his voice how the interception was proceeding. Sometimes, from the mental picture that was forming in my mind, I was able to anticipate the directions he was going to give me. As we got closer to the target and before I could see it, I would tell him where I wanted the target to be in relation to us. This would depend on the weather conditions and was intended to keep us unobserved as long as possible. The bond between pilot and radar/navigator was very important and was the reason why night fighter crews liked to stay together. For me, it was exciting to be led along blindly on a dark night and to suddenly see another aircraft appear. We had practiced interceptions for hours with other members of the squadron, taking turns being the fighter and the target, always hoping that some night our training would pay off. At 9:50pm the Controller told us to change altitude to 1,000 feet.

It was almost an hour later at 10:48pm that we were beginning to doubt we would encounter any enemy aircraft. We had patrolled back and forth and nothing had come within radar range of the *Ulster Queen*. We had been in the air nearly three hours and were beginning to get a little tired and depressed. Suddenly, as we were on our eastern leg I saw two green lights cross our path from port to starboard on a south-westerly course. I turned hard to starboard to investigate. 'Trademark' called and said there was a bogey in our vicinity. I replied that we had seen the bogey and were turning to intercept.

Again from 'Trademark' telling us to flash our weapon. He wanted me to push our IFF button that enlarged our radar blip, thereby allowing him to see which was the friendly and which was the bogey. This was often done to help the Controller when the blips were too close to tell one from the other. I told him we had the bogey on our radar and were intercepting. He would now monitor our progress and be ready to give us assistance if required. I could no longer see the lights, but Graham was directing me closer to a position where I could see and identify the other aircraft. We were slowly losing altitude and the target was coming closer. When we were 200 feet above the water, Graham said I should be able to see the other plane dead ahead. I turned my head from side to side, using my peripheral vision. Quite suddenly another plane came into view about 300 yards dead ahead, 100 feet above me. When the range was down to 250 yards it was not necessary to go any closer to obtain identification. It was a Dornier 24 flying boat. I could clearly see the three engines and the twin tails. The Dornier 24 had a wingspan of just over 100 feet and looked huge. To attack from optimum range the wingspan had to appear to be twice the width of the ring on my gunsight and we were at that position already. I told Graham to take a look and he confirmed the identity.

It was at this stage of the interception that we started to receive gunfire from the enemy and tracer shells seemed to be lazily curling over us. I centred the gunsight on the middle engine and fired three short bursts of about two seconds each. It was a relief when all the guns fired because I had often imagined being this close to the enemy and having the guns jam! I saw strikes on the port wing and engine and as our range was now reducing rapidly I turned away to port. The enemy glided down, struck the water and immediately burst into flames. The time was 10:50pm, two minutes after first sighting the enemy. I called 'Trademark' and told him there was a plane down with many people in the water and he told me to go to Angels One and vector zero nine zero. I turned on to our new heading, somehow reluctant to leave the scene. It did not seem possible that we had caused such devastation.

The Do 24T shot down by W/O Butler was 1M+RR of Seenotstaffel 7, which was on a flight from Athens to Suda Bay. Fw Hans Escher, the pilot, was lost with observer and Staffelkapitän Oblt Hans Glinkemann, plus four others.

We flew back and forth at the direction of the Controller for almost fifteen minutes. At 11:08pm we sighted two destroyers and I informed one. By the way he told me to keep clear of them I assumed they belonged to the Royal Navy and were probably acting as part of the escort for the *Ulster Queen*. A couple of minutes later we were on a northerly course when 'Trademark' called and said there was a bogey crossing port to starboard, range 5 miles. I quickly acknowledged and started a turn to starboard. As we continued to turn slowly, Graham obtained a contact at a range of 3½ miles. The bogey was still to starboard and much lower than we were. I kept turning and started to lose height while Graham continued to give me directions until we were down to a height of 100 feet on a heading of 150°. Although our airspeed was down to 140mph, we closed in on the target rapidly. When our range was down to 1,000 feet the other aircraft came into view. It was a 3-engine Junkers 52 land plane and we were closing very fast. I lowered the flaps a few degrees to give us more stability, but I could see that unless we acted quickly we were going to overshoot and probably lose the opportunity to get him. I told Graham to look and confirm my identification, while at the same time I lined up to attack. Graham agreed with me that it was a Junkers 52 and I immediately fired a long burst. We were now closer than 200 yards and the effect of our attack was terrifying. The enemy exploded in a huge ball of flame. There was no way to take violent evasive action and the fact that I had lowered some flap was a lifesaver because it allowed us to turn slightly quicker than normal. Without the flaps we probably would have gone into a stall because we were too low to dive to pick up speed. We flew right through the edge of the ball of fire expecting any second to be engulfed.

We circled the burning wreckage for about ten minutes but there was no sign of life, which was not surprising considering the violence of the explosion. Graham and I concluded we had seen enough action for one night and it would be a good thing if things remained quiet until it was time to return to base! At 11:28pm we had a call from 'Trademark'. There were two bogeys north of us. Vector 035° and investigate. The Controller gave us directions for about seven minutes and at 11:35pm Graham had a contact slightly to starboard and 3 miles ahead of us. We were just under 1,000 feet altitude and closing nicely at a range of 2,000 feet when the bogey disappeared hard to port. I went into a steep turn to port and called 'Trademark' and asked for help, but he had also lost contact and we had to give up the chase. We had barely gotten back to straight and level flying when 'Trademark' called again and said there was another target 18 miles west of us. He controlled us to within 2½ miles of the new bogey and Graham got a contact hard to starboard of us. The time was now 11:33pm and we had been under 'Trademark's' control over our allotted time of 1½ hours.

I turned hard to starboard and the range started to reduce rapidly. I again lowered some flap to reduce the speed, but now the target was only 100 feet ahead of us. It was a Junkers 52 seaplane flying very slowly. To avoid colliding I pulled along the right hand side of the enemy plane and could clearly see the unique corrugated skin and the swastikas painted on the side. The time was now 11:35pm and 'Trademark' called and told us it was time to return to base. I called back and told him we were in contact with an enemy plane and would talk to him later.

There was no way we could slow down enough to get behind the enemy so I told Graham that I was going to set my gyro compass to zero on our present heading and execute a 360° turn to starboard back to the same heading. If all went well we should pick him up again a few miles ahead of us and have a chance to do a more controlled interception. We agreed to try it, so I started the turn. As we completed our circle Graham picked him up at a range of 4 miles. We were both very excited because this was a manoeuvre we had not practiced. It was a great job by Graham to pick the target up so quickly. This time we made a good approach, but because of his slow airspeed we were still overtaking quite rapidly and I knew that we would probably only get one chance to attack him. The enemy was on an east-south-easterly course keeping about 3 miles off the coast of Trypete and slowly losing height to within 250 yards; I gave one short burst of fire. I observed strikes on the starboard engine, which caught fire. I gave another longer burst and then went into a hard climbing turn to port intending to try and come in for another attack. The enemy was losing height quite rapidly and as we completed our turn it struck the sea and burst into flames.

The time was 11:40pm and well past time to go home. We had been in the target area nearly two hours, destroyed three enemy aircraft and had come very close to being destroyed ourselves. It had been a busy night so far and we were still a long way from our base. I called the Controller and told him what had happened and that we were returning to base.

While chasing the seaplane, we had got in the middle of an area that was surrounded on three sides by land. We didn't have enough fuel to make our way home through the Straits of Kythera, so the only way back was to turn south from our present position and climb over the mountains that would confront us going across the Crete mainland. Graham would have to lead us through and over the terrain with the radar. Not the most pleasant thing to do at night but we had no choice. We were not supposed to fly overland, but it was a decision I had to make and was sure that our Flight Commander would back me up. The biggest worry was that if anti-aircraft batteries were deployed in the hills, we might get caught in crossfire.

I turned south and started to climb as fast as possible. Graham was reading off the distance to the enemy coast as indicated on the radar. If we could get to about 4,000 feet by the time we reached the coast, we should be able to reach the altitude required to clear the mountains. After a few minutes we were over land with the high ground a few miles ahead and I estimated that we still had another 1,500 feet to climb to be safe. I could vaguely see the ground beneath us in the moonlight and it looked ominously close. Graham kept assuring me that according to his radar all was well, so we pressed on. So far there had been no hostile response from the enemy. When we reached a height of 6,200 feet Graham announced that we should now be clear of the highest point and that from now on it was a piece of cake. After a few more minutes, I told Graham that if he was sure we had cleared the highest point I was going to put the nose down, build up speed and race for the southern shore and the comparative safety of the Mediterranean. He agreed and we made a run for it. As we were almost over the sea we faintly heard W/O Phelan, who had just entered the target area tell the Controller that he had a contact. Our Squadron was putting all their training to good use tonight!

When we were safely over the sea I kept the height at 50 feet until we were well clear of the enemy coast. We weren't particularly concerned about their night fighters because we believed we had a superior radar system. However, we had a long way to go to our base and as our fuel was getting low, we didn't want to get involved in any more action. We talked excitedly about the exploits of the last few hours and how we had managed the hat trick. Our score would be confirmed by the Controller because he had seen the blips disappear off his radar tube and it was possible that the crew of the *Ulster Queen* had seen the fire and explosions.

A few miles south of the coast of Crete, we saw a fairly large ship very well illuminated and we noted the position in order to report it to our IO. When we were about 70 miles away from the enemy coast I slowly climbed to 6,000 feet to conserve fuel. The remainder of the journey was uneventful and when we were 25 miles from base Graham picked up the beacon at Gambut and we changed course slightly to head for the airfield. The weather conditions were still good. The moon was visible, with 3/10ths cloud at 1,000 feet and visibility was 10 to 15 miles. I called Control and received permission to land and after a few minutes we could see the flares on the runway. The time was 1:05am and we had been airborne for 4hrs.55mins. We taxied to the dispersal area and switched off the engines. The ground crew could see that we had seen some action because the gun ports were exposed and they started to gather round.

Nobby Clark was the first to come up the hatch to help me out. I pulled the lever that retracted the seat back and unlocked the safety harness. The next thing was to grip the overhead rails and swing myself backwards onto the steps of the hatch. I was so stiff after sitting in one position for 5 hours that it was hard to do and Nobby helped me to get to the ground. Graham was already out and was surrounded by a group wanting to hear an account of our trip. Sonny Steele appeared out of the darkness grabbed me in a bear hug and wanted to know if we had been lucky. When I told him that we had gotten three he couldn't believe it. He said they had chased a lot of bogeys but had not got close enough to attack. I must admit the thought went through my mind that his lack of success could be due to not having time to practice with W/O Clay because they were both very experienced aircrew ... a good example why crews stayed together.

Joe Irwin was also there waiting for us, as we knew he would be. He already knew something had happened because of the excitement around the plane. When I told him the news it was like a tonic to him because the squadron had not had any success in many months. I broke Graham away from his group that were now discussing radar, (the usual subject when more than one radar/navigator got together) and went to report to the IO. We were given a small glass of brandy and started the debriefing.

By the time we were finished it was 2:45am. We heard that W/O Phelan and Flt/Sgt Baldwin had just landed at El Adam due to Gambut now being unserviceable because of a ground mist. There was more excitement...they had shot down another Junkers 52 [5 miles north of Maleme]. The total was mounting. We went back to the dispersal area where the ground crews were finishing servicing our plane. Nobby Clark told me I must have been pretty low at times because the windshield had dried salt spray on it. I told him not to tell Graham ... he wouldn't fly with me anymore! By now we were both feeling very fatigued and went off to our tent to try and sleep.

The next thing we knew it was daylight and there was a crowd of people outside the tent. I got up and looked and it was Terry Phelan and Denis Hammond with their navigators. They had both been diverted to El Adam and had just flown in from there. It felt like the middle of the night, but it was 10:00am. We quickly dressed and went to the Mess tent to get breakfast and compare notes. As we had heard, Phelan had destroyed one plane [5 miles north of Maleme] and Hammond had chased one but it had gotten away. The total score for the night was 4 aircraft destroyed.

26/27 September

W/O R. T. Butler/W/O R. F. Graham	ND243/Q	Do 24, Ju 52/3m See, Ju 52/3m damaged
W/O T. K. Phelan/Flt Sgt F. W. J. Baldwin	MM939/C	Ju 52/3m See

On September 27th, we spent the day trying to catch up on sleep. We were not flying that evening, so after dinner we relaxed and had a couple of Egyptian beers. There were four planes going again tonight and we went to the dispersal to see the first two off. The first one went at 6:55pm and there was the usual boisterous group giving advice! F/O Kirk was flying our plane of last night and we asked him not to scratch it. The ground crew had already painted three swastikas on the side of the cockpit. We didn't stay up to see them return and we found out the next morning that the score had increased. F/O Kirk and Flt Sgt Carr got a Junkers 52 and Flt Sgt Chapman and W/O Briginshaw also destroyed a Junkers 52 and damaged another. The Squadron score was now 6 aircraft destroyed and 1 damaged.

27/28 September

Flg Off. G. W. Kirk/Flt Sgt S. Carr	ND243/Q	Ju 52/3m
Flt Sgt E. G. Chapman/W/O W. Briginshaw	KV920/L	Ju 52/3m, J52/3m damaged

Their victims were apparently 8A+BJ (Hptm. August Meyer and crew) and 8A+NJ (Fw Hans Vorberg and crew) of 1.Seetr.St, which were shot down with the loss of both crews, and 8A+HJ of the same unit that survived with one crew member wounded.

On the morning of the 28th, Sqn Ldr Robbie Robertson flew in from Idku in a Hurricane. He asked to see Graham and me. We presented ourselves to him and saluted. He shook hands with us and told us that His Majesty King George VI had graciously awarded each of us the Distinguished Flying Cross. We were unprepared for this and at a loss for words. We managed to stammer our thanks and I thought it would be appropriate to salute again, so I did. When we thought about this afterwards we would burst out laughing. It was such an unlikely situation ... standing virtually in the middle of the desert being presented with a gong, and all sorts of saluting going on while the sand swirled around us!

After having a night off, it was our turn to fly again. We went into the flight tent and found that we were scheduled to fly ND243 again. We were going to be last off tonight, leaving around 10:30pm. Our take-off time would depend upon the crews before us being on time because we had to be 1½ hours apart in order not to have more than one plane at a time in the target area. Our plane was not ready for us to do our NFT, so we waited around the dispersal area. Even though we had always prided ourselves on having good morale in our squadron it was amazing what a little success had done. There was a different air about everybody and it was wonderful to be a part of it.

In spite of this, a few minutes later something occurred that scared the daylight out of all of us. Our dispersal area was directly across the airfield from 603 Squadron and they were arming their planes with rockets, which were attached on rails under the wings. Rockets were a new innovation and still quite unpredictable, so the armourer's were not supposed to connect up the firing mechanism until the plane was started and at the end of the runway ready for take-off. The reason for this precaution was because they had found that occasionally the action of starting the engines did something to the electrical system and caused the rockets to fire. On this particular day they had omitted to observe the precautionary measure and four rockets roared a few feet above our heads and landed in the desert with some beautiful explosions! Of course we had all flattened ourselves in the sand and we got up looking very sheepish!

The day dragged on, but as soon as it got dark and we had eaten dinner we prepared for flying and went to the dispersal area with Steele and Clay. Two crews had already gone, starting at 6:10pm and it looked as though we would all be leaving as scheduled. After Steele had gone we had 1½ hours to wait. We checked with the IO and discussed the possibility that we may run into more opposition in the form of German night fighters tonight. We refreshed our memory on the characteristics of the Junkers 88 (their standard night fighter) and the Junkers 188, which was a souped-up version of the 88. We must have been psychic because this discussion would stand us in good stead later that night.

We went to our plane and completed our pre-flight inspection and took off at 10:45pm. It was a beautiful night and the flight to the western end of Crete was uneventful. As on the first night, we reduced altitude to 50 feet as we approached the enemy coast. We made landfall at Cape Gramvansa and at 12 minutes after midnight we contacted 'Trademark.' We were told to patrol on a north/south course at 500 feet. We carried out this patrol for just over a half an hour and at 12:55am, we received a call from 'Trademark' telling us that there was a bogey approaching on a northerly course and we should go to Angels Five. I acknowledged and we started climbing as hard as we could. Shortly after, we were told to turn on to 150°, then a few seconds later to turn hard to starboard to 320°. At 1:05am we obtained a contact 3 miles ahead, to the right and very high above us. We immediately starting climbing and started our chase. Our speed was 200mph and we were slowly closing on the target. This was obviously not a slow moving Junkers 52. When we were at 6,700 feet and a range of 2,000 feet, I obtained a visual. The time was 1:10pm.

We kept gaining slowly until the range closed to 700 feet and I recognised it as a Junkers 188, one of the enemy's fast fighter/bombers that we had heard was being used as a night fighter. It was a very fast plane and could outrun us at heights over 6,000 feet. I opened fire from dead astern and saw numerous strikes on the fuselage and the starboard wing. We were getting some return fire from the enemy's tail, but it was not very accurate. The target turned to the right and started to lose height rapidly and I followed him into the turn and tried a long deflection shot. To my surprise it worked, because black smoke started pouring from the starboard engine.

It was at this crucial time of the attack that our radar was affected by the gunfire and stopped working. I kept turning in the direction that we had last seen the enemy and requested help form the Controller. He replied immediately that the target was two miles to the north of us. I kept reminding Graham to keep looking behind us because I was concerned that we may have encountered two night fighters working as a pair, which turned out to be not the case. We turned north and regained contact at 1:15am. The target was two miles away, below us and to starboard. We kept gaining steadily, following him down to 1,500 feet. We were 1,000 feet behind when I obtained visual contact again. He was now on an easterly course and appeared to be heading for the west coast of the island of Melos. I opened fire from dead astern scoring numerous strikes on the tailplane and starboard wing. Debris was breaking off the enemy and floating past us, and then the starboard engine caught fire. I broke away when we were directly above the badly damaged plane and turned to starboard. He was diving steeply toward the sea just off the coast of Melos. When we had completed our orbit we could see no further sign of him and I assumed that he must have dived straight into the water. I talked to 'Trademark' and he said that the enemy blip had disappeared off his radar screen, which backed up our belief that he had gone in the water.

Their victim was apparently a He 111 (701711) of 2./KG4 that was reported shot down by a night fighter off Melos, in which the pilot Uffz Hans-Joachim Schneider and Obfw Erich Grün were killed, and Gfr Fritz Berger wounded.

We resumed patrol at 1:20am. Five minutes later 'Trademark' called and reported more trade coming in from the south and we were to go to Angels Five and vector 180°. We started climbing and heading south. We knew that if the bogey was coming from the south we were on intercepting courses and we would soon have to reverse direction. 'Trademark' called and told us to turn onto 290° and keep climbing. At 1:30am, Graham got a contact directly above us as the bogey crossed our path. We started to turn and regained contact hard above us, but he again disappeared. I requested help from 'Trademark' but he couldn't give assistance. Graham and I decided that it was probably another night fighter using his radar to take evasive action. By this time we were at 8,000 feet and the Controller called and told us to resume patrol southward at our present height.

It was an extremely clear night and at 1:35am I saw another plane cross the moon track on a course of about 020°. I could clearly see his shadow on the water, so deduced his height to be about 50 feet. I turned to the right and started a steep dive to go after him; at the same time I called 'Trademark' and asked for help. Again they could not help me. We went down to 100 feet and turned from side to side to try and pick up the contact, to no avail. After a while we gave up the search and resumed patrol. At 1:51am 'Trademark' called and told us to vector 180° at Angels Ten for base.

The journey back to Gambut was uneventful, although I did ask Graham to watch our rear until we were well clear of Crete! We discussed the fact that we did not think it was going to be a piece of cake from now on because it appeared the enemy was deploying opposition in the form of night fighters with some type of radar on board. We were lucky to have gotten the Junkers 188 as it had been taking some quite violent evasive action indicative of radar control. However, every time we needed help the Controller stepped in, which of course was how it was supposed to work.

As Graham picked up the Gambut beacon about 50 miles out, we started losing height, ready for landing. The weather was still fine with a slight haze, the moon had almost set and there were some strata cumulus clouds at 5,000 feet. Visibility was about 10 miles. We touched down on the runway at 3:30am having been in the air for 4¾ hours … the last plane to return.

We got our glass of brandy from the IO before we started the debriefing. He told us that Phelan and Baldwin had got a Junkers 52 [60 miles north-north-east of Heraklion]. We found out later in talking to Phelan, that all the time he was in the target area his starboard engine had been acting up. It had been cutting out for no apparent reason, but he stayed there and pressed home his attack. This was very commendable because being that far from base with only one good engine could be a very nervous situation. A lot of pilots would have headed for base immediately and would not have been criticised for doing so. We also learned that Steele had chased what he thought was a 188, but wasn't successful in getting close enough to attack.

We went over our attacks with the IO. He was especially interested in the head-on interception because these were the most difficult to accomplish, requiring a lot of trust and cooperation between the pilot, controller and navigator. We finished our debriefing about 5:00am and it was time for bed. The Squadron score was mounting. It was now 8 destroyed and 1 damaged.

28/29 September

W/O R. T. Butler/W/O R. F. Graham	ND243/Q	Ju 188
W/O T. K. Phelan/Flt Sgt F. W. J. Baldwin	MM939/C	Ju 52/3m

We were not scheduled for flying the night of September 29th having just returned that morning. The crews going tonight were W/O Griffin and Flt Sgt Green, W/O Hammond and Flt Sgt Harrison, W/O Bays and Flt Sgt Battise [*sic* – Battiste], and lastly F/O Kirk and Flt Sgt Carr. Flt Lt Bradley and Flt Sgt Forrester flew in from Idku bringing another Beaufighter, but did not go on operations that night. Griffin and Green claimed a probable Ju 52, Hammond and Harrison destroyed two Ju 52s [30 miles north-west of Trypimei and 4 miles north of Maleme] and damaged one other [north of Crete], Bays and Battise [Battiste] damaged a Ju 52 [south of Melos], while Kirk and Carr were unlucky. It was September 30th, and the Squadron total had grown to 10 destroyed, 1 probable and 3 damaged.

108 Squadron was also flying sorties seeking the evacuating aircraft and had begun detaching sections of three aircraft to Gambut for night operations, returning to Idku in the morning. W/O John Burleton/Flt Sgt Graham in 108/P claimed the unit's first kill operating from Gambut, a Ju 52/3m, on this night.

29/30 September

W/O D. Griffin/Flt Sgt A. D. Green	ND299/G	Ju 52 probable
W/O D. V. Hammond/Flt Sgt D. A. Harrison	KV920/L	2 Ju 52, Ju 52 damaged
W/O H. J. Bays/Flt Sgt C. T. W. Battiste	KW153/V	Ju 52 damaged
W/O J. L. Burleton/Flt Sgt Graham	108	Ju 52

Four Ju 52s of IV/TG1 were reported lost. W/O Roy Butler continued:

We awoke the next morning to a blinding sandstorm. Sand was piled on our beds and blowing through every crack in the tent. The journey to the Mess for breakfast was an ordeal. Visibility was down to a few feet and sand was blowing in our mouths and eyes. Upon reaching the Mess tent, the situation was not much better; there was sand on the tables and in the food. We stayed in the Mess tent most of the morning.

Four crews were scheduled for operations that evening of the 30th. They were Flt Sgt Chapman and W/O Briginshaw, Flt Sgt Grimshaw and Flt Sgt Waller, Flt Lt Bradley and Flt Sgt Forrester and lastly P/O Steele and W/O Clay. The ground staff was not able to work on the planes to get them ready for air testing and flying was out of the question. There was nothing to do but wait for the weather to improve. In the afternoon the wind dropped and everything was back to normal and work was hurriedly resumed to get the planes ready. Our ground crews were doing a wonderful job, especially with the radar because it was so susceptible to damage from sand. We were lucky because sometimes sandstorms went on for days and there was nothing we could do but wait it out.

The planes went off as scheduled, Chapman being first off at 9:50pm and Steele was the last to land at 6:10am on the morning of October 1st. The crew of Bradley and Forrester destroyed a Dornier 24 seaplane, which brought the Squadron score to 11 destroyed, 1 probable and 3 damaged.

30 September/1 October
Flt Lt A. J. Bradley/Flt Sgt J. Forrester KW160/W   Do 24

W/O Roy Butler continued:

Some of the other crews taking part in the night's operation had intercepted the enemy but had opened fire before they were close enough to do real damage. It had become obvious to the crews that it was very important to get within 250 yards before opening fire. Hammond and I had compared notes and had agreed that the best attack was to get as close as possible and move the control column around slightly while firing. This had the effect of spraying the shells and meant that the cone of fire was larger. Crude but effective, as was borne out by the results we were getting!

There was one sad note about the night's operations. 108 Squadron had sent three planes into the target area; one of them crewed by W/O Knight and Flt Sgt Harwood. We all knew this crew because they had been with 46 Squadron before being posted to 108. They failed to return. The *Ulster Queen* last heard from them as they chased a bandit toward the island of Melos. This turned out to be the only casualty of the whole operation.

On the evening of October 1st, Graham and I were first off and we were airborne at 8:05pm, followed by Joe Irwin and his radar operator P/O Watson. This was their first patrol and we were all hoping they would have success. They would be followed by three more crews, which meant that this would be our busiest night with a total of five aircraft being used. As we left the dispersal area, it was a hive of activity, with planes being readied for take-off. Once airborne, we started climbing to our cruising altitude of 6,000 feet and headed for the western end of Crete on a course of 343°. This was our third night on patrol and I kept reminding myself not to get too complacent because we had been very lucky so far. It didn't seem possible that we could dominate the enemy airspace night after night without some kind of opposition.

We were in a different plane tonight, our usual having been returned to Idku for service. It was easy to get attached to an aeroplane and I hoped that this one would serve us as well. As usual we lost altitude as we approached the enemy coast and I went through my routine of setting the controls for very low flying. Graham turned on the radar while I armed the guns and set the rheostat on the gun sight. We were as ready as we could be when we made landfall at Elaphonisi on the coast of Crete. We turned on to a course of 50°, which would take us toward the *Ulster Queen*. After a few minutes I made contact with 'Trademark' and was told to patrol east/west at Angels One.

The time was 9:35pm. There was thunder and a lot of lightning flashes in the patrol area. At 1,000 feet there was a layer of strata-cumulus cloud and the moon was full. Lightning was illuminating the clouds, creating a beautiful but eerie scene. We flew back and forth under the Controller's direction for the next 30 minutes, during which time we had been increasing altitude to 4,000 feet. At 10:05pm 'Trademark' informed us of a bogey on a course of 330°. Range 12 miles. Speed 150 and height 4,500 feet. Vector 310° to intercept. This indicated we would be on a slightly converging course and the bogey would be on our right hand side as we got closer. At 10:13pm we obtained a contact on our radar 4 miles ahead and closed in slowly. Three minutes later we still had not gotten a visual contact when the Controller told us to break off pursuit. The target had broken away and he didn't think we could catch him. There was another bandit coming north at low level. He told us to reduce height to 500 feet as quickly as we could and watch for target to cross from port to starboard.

We dived down to 500 feet and at 10:16pm we again obtained radar contact at a range of 5 miles and I informed the Controller we were taking over the interception. The target was still slightly below us. Graham directed me to turn on to 330°. Our airspeed was 220mph and we were closing slowly. At 10:24pm I got a visual contact at a range of one mile, slightly above us. We were about 10 miles west of the island of Melos.

We closed to 700 feet and I recognised the target as a Heinkel 111. He was on a course of 330°, speed around 200mph. and his height was 250 feet. I asked Graham to look and confirm my identification. He agreed with me and we commented on how we could clearly see the unusual design of the joint where the rear edge of the wings met the body. Just as the instructor in aircraft identification class had stressed! We closed to 200 yards and I gave a three-second burst from dead astern. I saw strikes on the tailplane and pieces started breaking off and floating past us. Fire started at the starboard wing root and smoke began to pour from the starboard engine. The He 111 had a top waist turret but they did not return our fire, probably because of the damage that we had already done to them. We broke away to port and watched the enemy glide down and strike the sea with a momentary burst of flame and then the water engulfed the wreckage. We did not observe any survivors as it disappeared. The time was 10:30pm.

For the next 35 minutes we patrolled under the direction of 'Trademark' with no further incidents and at 11:05pm we were told to return to base. We faintly heard our replacement calling as they came into the area. The weather was still very threatening as we turned onto 180° and started our journey back to base. The flight back was uneventful, with the weather improving the further south we went. When we approached Gambut, the visibility was 15 to 20 miles with a full moon and we could have almost landed without the aid of flares. We touched down at 12:40am having been airborne for 4hrs.35 mins.

Later on that morning we learned that Hammond and Harrison had destroyed a Ju 88, and Bays and Battiste had got a Ju 52 [10-12 miles south of Melos] and a Do 24 [Anaphi area]. They were the last plane to return from the previous evening's operations, landing at 8:25am. The Squadron count had increased to 15 destroyed, 1 probable and 3 damaged.

Flt Sgt J. P. Underwood (108/Y) claimed on the night of 1/2 October: At 21:00 he was vectored by the *Ulster Queen* on to a bogey and then gained a visual, believing that it was a Ju 88, flying north-east of Dhia at 700 feet. One quick and unexpected burst of cannon sent the aircraft down in flames, the pilot attempting to ditch but it burst into flames. But 108 Squadron also lost a crew on this night, when W/O Reg Knight and Flt Sgt Len Harwood failed to return in 108/C, having taken-off from Gambut at 03:20. They were last heard to report that they were chasing a bandit, so presumably fell to return fire.

1/2 October

W/O R.T.Butler/W/O R.F.Graham	KW160/W	He 111
W/O D.V. Hammond/Flt Sgt D.A.Harrison	KV920/L	Ju 88
		(actually He 111)
W/O H.J. Bays/Flt Sgt C.T.W.Battiste	MM910/E	Ju 52, Do 24
Flt Sgt J.P. Underwood/Flt Sgt J.I. Hall	108/Y	Ju 88
		(actually He 111)

III/KG27 reported the loss of three Heinkels (see following night), 1G+CS (701657) of 8 Staffel in which Fw Friedhard Nierdergesäss and crew were all lost. The second was 1G+MR of 7 Staffel, flown by Fw Alfred Jobst, who recalled:

We [including observer Ltn Gombert and Fw Eduard Fischer] took off at 19:35 [on 1 October] from Athens-Kalamaki into the great adventure with a target of Heraklion harbour and airfield at Crete's north coast and the antique harbour of Knossos situated only 5 km to the southeast, the sovereign seat of the legendary King Minos, setting of the stories of Theseus and Ariadne – the one with the famous thread – and thus the second treasure trove of childlike fantasies, that was admittedly now largely subdued by bitterly serious reality.

A beautiful Mediterranean autumn day extended an almost abstract picture of flawless beauty with a cloudless sky, a grand mountain-panorama dipped in pastel-like ocher and, before us, a sea wide in the shine of the evening sun, gleaming indefinitely. The reality was quite something different! We had no binding strategy in expectation of the British night-hunters that were lying in wait, neither for the flight-course, nor for the cruising altitude. Each pilot had to decide in for himself, whether to fly in an arc east of Rhodes, an obviously extended duration of flight, over the islands of the Cyclades, with Syros, Paros and Santorini. Thus the decision was between flying for the longest possible amount of time in close proximity to the islands, or the direct route over the island Melos. Since the British Beaufighters were equipped already with radar, flying low, at about 5 to 10 meters altitude with calm sea conditions seemed hardly any risk, in order to remain below the radar. There were only strict instructions respecting the formation of the aeroplanes. We were supposed to stay as far from each other as possible, preferably avoiding visibility, in order to exclude accidental friendly fire.

I decided on the course over the Cyclades and a low altitude after the flight over the island of Santorini. At first, it appeared that we had a splendid flight in store for us, over a peaceful dreamy island panorama in the dusk over Odysseus' wide sea. After approximately one hour of flight time, the clock showed 20:40. I suddenly noticed the silhouette of an aeroplane against the moon as it rose out of the sea. It was slowly passing mine at a close distance on the starboard side, twin-engine, but evidently smaller and faster than our Heinkel and was clearly recognisable, equipped with its star motors instead of row-motors. It quickly became clear to me that we were not dealing with a He 111 here, although the radio operator, the one delegated for a few missions with the squadron and among other things the lieutenant responsible for the aeroplane-recognition service, believed that that was unequivocally what he had identified. In response to my pressing question of the further behavior of the object that had meanwhile disappeared from my view came the ominous answer: "Now it's right behind us!" At the same moment, the first streak of light swept over the right wing on the level of the fuel tank, which immediately caught fire. A second followed which accurately ripped open the left wing at nearly same place and also began to burn. Then, the spook was gone. The Beaufighter had turned away under fire from our aircraft's weapons, even though we were much too late. Whether he was hit or not, we could not tell.

Now both wings were ablaze behind the motors with eerie red-black flames. The aeroplane, so it seemed, could explode at any moment, but I was still able to steer. And the motors were still performing sufficiently to climb 80 to 100 meters so that we could get our bearings and to keep the machine in the air for as long as possible because every minute in flight shortened the distance to Heraklion's harbour, whose blinking beacons we had already seen from afar.

All of this lasted only few moments and then the dream of flying was all over. I could only concentrate on 'starving' out my aeroplane in the descent to get to the border, i.e. to reduce the landing and touch-down speed, and attempt a gentle belly-landing on the water. With the splash of the fuselage, the airscrews and the disks of the bow-cockpit burst. The fire suddenly had gone out, but immediately the water began to come through the hole into the wreck gurgling and gargling and quickly rose into the entire fuselage. The rubber dinghy mechanism had worked perfectly, and the men were able to leave the wreck through the opening however possible and escape into the rubber dinghy. I was the last one standing on the left wing, already up to my stomach in water and my comrades, not without effort pulled me into the boat. The stern of the aeroplane with its pitch and yaw rudders stood up steeply and sank almost vertically in the sea, leaving no trace. (see Appendix II)

The Do 24 shot down by W/O Jim Bays was J9+CA flown by Obfw Wilhelm Lange, as recalled by Uffz Karl-Heinz Lüdtke, one of the flight mechanics:

When things got hectic we had to clear all the islands of German troops and this wasn't easy. Lange and crew were ordered to help in clearing Crete. We started on October 1st from Phaleron and we arrived in the Suda Bight without an enemy encounter, which was rare in those days. It was also my first flight as an Unteroffizier as I got promoted a few days earlier. Unteroffizier Meissner and I readied the Do 24 to take on the soldiers for the return flight. 22 soldiers entered the aircraft and we handed them a lifejacket. The last one to enter was an officer carrying a crate with documents. This was too much for Lange who said that the crate had to be left behind, something which the officer declined to do and he stated that he was the higher ranking officer and Lange had to what he was told. Lange on the other hand was the Flugzeugführer and was in command of the aeroplane regardless of the rank of anybody on board. Things got so bad that the airport commander had to intervene. The Oberleutnant had to open the crate to his embarrassment and was ordered to stay behind and catch the next flight. Due to all this delay it was dark by the time we were ready for the return flight to Phaleron. To make things worse we received a message that allied night fighters were reported in the neighbourhood. After consultation with the higher command they told us that despite everything we had to take-off for Phaleron. Fate was taking its course!

Just short of the island Melos we were shot down by an Allied night fighter and Lange managed to land the crippled aircraft on the water, not without hitting the water with the right wing. Thank god almost everybody got out alive. During the attack however the tail gunner Feldwebel Wüstenfeld and radio-operator Feldwebel Lind were badly hurt or killed in the action, we don't know as the aircraft sunk taking both of them down into the deep waters. All the soldiers, as far as we could see, were able to get out and had on their life vests, which was a good thing. However those vests were made of kapok, which was good stuff, but after 4 to 5 hours it starts to suck up water and thus lose its floating capacity. The remainder of the original crew had inflatable life vests on and this was our rescue. I don't know if any of the 22 soldiers was saved by the German navy, which was still on the island of Melos because they were afraid to leave the harbour in fear of getting shot at. I thus doubt that any of the soldiers survived. Lange was unfortunate because during the escape from the cockpit hatch he ripped his one-man dinghy off and thus only had his life vest. When he noticed me in my dinghy he swam over and asked if he could join me, something which I could not deny. But would a one-man dinghy hold two people? I let Lange enter the dinghy first (as a good host should) and he started blowing the tube to get more air in, after that I entered. In that way we floated for about 19 hours under the blazing sun in the Mediterranean. The dinghy was of excellent quality to hold us both for such a long time. We closed in faster on the coast than our Meissner as we used our scarf as a sail. We had great difficulty covering the last part of the journey, as we were both unable to move for so long our joints were stiff. When we were on land we immediately fell into a deep sleep, we were so very tired.' (see Appendix II)

W/O Roy Butler continued:

[Ray] Graham and I were not scheduled to go on operations the coming evening of October 2nd. There were six planes being prepared, the first to take off at 5:55pm. Our CO Robbie Robertson had flown in from Idku and was going for the first time. In the evening, we went to the dispersal area and watched the first few planes take-off. First off were Chapman and Briginshaw and we decided to wait for their return. They landed back at Gambut at 11:25pm, having damaged a Do 24. This turned out to be the only claim that night. The last plane to land came in at 7:45am. The squadron score now stood at 15 destroyed, 1 probable and 4 damaged.

108 Squadron was also successful, two Heinkels being claimed shot down. Wg Cdr John Young AFC, the CO in MM929/H was vectored on to a bandit by *Ulster Queen*, gained a contact and then a visual on a Heinkel flying at 6,500 feet. This was shot down into the sea whereupon it burst into flames and exploded. A second Heinkel fell this night, W/O O'Malley (with Flt Sgt Thomas in ND290/E) catching one at 00:15, heading northwards at 8,500 feet, which was also shot down in flames, falling just west of Parapola.

2/3 October

Flt Sgt E.G. Chapman/W/O W. Briginshaw	KV920/L	Do 24 damaged
Wg Cdr J.R.C. Young (108 Sqn)	MM929	He 111
W/O P.J. O'Malley/Flt Sgt D.G. Thomas	108Sqn	He 111

III/KG27 reported the loss of two Heinkels (three shown below one obviously related to the previous night.) The losses were recorded as 1G+CR of 7 Staffel flown by Oblt Claus-Wilhelm Henkel (pilot); 1G+HR also of 7 Staffel flown by Obfw Hans Ospel; and 1G+L of 8 Staffel that fell 20 miles south of Athens, killing Oblt Günter Lecke and his crew. There were no survivors from any of the three aircraft. W/O Roy Butler continued:

> On the night of October 3rd, five aircraft were due to go on operations. Sqn Ldr Robertson scheduled himself to fly again, even though he had not returned from the previous night until 4:15am. Our Flight Commander, Joe Irwin would also be in the air again. The first plane took off at 5:00pm and we were to be the last off. We took off at 12:29am and two planes had already returned by that time, one of them being Robbie Robertson, who, once again, had not had any luck.
>
> We contacted the *Ulster Queen* at 1:55am and then patrolled on an east and west pattern at 500 feet from 2:15am until 3:30am without any sign of the enemy. At the end of our allotted time 'Trademark' called and wished us goodnight. I did not realise that it would be the last time that anyone from our Squadron would be talking to them because it was not until later that we learned that the *Ulster Queen* would be leaving the Aegean. They had done a wonderful job and it was a tribute to the Royal Navy for having kept them safe, especially during the daylight hours. As they had played such a key role in all that we had accomplished, it would have been nice to meet them personally and compare stories.
>
> We decided we would make our return by flying over Crete, the way we had the first night… but without the urgency of having to gain height quickly as on that occasion. It was a beautiful clear night and I didn't know at the time that it would be the last time I would see the island of Crete until many years after the war. We arrived back to Gambut without incident and landed at 5:14am. We learned that all our aircraft had returned safely without encountering the enemy except Flt Lt Irwin and P/O Watson. They had shot down a Ju 52 landplane. At this point, the No 46 Squadron Gambut Detachment final score was 16 destroyed, 1 probable and 4 damaged.

3/4 October

Flt Lt J. Irwin/Plt Off. G. H. Watson	ND122/Z	Ju 52

On October 4th, the *Ulster Queen* was withdrawn from the target area. From then on, until the 10th, two planes were deployed every night. Unfortunately, without the support of Ground Control, the chance of locating enemy planes was very small. On the last two nights a Royal Naval vessel, HMS *Colombo* was used as a Control, but still without success. The moon was waning and there was barely enough moonlight to sustain two intruder patrols each night. The aircrews were gradually being returned to Idku ... the operation was coming to an end. Graham and I flew a plane back to Idku on October 5th. We were taking an army officer with us who needed to get to Alexandria in a hurry. There was no room for a passenger to sit in a Beaufighter, so he had to stand behind me in the cockpit.

Mosquito XIIIs of 256 Squadron operating from Foggia, Italy, took over from 46 Squadron the main role of hunting down the evacuating aircraft with immediate success. On the night of 4/5 October, the newly appointed CO Wg Cdr Hugh Eliot DFC[86] shot down a Ju 52/3m of IV/TG1 at 21:55 near Salonika. Flying HK507 with R/Op Flt Lt Denis Ibbotson, he sighted the transport aircraft at 500 feet with its navigation lights on, on its final approach to Salonika/Sedes. He gave two short bursts and it burst into flames and crashed at the end of the runway. This was probably an aircraft of 13./TG1 flown by Obfw Günther Dörrfeldt who was killed with his crew.

Another Mosquito, MM527 crewed by Flt Sgt John McEwan and Flt Sgt Sid Coles, engaged a Heinkel at 22:57 at 2,000 feet over Eponomi. They closed in and gained a visual whereupon a quarter beam attack was carried out. The Heinkel's starboard engine caught fire and the aircraft went into a starboard diving spiral. It crashed into the ground leaving a trail of sparks before it burst into flames. A second Heinkel fell to Sqn Ldr Richard Mumford (in HK437 with Flg Off. R. B. Joynson) shortly after 23:50. Having gained a radar contact, Mumford closed in and engaged the aircraft at 1,500 feet. He fired a short burst from astern whereupon it caught fire and crashed in flames. The Mosquito was hit by two small pieces of debris but returned safely.

The Heinkels were believed to have been 5J+FK of 2./KG4 that fell in the Athens area with the loss of Obfw Günther Döring and crew while 1G+AD of 8./KG27 crashed at Kalamaki on a return flight from Crete having been attacked by a night fighter. The crew survived apart from the observer. A third Heinkel was lost when 1G+BN of 5./KG27 crashed after take-off for Salonika/Mega airfield. Uffz Eugen Ott, his crew and fourteen passengers were killed.

Two nights later (6/7 October), three Mosquitoes of 256 Squadron flew from Foggia to Brindisi where they refuelled before carrying out patrols off southern Greece. Wg Cdr Eliot (HK435 with Flt Lt Ibbotson) sighted an aircraft burning its navigation lights. He closed and fired but observed no results. A second attack was made, again without result, so he orbited and carried out a third attack on what he now identified as a Do 24. Its port engine burst into flames and the pilot, Obfw Karl Büge, attempted to ditch but crashed on the water's edge south of Kalamaki whereupon it burst into flames. The seaplane was totally destroyed and its pilot and crew were killed.

On 9 October, 108 Squadron lost another Beaufighter. Plt Off. C. E. Baldry and Flg Off. Jack Watson had been vectored on to a bogey by HMS *Colombo* and were last heard chasing an aircraft but the Beaufighter (ND???) crashed into the sea as Baldry attempted a steep turn with flaps and wheels down. Fortunately, the Beaufighter splashed down not far from HMS *Colombo* that rescued Baldry but Watson was lost. Another Heinkel fell on 12 October, 1G+EM of 4./KG27, about fifteen miles north of Heraklion in which the pilot, Fw Herbert Mittrach, was killed though his crew was rescued. This aircraft may have been the victim of Flt Sgt John McEwan and Flt Sgt Sid Coles in 256 Squadron's HK509 that failed to return from its sortie. Two nights later (14 October), 5J+CP of 6./KG4 was shot down by a night fighter in the northern part of Gulf of Salonika at 21:03. The crew was rescued by minesweeper.

On 16 October, the advance party of 108 Squadron arrived at Araxos followed by the remainder of the squadron within the next couple of days. From there the Beaufighters carried out intruder operations over northern Greece, mainly strafing transport and other ground targets. 6./KG4 lost another Heinkel on 22 October, 5J+CP crashing into the sea about forty miles east of Euboea. Hptm. Johannes Schumm and crew were all lost. Flg Off. Wally Cunningham of 108 Squadron (with Flg Off. Bob Common in ND145/W) reported an AI contact and pursued a Heinkel that he attacked from astern setting its starboard engine on fire. It went down in a 'screaming dive' into the sea. A Ju 188D 8H+EL of 3.(F)/33 took-off from Salonika/Sedes at 10:45 on the same date. One engine began to give trouble and the pilot turned back but the aircraft blew up and crashed near Kymi (Euboea) at 13:00. Uffz Gerhard Eckert (pilot) and the W/Op baled out and were taken prisoner; one of A/Gs baled out but his parachute failed. The POWs apparently heard over the radio that a Beaufighter had claimed with shooting them down but they had seen no hostile aircraft.

One of the last, if not the last aircraft to be lost during the evacuation period was He 111 5J+CM of 4./KG4 that failed to arrive at its destination on Christmas Eve. Uffz Heinz Kiehling and crew were all lost.

CHAPTER XI

Spitfires vs. The High Flyers – 1942-44

With the major action in the Eastern Mediterranean from mid-1943 onwards occurring mainly over the Aegean, aerial encounters for Libyan and Egyptian-based fighter units were few and far between. With RAF air strength ever increasing in North Africa, the Luftwaffe found that the task of reconnoitring British ground movements, searching for shipping and keeping an eye on the arrival of reinforcements ever more demanding. Its main reconnaissance aircraft, the Ju 88T, was no longer free to fly over the coast without interference since Spitfires had begun arriving in Egypt. Even earlier, in late May 1942, to help counter this failing, 2.(F)/123 at Kastelli on Crete had received four pressurised high-altitude Ju 86R-1s (WrkNr. 292, 479, 5101, 5144) for operations over Egypt. By August, they were flying along the Nile from Port Said to Suez and brought back evidence of the huge build-up of Allied equipment and supplies. Grp Capt. Kenneth 'Bing' Cross, OC 219 (F) Group, wrote:

> Without warning from Intelligence or from England, a new problem faced our air defence. Early one morning … the controller said: "We have a high flying aircraft plotted 70 miles north-west and heading for Alexandria. I have a section of 274 Squadron Hurricane IIs airborne and, barring changes of heading by the enemy, should make an interception some 5 miles out."
>
> Shortly afterwards a high flying aircraft appeared to the north-west with a very long condensation trail behind it. The trail was so conspicuous that I knew the Hurricane pilots would have no difficulty in spotting the aircraft and I waited for the inevitable combat. Nothing happened.[87]

The Hurricanes had climbed to 36,000 feet, their maximum service altitude and reported that the enemy aircraft was still above them at an estimated 42,000 feet.

This really was a problem. I discussed the problem with the staff at Air HQ Egypt and signals were sent to England for any information they had about this flyer. The answer was soon with us. The Air Ministry believed the aircraft to be a special high-flying Ju 86 used solely for reconnaissance. It was assumed that it had a pressurised fuselage or cabin since it remained at altitude for many hours. It was not a fast aircraft, nor was it armed.

My best aircraft was just not up to the task but fortunately there were a few Spitfire Vs at Aboukir being modified for the Desert Air Force and two were allotted to us. It was apparent to me that though the Spitfire V was superior in performance to the Hurricane II, it would have difficulty in climbing above 40,000 feet quickly enough to intercept the Ju 86 before it turned for home. It was decided therefore to lighten the Spitfires by removing everything but essential equipment for this particular role. As a start, because the Ju 86 was unarmed, the heavy protective armour was unnecessary and so removed. Also, as the Ju 86 was a large aircraft it would be an easy target so the Browning guns were removed, leaving just 20mm cannons as the only armament. It was argued, rightly I thought, that with the Ju 86's cabin being pressurised, one strike by a cannon shell would be enough to de-pressurise the cabin and force rapid descent to a lower altitude where if necessary it could be dealt with by the Hurricanes. Other items removed included the IFF responder, survival kit and Browning ammunition chutes.[88]

No.103 Maintenance Unit at Aboukir (the Middle East's major maintenance, repair and testing unit established in November 1939) had recently received Spitfire VCs BP985, BR114 and BR234 from the UK. More Spitfires would arrive shortly thereafter. On 16 June, instruction was received for the MU to use the Spitfires for the defence of Alexandria and specifically to deter the daily reconnaissance flights. As these flights had proved beyond the means of the Hurricanes, the standard Spitfire V would also be unable to reach the heights required. Thus, the three Spitfires were stripped of all unnecessary equipment. Radio, armour and normal armament were removed and the engines specially tuned and locally fabricated extended wingtips fitted. Grp Capt. Cross continued:

Meanwhile, the Ju 86 came again and completed what was to become in the following weeks a regular route. It appeared on the radar screen well out to sea from Alexandria, flew over the harbour, down the road to Cairo, across the Suez up the Canal to Port Said and then away to the north, back to Crete. Such comprehensive photographic coverage of every sensitive area in Egypt was plainly of great value to the enemy and would nullify any attempt we make at deception and greatly lessen the value of camouflage.

The first interceptions were failures, the Spitfire's rate of climb being insufficient to make the required height before the enemy got too far ahead. There were urgent consultations with the test pilots after each sortie. They said they must lighten the Spitfire even more. The heavy cannons were removed and two of the lighter Brownings substituted. Ammunition was limited to 150 rounds per gun, and later reduced to 50 rounds. The heavy-duty battery was removed and a small radio battery put in its place. Even so, on the next sortie though the Spitfire got within 2,000 feet immediately below the Ju 86, it could not get any higher and raising the nose for a long-range shot led to an immediate stall. The pilot reported that he was at 43,000 feet with the Ju 86 going away when he broke off the attack.

We needed to increase the performance of the Spitfire somehow, so the engineers turned their attention to the Rolls-Royce Merlin. It was decided that the only measure within the competence of the engineering resources in Egypt was to increase the compression by taking a sixteenth of an inch off the cylinder head. It had to be done and it is a measure of the skill that had been built up over the years in the work force at Aboukir that the task caused little concern. Most of the artisans at Aboukir were civilians, the highest proportion being Maltese, but there were also Greeks, Egyptians and other nationalities employed there, and had been for years. The supervisory staff were all RAF officers and senior NCOs.

Even with the increase in power, though, it was still impossible to reach the height the Ju 86 flew at. On one attempt the pilot flew to within a few hundred feet but with his fuel down to a few gallons he had to give up the chase. The last remaining heavy piece of equipment was the R/T set, but if this was removed how was the pilot to be directed by the ground controller to make an interception? In discussion with the pilots it was decided that the set should be taken out and that the lightened Spitfire would take off and climb in formation with a standard Spitfire until a visual sighting was obtained when the lightened aircraft would continue on its own.[89]

Tactics were developed whereupon the aircraft operated in pairs. One Spitfire was to fly as 'Striker' aircraft, accompanied by either another Spitfire or Hurricane as 'Marker' aircraft that was to remain at a lower altitude, shadowing the enemy aircraft from below and provide information to both the 'Striker' and ground control as the enemy aircraft was often invisible both visually and to radar at high altitudes.

Above 35,000 feet without a pressure cabin a man struggles to remain conscious even with the help of oxygen. He can suffer not only from intense cold but also from temporary paralysis of the limbs, expanding gasses which distend the intestines, and sometimes from 'the bends', an affliction which deep-sea divers can also know, in which all the joints of the body are gripped in a pain said to be more intense than any other. Great height also has a temporary effect on a man's mind, plunging him into despondency against his will.[90]

So concluded an assessment by RAF doctors into the difficulties of high altitude flying without adequate safeguards. These circumstances were those faced by 103 MU's resident test pilots, thirty-eight-year-old Flg Off. George Reynolds and thirty-three-year-old Plt Off. Arthur Gold AFC. Both were pre-war regulars, Gold having joined the RAF as a Boy Entrant aged fifteen. However, they were soon to be joined by other younger pilots including Plt Off. Eric Genders DFM who had fought with 33 Squadron in Greece (in 1941) and a detachment of pilots from 123 Squadron who had recently arrived from the UK sans aircraft. Genders had been posted to the unit as a test pilot and later wrote home about his new assignment:

> It is a great thrill to put a fast fighter through the maximum speed test and to open the throttles fully for five minutes. In the diving test we can get to terrific speeds. I was once in the middle of a fast dive with a Hurricane when suddenly the cockpit hood blew off, the side of the cockpit was torn away and the fabric on top of the fuselage was stripped. Luckily nothing else went and I got her down safely ... [and, on another occasion] ... Once, in the Cairo area, when I had tested a twin-engined plane and was bringing it in to land, one of the engines failed. I had to throttle back the other engine. I shot over the airfield with the plane partly out of control and managed to pancake her down on a roadway in the middle of an Army camp. There were huts all round, so I was pretty lucky. One of the engines was torn off and left on a telegraph post and the tail unit was left on another. Fortunately, no-one was hurt.

On 18 June, three high-altitude flights were undertaken but without success. Four more followed on 19 and 20 June, one the next day and three on 23 June. Five flights were made on 27 June and during one of these Plt Off. Genders reported damaging a Ju 86 at 40,000 feet, but was unable to shoot it down. In fact, the first success for the unit was claimed by 123 Squadron's Plt Off. Alastair Wilson (BP852) on 26 July when he managed to shoot down Ltn Gustav Stich's Ju 88A of 1.(F)/122 north of Alamein. The crew was rescued from the sea including observer Hptm. Heinrich Beysiegel who was Chief Weatherman and Staffelkapitän of Wekusta 26.

Daily flights in pursuit of the high-flying quarry continued unabated, Plt Off. Genders attacking a Ju 86 on 2 August while Plt Off. Wilson managed to close to within 800 yards of another on 5 August, both without observed results. Both Flg Off. Reynolds and Plt Off. Gold opened fire on a Ju 86 on

7 August, Reynolds engaging initially at 46,000 feet, but with the same inconclusive result.

145 Squadron, which had been operating Spitfires during the recent heavy action, was withdrawn to Idku for a brief rest for its pilots, although they were tasked to assist the pilots of 103 MU in keeping the ubiquitous recce aircraft at bay. Its first success came on 8 August when Flt Lt Wally Conrad RCAF (BR467) and Sgt R. A. Cunningham damaged a Ju 88.

Almost a week later (14 August), Flg Off. Reynolds engaged a Ju 86 at 47,000 feet and another on 20 August, both without success. Sgt Duigan of 145 Squadron was also scrambled to intercept the latter intruder. Flying one of 103 MU's Spitfires, he got to within ten yards of the intruder at 40,000 feet but his guns froze after firing only one round. He tried to ram its tailplane but got caught in the slipstream and lost 1,000 feet, after which he gave up the chase. Later, on 22 August, Flt Lt John Taylor of 145 Squadron claimed damage to a Ju 88.

Although the pilots believed they were gaining strikes during these brief engagements, frustratingly the reconnaissance aircraft escaped destruction. But finally, on 24 August, Reynolds was credited with shooting down a Ju 86:

> It fell to 38-year-old Reynolds to make the first interception at 37,000 feet, north of Cairo. The Junkers crew sighted the Spitfire and strove for more height, but Reynolds followed doggedly, levelled off at around 42,000 feet. Opening fire, he had the satisfaction of seeing the Ju 86 bank and dive with smoke pouring from one engine. By then Reynolds had reached the limit of his physical endurance. For the second time during the flight he blacked out, to regain consciousness after his Spitfire had dropped 10,000 feet out of control. Regaining control he landed with a mere 5 gallons in his tank to learn that the Ju 86 was down in the desert.[91]

However, the report – written retrospectively by another hand – was partially erroneous. It transpired that the Ju 86 credited to Reynolds did not in fact crash. The confusion arose following the shooting down of Ju 88 L1+NL by a pilot of 73 Squadron on this date and the later crash-landing of a Ju 86 in the desert on 6 September. Of the difficulties experienced during this flight, Reynolds commented:

> I had been experiencing great pain at that height, as I was over 40,000 feet for nearly half an hour and felt rather ill. Added to this, my petrol and oxygen were low and wished to get home as quickly as possible. I landed at base with five gallons of petrol left.[92]

Reynolds came close to gaining another success on 27 August, claiming damage to another Ju 86 he attacked at 49,500 feet before it escaped. Meanwhile, Sgts M. A. Powers and G. W. Small of 145 Squadron engaged and damaged a Ju 88. However, two days later on 29 August, a Ju 86R (865144) of 2.(F)/123 crewed by Hptm. Helmut Rammig and observer Ltn Günther Kolw ditched following 'engine problems' while returning from a recce flight to photograph the Suez Canal. The crew reported that on the return flight, about 100 miles north of Alexandria, one engine failed at 32,000-33,000 feet. About 1,000 feet below, a Spitfire was seen but the crew did not observe any gunfire. The Junkers rapidly lost height and ditched about seventy miles south of Crete. A Do 24 of Seenotstfl.7 responded with Ltn Phillip Barbinger at the controls. When they were being pulled onboard, the Dornier crew enquired about the remaining crew and could not believe that only two crew flew the Ju 86. Plt Off. Genders was the pilot of the Spitfire but reported that his guns jammed after a short burst, but he may have been responsible the Ju 86's demise.

2 September saw Plt Off. Alastair Wilson and Flg Off. Reynolds scramble when a contact appeared on the radar screens, Wilson climbing to 41,000 feet where he opened fire on a Ju 86. Unfortunately, his aircraft developed engine problems and was forced to break away and leave the reconnaissance aircraft to complete another successful sortie. Next day, Reynolds was advised of the award of the DFC:

> In addition to normal duties, this officer has completed numerous sorties in the Middle East against enemy reconnaissance aircraft flying at great altitudes. In one of these he engaged an enemy aeroplane and probably caused its destruction. On four previous occasions, he had damaged enemy aircraft. Flying Officer Reynolds has displayed a high standard of skill and devotion to duty.

Not all of the recce intruders came 103 MU's way. On 2 September, two of 94 Squadron's Hurricane pilots, Plt Off. Alan 'Blondie' Walker (BP346/C) and Sgt Alderdice (BP339/F), were patrolling over Suez when they were vectored on to a Ju 88. Walker hit it with his first shots and pursued it to low level where another burst set one of the engines on fire. The 1.(F)/121 aircraft, 7A+BH flown by Obfw Adolf Hauhoff, crash-landed in the desert. By this time, Walker had almost run out of fuel only just managing to land at an RAF airfield. As he turned off the runway, the engine of his Hurricane died. Later in the day he took a light aircraft and landed alongside the German aircraft to examine the effects of his shooting. He also met the pilot, Obfw Hauhoff, who was taken prisoner together with the rest of his crew.

Further along the coast at Port Said's el-Gamil airfield, 252 Wing had established a small unit dubbed the Delta Defence Flight formed with a few of 94 Squadron's redundant pilots under the command of Flt Lt Richard Webb RNZAF and equipped with four Spitfire Vs. Their role was local air defence against recce intruders and on 3 September, gained a success when Flt Lt Webb (BR487) and Sgt Ross (BP985) shot down a Z.1007 of 191ª Squadriglia BT at 18:45, the aircraft crashing at Burg el-Arab close to Alexandria. Two of Sottoten Achille Scaduto's crew were captured.

But a confirmed success did come 103 MU's way on 6 September when Plt Off. Genders (BR234) and Plt Off. Gold (BR202) were scrambled on the approach of another Ju 86. Genders was the 'Striker' and climbed to 43,000 feet where he attacked '5101' some sixty miles off the coast. His fire struck home and the recce machine fell away, believed to have been badly damaged. Plt Off. Gold also managed to get in an effective attack and '5101' carried out a forced landing in the desert behind German lines at Bir el-Abd landing ground. It was assessed to have been sixty per cent damaged although the crew survived unhurt.[93]

Genders' subsequent report revealed:

Plt Off Gold and I took off together. We sighted the aircraft about 50 miles east of Alexandria and the Germans must have seen us as they began to fly back again over the sea. I caught up with it when about 100 miles from land and with my two machine-guns stopped one of the Junker's engines. I now turned back as I had only about three gallons of petrol left.

Gold, who was with the heavier Spitfire was 2,000 or 3,000 feet below, waited until the Junkers lost height and then give it the coup de grâce. Gold got back to the airfield with a few gallons to spare, but I ran out when still a long way from the coast.

Genders continued his account in a letter home:

…On my way back to shore my engine failed so I had to bale out over the sea. I did this at 1,000 feet and the parachute opened quite quickly, but I did not have time to get any sensations of the descent, as I had to get the release gear ready for when I hit the water. I do not think I went under the water. I got rid of the parachute harness as quickly as possible and then blew my Mae West up. We do not fill our Mae Wests on the ground as any air in them expands to about six times its volume at very high altitudes, and this would explode the thing.

When I had blown the Mae West up, I discarded my helmet, shoes and socks, but to have got my flying kit off I would have had to have taken off my Mae West, and, as this is put on like a jacket, I do not think I would have got it on again, so I had to keep my flying suit on. When I was in the water, I realised I was in an awful fix. I was ten or more miles from the coast and I thought my only hope was for a searching aircraft to find me. I learned later that 12 aircraft searched for me and I saw five of these. Two of them had come fairly near to me but they had not seen me although I splashed about as much as possible.

After the aircraft that were looking for me disappeared, I became very despondent. But I thought of one of your sentences in a letter, 'God who has protected you for so long will continue to do so'. I decided I would try to swim to shore even if it took me several days. I was on my back with the Mae West supporting my head, and I did a kind of back stroke with my arms and scissors kick with my legs. The swimming kept me warm but my movements seemed very slow and I soon became tired, my arms particularly. I wondered if it was a hopeless task and then realised nothing is impossible to God, and I recollected Hymn No.10 we had at a service I attended at Athens. I seemed to get renewed strength after that and continued swimming all the afternoon and night. At about 8:30 in the morning I saw telephone posts on shore, and I finally got to land about 10 o'clock. I had been in the water 21 hours.

Two natives who were shooting sea birds came up to me. I undressed and dried in the sun. One of the natives lent me one of his undergarments to wear whilst my shorts and shirt dried and we talked to a coastguard camp about two miles away. I phoned up my CO to tell him I was OK and asked for transport, and then I had some food. The first thing I ate was a small piece of bread and cheese. I had hardly swallowed this when I felt sick, so I went outside and got rid of four or five pints of sea water, plus the small piece of bread and cheese. I then went back and had a hearty meal of boiled eggs and home-made bread...

Flg Off. Reynolds (BR114/B) was in action again on 9 September when he fired at a 'Ju 86' at 44,000 feet that he claimed damaged. An official report – probably a press release – revealed:

The enemy came at always greater and greater heights; the last one [sic] was pursued to nearly 50,000 feet. This fell also to Reynolds, he had been for more than an hour higher than 45,000 feet. His whole cockpit, instrument panel, control column, Perspex, were coated thickly in ice. His body was wrenched with pain, his arms were temporarily paralysed and his eyesight for the moment almost failed with weakness.

When he met the Ju 86 at a distance of only 100 yards but at a height of 50,000 feet, he was physically incapable of firing his guns; the enemy turned and fled towards the sea. Reynolds manoeuvred his Spitfire to follow it by moving the position of his body in the delicately-balanced aircraft. He caught the Junkers once more, far out over the Mediterranean, and managed to move his hands sufficiently to press the firing button. The Ju 86 was destroyed [*sic*].'[94]

No Ju 86 was lost on this occasion but a Ju 88D of 2.(F)/123 (4U+FK 430166) failed to return from a sortie over Port Said in which Ltn Gerhard Pichler and crew were posted missing. The RAF press release continued:

> The Spitfire completed much of the return journey back to base in a powerless glide. When the pilot started to glide home on that flight he glanced round and below him at a remarkable panorama. He could see the whole of the eastern Mediterranean spread out like a map beneath him. To the west, he could see past Benghazi into the Gulf of Sirte; to the east, the coastline of Palestine and Syria with the mountains beyond. Behind him lay unrolled the island-sprinkled Aegean. In the front lay Egypt revealed at one glance from the coast to beyond Cairo, and the length of the Suez Canal from Port Said to Suez.[95]

Plt Off. Gold reported intercepting another Ju 86 on 15 September, climbing to 44,000 feet to engage. He opened fire and claimed damage before it dived away and escaped, but not before he had taken photographs of his victim. Gold received a second AFC for his work with 103 MU, one of the few to gain two AFCs.

A new Hurricane unit had recently arrived at Shandur, 417 RCAF Squadron, and on 26 September, opened its account when Flt Sgt Gil Leguerier RCAF shot down Ju 88D 7A+AH of 1.(F)/121 over the Suez Canal. The French-Canadian pilot was on standing patrol 28,000 feet above Suez at noon when ground control directed him to intercept 'an enemy machine'. Ten miles to the south-east, he sighted a Ju 88 and carried out two attacks at close range. The Ju 88 spun down into the sea and exploded, Leguerier observing three parachutes, but all four of the crew managed to bale out and were rescued from the sea. Oblt Hermann Meier and crew were all taken prisoner.

1 October opened with the shooting down, probably by AA fire, over Alexandria of a Bf 109 reconnaissance aircraft of 4.(H)/12 in which Uffz Ernst Depke was killed. It was Plt Off. Genders' turn to claim a success on 21 October when he intercepted a Ju 88D – 7A+?H of 1.(F)/121 – north-east of Alexandria flying EP407. The badly damaged aircraft managed to escape and returned to its base with the observer wounded. The following week (on 29 October), Plt Off. Blondie Walker and his No.2 of 94 Squadron had the unfortunate experience of shooting down an American aircraft, a US C-47 of Air Transport Command on a courier flight to 9th Air Force HQ in Cairo. The Hurricane pilots had been ordered to intercept a low-flying

aircraft that was approaching a convoy north-west of Port Said. With no Allied activity reported in the area, Walker was given clearance to attack in hazy conditions and he sent the aircraft spiralling into the sea. Capt. Paul F. Roth and 1/Lt Jens H. Hansen were killed.[96] At the subsequent court martial, Walker was completely exonerated as the American aircraft was 150 miles off course and had failed to display the mandatory identification codes.

October also saw the arrival at Aboukir of Flt Lt Tom Cooper-Slipper DFC who took command of 103 MU's Special Performance Flight. The former Battle of Britain pilot who had also participated in the fighting at Singapore was appointed Chief Test Pilot. Another new arrival was American Flg Off. Wendell Nelson RCAF who had been flying Hurricanes with 6 Squadron in the desert.

At about this time the Luftwaffe was not only using the Ju 86P and Ju 88T for high-flying reconnaissance but also introduced the prototype Ju 88C-7 (K9+VH) fitted with two BMW801J engines. The aircraft arrived at Kastelli, Crete, in the hands of Oblt Siegfried Knemeyer:

With the Ju 88 prototype and the BMW801 engines the performance was so good that fighters could not touch her despite at that time Spitfires were available around Alexandria. One morning I flew the aircraft around Cyprus, down along the Palestinian coast to Port Said, reaching 9,000m (29,000 feet) in a slow climb but holding speed. I then turned along the Suez Canal to the town of Suez, and returned along the same route back to Port Said. Several fighters were seen below us but they were slower and could not match our altitude.

Late in the afternoon of that day I flew another mission from Crete direct to Port Said and Alexandria harbours where we took pictures of ships assembled there. The total tonnage of the ships photographed that day exceeded one and a half million tons. Two days later [Generalfeldmarschall] Kesselring came especially to Crete to talk to me about it.

Next day I made another sortie over Alexandria, but this time my port engine acted up over the harbour but, fortunately, I was at about 10,000m (33,000 feet) when it happened. That meant that I could head back parallel with the North African coast to Tobruk without losing too much height. From there I headed directly back to Crete and made a good landing on one engine. After a replacement component had been brought out for the damaged engine, I flew back to Oranienburg.

November was not a good month for 2.(F)/123 at Kastelli losing Ju 88D 4U+EK on the first day during a recce of Alexandria, the aircraft crashing into the sea due to engine problems killing Uffz Alfred Kleinschmidt and his crew. On 11 November, the unit temporarily lost the service of Ju 86 (860479) when it was damaged in a crash-landing at Calato, Rhodes, and five days later, on 16 November, Ju 88 L1+DN of 5./LG1 was shot down by two Hurricanes flown by Sgt Bill Imrie and Sgt Geoff Grove of 94 Squadron operating from el-Gamil. Hptm. Heinrich Kohl and his crew were taken prisoner.

The Canadian 417 Squadron, awaiting its turn to convert to Spitfires, continued patrolling with Hurricanes over the Nile delta and escorting convoys. On 4 December, Flt Lt Bill Pentland RCAF and Wt Off. H. G. Conn RCAF patrolled sixty miles north-west of Alexandria in poor visibility when they suddenly caught sight of a Ju 88 low over the water. Together they dived upon it firing and black smoke began to stream from its port engine before it escaped into a rain cloud and was lost.

The four Spitfires of the Delta Defence Flight arrived at el-Gamil on 30 November from Shandur. Its pilots soon claimed a second success when, on 20 December, Flt Lt Richard Webb (BR487) and his New Zealand fellow countryman, Flg Off. Monty Rowland (BP985), shot down a Ju 88D of 2.(F)/123 north-west of Port Said. Uffz Hans Zweigert and his crew of 4U+KK were all posted missing.

With the Axis forces currently retreating across Libya towards Tunisia, aerial activity in the Eastern Mediterranean decreased although Greek, Cretan and Aegean-based reconnaissance units continued to test British radar defences along the Egyptian and Libyan coasts. The high-flying crews of the remaining Ju 86s and Ju 88Ts were still generally cocking a snook as Spitfires struggled to reach their altitude, as noted by Wg Cdr John Kent DFC AFC, who had arrived from the UK earlier in the year to take command of 17 Sector, 212 Group, which had its HQ at Benina (see Chapter III). The three squadrons under his control, 89 on Beaufighters, 33 and 7SAAF with Hurricanes, were based at Brecis LG near the Tocra. He wrote:

> By now the Germans and Italians had been driven out of Africa and activity died away almost completely except for high-flying reconnaissance Ju 88s and Ju 86Ps ... the Hurricanes with which the squadrons were equipped were virtually useless when it came to try to deal with the high-flying German machines and interceptions were continually being missed. Eventually three Spitfires were allotted to each squadron and these aircraft we stripped of all equipment that could be spared in our endeavour to increase their ceiling.
>
> On one occasion, after a long chase, I managed to coax my Spitfire up to an indicated 41,500 feet but was still about 1,000 feet below and slightly behind a Ju 86P. Whilst the Spit appeared to have reached its absolute ceiling, the German aircraft was still slowly climbing away so, in desperation, I pulled up the nose of my aircraft and fired a burst hoping that a lucky shot might bring down the enemy aircraft.

I do not know what became of the Junkers but, as I fired, my machine shuddered, stalled and flicked into a spin from which I was unable to recover until we had reached 20,000 feet. Although this sort of thing was repeated by various pilots, without strikes being seen, we must have been hitting these exasperating machines as at one time, according to an intelligence report, all the Ju 86Ps based on Crete were unserviceable with bullet-perforated cabins.[97] (see Appendix V)

The first few months of 1943 were relatively quiet operationally-wise for 103 MU with the Luftwaffe heavily involved in the fighting over Tunisia, but following their eviction from North Africa, German thoughts returned to the Aegean. Thus, the pilots of the high-flying Spitfire IXs (which included BS342, EN399, JK980 and JL228) found themselves again confronting the Ju 86s and recce Ju 88s. Flt Lt Tom Cooper-Slipper, now the MU's Chief Test Pilot, made contact with a Ju 86 some forty-five miles north of Aboukir on 7 June. He sighted it at 30,000 feet but on spotting the Spitfire, the Ju 86 climbed to 40,000 feet. Cooper-Slipper fired 100 rounds from each cannon to lighten his load and climbed to 43,000 feet but the recce aircraft remained 300 feet higher. He lifted the nose of the Spitfire and fired his remaining ammunition, but no hits were observed and he was unable to retain contact. With his machine-guns frozen he gave up the pursuit and returned to base.

Flt Lt Monty Rowland fared better on 12 June when he intercepted a Ju 88 at 31,000 feet. He climbed at a speed of 310 mph and gained 500 feet on his opponent. The recce aircraft started violent evasive action although the New Zealander was able to score hits with his first burst and pieces fell off after his third burst; however, his cannons jammed and he was forced to let the Ju 88 escape. Flt Lt Cooper-Slipper was in action again on 15 June making a claim for an aircraft he identified as a Ju 188. The aircraft was sighted over Alexandria, 4,000 above. He climbed and closed in to fifty yards, hitting its port engine and fuselage causing the port undercarriage leg to fall down. The Junkers rolled to its left and he got in another burst, following which it dived to 10,000 feet. Cooper-Slipper followed and again closed in to fifty yards but his port cannon failed to fire. He followed it down to sea level by which time the port leg had retracted and fired short bursts with his starboard cannon. However, the lucky German crew survived to return to base.

Service pilots were coming and going to fly the converted Spitfires and included at the beginning of July four Australians: Flg Off. Ken Watts, Flg Off. Harry Freckelton, Flg Off. Hal Rowlands and Flg Off. Alec Arnel. Two of these were in action on 2 July, north-east of Aboukir, Freckelton (BS342) and Rowlands (JL228) climbing to intercept a Ju 86, 4U+IK of 2.(F)/123, at 42,300 feet that was apparently photographing a convoy. Freckelton made the initial attack followed by Rowlands, and as the reconnaissance machine dived away damaged, it was caught at 31,000 feet by two pilots of 80 Squadron, Flg Off. J. Hunter (EE839) and Plt Off. G. T. Pratley (EE840), who applied the coup de grâce. Neither Ltn Franz Stock nor Ltn Udo Kannenberg survived when their burning and disintegrating machine crashed into the sea. Pratley's Spitfire developed engine problems during the encounter and he was obliged to bale out but was soon picked up by a ship of the convoy having suffered slight burns.

On July, Flg Off. Ken Watts scrambled from Bu Amud in JL228 and intercepted a Ju 86 at 42,800 feet about twenty miles north-west of Benghazi.

> I climbed to 40,000 feet, balls out, hanging on the prop. Up there it was a new world and the sky was an intense indigo, the darkest deep blue I have seen. The outside temperature was minus 45 degrees. The Spits had no cabin heating and my breath iced the windscreen and Perspex canopy. The curvature of the earth was quite apparent.
>
> After what seemed and age I saw the vapour trail approaching about 20 miles north-west of Benghazi. It climbed right over the top of my kite and with chagrin and admiration for the technology of this large slotted-wing aircraft, I tried to lift the nose of the Spit to fire the single machine-gun, but in the thin air the kite spun off.

In his logbook he added '...had three squirts from port quarter. No strikes observed.'

> I felt hazy and dozy because of the oxygen lack, so straightened out and went for the deck. Two blood wagon bods from the ambulance lifted me out and took me to the Ops room, where Air Vice-Marshal Sir Sholto Douglas and Group Captain Bain had witnessed the 'do'.

Flt Lt Jeff West DFM, an experienced New Zealander arrived to take charge of the Special Performance Flight at Aboukir while other new arrivals included Australians Flg Off. Don McQueen and Flg Off. George Purdy. Flt Lt West was soon in action being scrambled on 19 July together with Flg Off. Harry Freckelton as Pink Section. They sighted a Ju 88 at 32,000 feet, some four miles north of Alexandria. West attacked first:

> Opened fire, one-second burst from half to head-on at 200 yards. Saw flashes just out from port engine. E/a was diving slightly and flying very fast. Had 100 yards lead. Jettisoned my overload tank; maximum boost and throttle

but could close only very slowly. E/a's port engine was discharging slight black smoke. Did not appear to be gaining appreciably on the e/a. Spit was indicating approximately 350mph. Lifted nose and gave a few short bursts at between 300/400 yards. E/a was jinking and appeared to be taking evasive action just as incendiaries looked like striking. E/a seemed to lose speed quite suddenly and [I] fired last burst of one-second at approximately 200 yards. No hits observed. Ammunition and petrol low. Was ordered to return to base.[98]

Pink 2, Freckelton, similarly reported:

Made an attack from about 45° ahead, starboard beam. Saw one strike on port wing. E/a turned, diving slightly at high speed. Endeavoured to close range. E/a continued to lose height gradually, in stages. Closed in to about 300 yards at sea level. Fired one burst. Shots fell all round e/a, which was right down on the deck, but no strikes observed. Expended last ammunition from about 300/400 yards.[99]

No joy for the streamlined Spitfires on this occasion. The pressure of continuous high-altitude flights remained a problem, Plt Off. E. J. Sidney becoming unwell on 29 July while flying at 40,500 feet in pursuit of a bandit and being forced to return. Flt Lt West was airborne after the same aircraft, a Ju 86, and climbed to 42,300 feet with the intruder at least 1,000 feet above. At about 300 yards astern and still below, West eased the Spitfire's nose up and fired a one-second burst, but the port cannon failed. He again manoeuvred into position but as soon as he fired the recoil pulled the Spitfire to one side and lost height. And so another high-flyer made its escape.

Plt Off. Sidney was again unlucky when, on 6 August, he scrambled to intercept a bandit at 36,000 feet, fifteen miles north of Appolonia. He spotted the intruder's give-away condensation trail some 6,000 feet above, but when he attempted to jettison his overload tank, he found the gear to be jammed. Unable to gain sufficient height he was ordered to return to base. However, his section leader, Flt Lt West, was able to climb to 38,000 feet having successfully jettisoned his tank and closed in on the Ju 86, only to be seen by the crew, the recce aircraft then climbing even higher. West followed until he reached the Spitfire's ceiling height of 41,900 feet:

E/a was then 500 feet above. The Spitfire's hood and side panels had completely frosted up and the only vision was through the armour-plated glass windshield. I eased up the nose and fired a short burst in the hope of damaging the e/a, and also lighten the aircraft. The starboard cannon stopped after the second short burst. On a subsequent attack, a few minutes later, I was 300 feet below and 300 yards behind and observed a strike on the starboard tail unit. E/a turned sharply to port and edged back to north. I got in position again about 200 feet below and 200 yards behind, but on pressing the gun button the gun failed to fire a single shot.[100]

There was more action on 12 August, two Spitfires being scrambled at 17:52 on the approach of two PR Bf 109s heading for Derna. As Flt Lt West and Flt Sgt Stott climbed to engage, one Messerschmitt turned across their line and West opened fire. No strikes were observed and the German fired at West's aircraft but his fire fell way behind. At this point West momentarily blacked out and the Messerschmitts made their escape. Flt Sgt Stott was late in making an interception on the second fighter that performed a half-roll and dived away.

Flg Off. George Purdy had better luck when he was scrambled at 18:30 on 14 August sighting a Ju 88 at 28,000 feet. He carried out an attack from quarter to astern, closing to 150 yards: strikes were observed on its port engine and pieces fell away. The Spitfire's windscreen was immediately thickly coated in oil from his victim and the Australian was forced to break away and return to base. It would seem that his shooting was better than he thought since 4U+IK of 2.(F)/123 failed to return with the loss of Ltn Hans Peters and his crew.

Flt Lt West claimed damage to a Bf 109G reconnaissance machine he engaged over the Nile area on 13 August and six days later pursued two more but was unable to close. The New Zealander, who had flown as Wg Cdr Bader's regular No.2 in 1941, was certainly earning his flying pay. On 24 August, he claimed another Bf 109 shot down off the Egyptian coast. Having been scrambled with W/O White of 94 Squadron as his wingman, and having followed various vectors, they suddenly spotted two Bf 109s about half a mile ahead.

I dived to attack and came up under the starboard of the Messerschmitt, and fired three bursts. Both e/a seen to dive vertically, the one attacked giving white smoke from 6,000 feet to sea level. Only one hostile seemed to flatten out. No.2 was able to attack when hostile dived but did not get a chance to fire. Saw splash in sea and only one Messerschmitt seen to make off. Claim one Messerschmitt destroyed.[101]

2.(F)/123 reported no loss on this date. The splash may have been the result of an overload tank being jettisoned.

Another experienced pilot was attached to 103 MU when former Battle of France pilot and more recently CO of 94 Squadron, Sqn Ldr Darky

Clowes DFM, arrived. He was soon in action being scrambled to intercept two 'hostiles' north of Derna on 3 September. These were Bf 109s which he pursued according to instructions, but they suddenly attacked him from out of the sun. He turned into them, pulled up the Spitfire's nose and opened fire. The Messerschmitts weaved violently and dived away. Clowes followed for 100 miles but was unable to close and shortage of fuel forced him to break away and return to base.

The final success for 103 MU pilots occurred on 13 September when Flg Off. Don McQueen claimed damage to a Ju 88 off Alexandria. He pursued the Ju 88 with two aircraft of 74 Squadron. He finally closed in and carried out attacks from the rear quarter, astern and below, strikes being observed and an explosion occurred half way along the fuselage. McQueen was compelled to pull away violently to avoid debris. In the meantime, the rear gunner of the Ju 88 was active but failed to hit his pursuer. Another attack was made from the starboard rear quarter, but his guns jammed and engine coughed, and lost sight of the intruder. However, Ju 88T-1 4U+7K of 2.(F)/123 failed to return from a sortie to the Alexandria area with the loss of Ltn Werner Schiller and crew. The two Spitfires of 74 Squadron managed to close with Sgt Barrett firing from long distance only to realise he had fired his machine-guns and not cannons.

With the effective demise of the Ju 86R flight operating from Crete and with regular squadrons now operating Spitfire IXs, the Luftwaffe struggled to maintain recce flights without fear of being intercepted allowing 103 MU to revert to its main role of maintenance and repair while the Special Flight continued to modify and experiment. Inevitably, accidents occurred from time to time. Flt Lt S. E. Zeitoun of the Royal Egyptian Air Force lost his life in a clipped-wing Spitfire VB (ER224) on 8 January 1944, his aircraft colliding with a wind indicator on taking-off from Aboukir.

CHAPTER XII

Luftwaffe Reconnaissance Operations in the Eastern Mediterranean – 1943-44

The eastern North African coastline, with its almost continuous chain of radar sites, was becoming near impregnable and impenetrable for all but the most fortunate of Luftwaffe reconnaissance crews crossing the sea from the direction of Greece, Crete or Rhodes. There was the odd chink in the armour, areas where radar coverage did not quite overlap, which the Germans soon discovered and used to their advantage, but generally the RAF day and night fighters held air superiority.

With 103 MU dealing effectively with the high-flying Ju 86s and Ju 88s, it was left to regular RAF squadrons to deal with lower-flying recce aircraft with mixed success. On 11 January 1943, 2.(F)/123 reported that 4U+GK had failed to return from a sortie to Alexandria in which Fw Rudolf Grossmeyer and his crew were lost. The Italians were still probing the defences and occasionally carried out small-scale nocturnal bombing raids from Rhodes against Lebanese/Palestinian coastal targets as witnessed on the night of 20 February. That night the targets for Z.1007bis of 30°Stormo were the oil refineries and fuel depot at Beirut. A Beaufighter (46/L) of 46 Squadron detachment at Idku was scrambled and Flg Off. Alan Olley (with Sgt E. W. Baldwin) was directed onto a Z.1007bis over Alexandria that had presumably lost it bearings. On gaining a visual, Olley opened fire at 200 yards. The Cant's port engine caught fire and soon the blazing machine crashed into the sea. There were no survivors of Cap. Vincenzo Guidi's 193ª Squadriglia aircraft.

238 Squadron was one of several former Hurricane units that had been withdrawn to re-equip with Spitfires. Currently at el-Gamil, four Hurricanes and a single Spitfire were scrambled at 15:25 on 27 March when a Ju 88 was reported in the area. The Spitfire was flown by Flg Off. George Aylott who spotted the intruder over Port Said. He pursued it out to sea and carried out three attacks before a large section of its port wing broke away and the

aircraft crashed into the sea, 4U+IK taking Uffz Johann Holzer and his crew with it.

7SAAF was currently based at Bersis and most of its recent sorties had encountered friendly aircraft:

> There was one scramble today [2 April] for a genuine bandit. Unfortunately, the bandit was at thirty-thousand feet overhead before the section was scrambled, and it was quite impossible to hope for an interception. Spitfires of 33 Squadron, which had been scrambled before us, also failed to intercept.

Another Ju 88 was lost on 16 April, II/KG1 reporting the non-return of one of its aircraft (L1+IP) south of Rhodes. This possibly suffered a mechanical malfunction. Uffz Herbert Stucklik and his crew were lost.

30°Stormo mounted another of its small-scale nocturnal raids on the night of 24 April, on this occasion Z.1007bis targeting the oil refineries and fuel depot at Haifa. Again, a 46 Squadron Beaufighter was scrambled and Flt Sgt Les Holmes (with Flt Sgt Mark Bell in 46/Q) was directed onto a Cant at 19,000 feet some thirty miles out to sea. He fired a two-second burst at 150 yards, this causing a terrific sheet of flame as Cap. Pietro Bertozzi's 193ª Squadriglia aircraft dived into the sea. There were no survivors. Shortly thereafter, the crew gained a second contact. Holmes closed in from astern and fired a two-second burst, observing strikes on both port and starboard engines. He fired two more bursts before the aircraft entered cloud. Despite severe damage, the bomber reached its base at Gadurra.

2.(F)/123 despatched one of its Bf 109G reconnaissance aircraft to Cyprus to check on shipping off the south coast of the island on 29 April, but 4U+WK piloted by Oblt Richard Rapp failed to return. It had possibly run out of fuel since two days later another Bf 109G from this unit crash-landed at Gadurra on return from a sortie due to fuel shortage. The aircraft was written-off but the pilot survived. That the RAF was aware of Bf 109s being used for high-flying recce purposes was revealed in 7SAAF's ORB entry for 31 May:

> The readiness section was scrambled [from Derna] at 10:57 for the interception of two 109 recce kites which were at plus thirty thousand over Tobruk. They were ordered to pancake when they were at twenty-five thousand feet, as the bandits turned away north-east before coming into range. We all wondered just how many hundred miles an hour faster than the Hurries the recces were.

At 07:10 on 6 June, a Z.1007bis of the 195ª Squadriglia, 90°Gruppo, took-off from Rhodes for a reconnaissance sortie to the south of Cyprus only to be intercepted and shot down by a Beaufighter of 46 Squadron two hours later. Flt Lt Owen Hooker RNZAF (with Sgt E. H. Chambers in V8505/E) reported:

> E/a sighted below. Our aircraft at 9,000 feet, e/a at 700-800 feet. Identified as Z.1007bis. He took no evasive action. We opened fire at 300 yards closing to 200 feet. Four or five bursts. The first missed but others found strikes, blowing off port fin and port motor was put out of action. E/a did a slow turn to port and pulled up his nose as our aircraft passed. He side-slipped into the sea. There was a lot of wreckage but no survivors were seen. Our aircraft received two hits in starboard motor.

Ten.Arrigo Zorzut was killed with his crew. Two more aircraft of the same unit took-off from Gadurra at 13:00 in order to search the missing airmen. They spotted the wreck at 15:00 and forty minutes later were attacked by, according to the crew, a Beaufighter and two Spitfires. One of the Cants was hit, two crewmembers being wounded. The Spitfires were from 127 Squadron, Flg Off. J. P. McDonnell (AP656) and Flt Sgt G. M. James (EL335) claiming damage to the aircraft.

At 16:30, the bombers were attacked by two more Spitfires, following which Cant MM24758 was seen falling away with the starboard engine in flames and failed to return. Ten. Alessandro Marri and crew were lost: Marri was found dead in a lifeboat on the Turkish beach at Karatasc (about forty miles from Adana) during the night of 15/16 June. The Cant had fallen to Plt Off. R. W. Bunyan and Flt Sgt Hilton Rayment RNZAF of 238 Squadron from Cyprus.

Plt Off. John Watton of 123 Squadron caught one of the elusive photo-recce Bf 109Gs of 2.(F)/123 in Bu Amud area on 12 June. Oblt Justus Lindemann baled out of 4U+IK and was taken prisoner. Four days later, Flg Off. Alan Olley of 46 Squadron again found himself in combat with a Z.1007. He and Sgt Baldwin in X8165/G had been scrambled at 15:25:

> Z.1007bis flying almost due south at less than 1,000 feet and slightly to port of our aircraft. Our aircraft made head-on attack, opening fire at about 800 yards closing to 250 yards. No results observed. E/a evaded by turning starboard and returned fire from upper gun position but failed to hit our aircraft. We turned to port and made height. Dived on e/a, which was travelling fast. Opened fire at about 600 yards closing to 150 yards and fire broke out in e/a between fuselage and starboard engine. No return fire experienced during this attack but e/a broke away. Only one machine-gun firing and all cannons stopped. The Cant did a starboard diving turn, skimmed along the water and tail unit broke away. Orbited position twice and saw five survivors on the mainplane, which was about quarter mile off Khelidosia Rocks (Turkey).

Ten.Col. Grimaldo Castelnuovo and crew took to their life raft and made land at Antala, Turkey, where they were interned.

A Spitfire of 80 Squadron made the next successful interception off the coast on 21 July, Flt Sgt H. F. Ross (ES140) shooting down in flames a Ju 88 of 2.(F)/123. 4U+XK that crashed into the sea with the loss of Obfw Erwin Freudig and his crew. A Walrus searched in vain for the crew. On 29 July, two Hurricanes of the Greek 335 Squadron scrambled from LG121 to investigate a bogey off the North African coast and Plt Off. Eleutherios Hajioannu (BP606) claimed a Ju 88 damaged. It seems that his victim was Ju 88 KQ+KR of 1./E-KGr.Ju 88/Gen.d.Fl.Ausb. The badly damaged aircraft crashed at Larissa on return, the crew having reported combat with Hurricanes over the sea. Ltn Alfred Kubeil and crew were killed. Another of 2.(F)/123's Ju 88s failed to return on 31 August, 4U+6K having been despatched to recce the airfields on Cyprus. The cause of its loss is unknown but probably due to mechanical problems. Uffz Helmuth Danders and crew were lost.

During the first part of September, 2.(F)/123 lost two of its Bf 109Gs, the first ditching on 4 September due to 'engine failure', its pilot being rescued. It seems possible that the reconnaissance machine 4U+HK had been intercepted by a Spitfire V of 7SAAF flying from el-Gamil. At 17:02, Yellow Section was scrambled to intercept 'a high-flying enemy aircraft'. Black Section followed a few minutes later. These two pilots became separated but, at 17:50, Black 1 (Lt Harold Boyer in ER335) was heard over the R/T to call 'Tally-ho!' followed by silence. Rescue craft and other Spitfires were sent to the relevant area about fifty-five miles out to sea to carry out a search but no sightings were made. The twenty-one-year-old from Johannesburg was presumed lost. A second Bf 109G (4U+ZK) crashed west of Kastelli on 10 September due to 'pilot error'. Ltn Heinz Gruttke was killed.

A Ju 88T-1 of 2.(F)/123 was lost on 15 September, Sgt John Stephen (EN399) of 80 Squadron shooting down 4U+IK into the sea 150 miles south-west of Crete at 11:30. The subsequent interrogation report revealed:

This aircraft was flying at 30,000 feet at a speed of 380kmph, presumably on its return from the target [a photographic reconnaissance of Benghazi] when it was attacked and shot down by a Spitfire. The pilot [Obfw Alfred Nitsch] was picked and is in hospital, but the observer and W/T operator are missing. This was an unusually distinguished crew, which will be great loss to the unit. The pilot was a man of vast experience and was regarded as the best pilot in the Staffel; he was awarded the Ritterkraus at the beginning of July 1943, by which time he had made over 200 war-flights in the Mediterranean theatre. Although an NCO he was treated as an equal by the officers of his Staffel and was allowed to use the officers' mess. The observer, Oblt Peter Schug [aged 37] was either Staffelkapitän or acting Staffelkapitän of 2.(F)/123. He had been a Brigadeführer in the SA. The W/T operator [Obfw Herbert Richter] is stated to have held the Deutches Kreuz in gold.'

Mystery surrounds the loss of several recce aircraft over the ensuing few weeks, although mechanical problems were probably the cause, except for one. On 19 September, a PR Bf 109G-6 (4U+IK) flown by Obfw Josef Hofmeister of 2.(F)/123 failed to return from a sortie over the Mersa Matruh area. On 10 October, Ju 88A K5+AH of 1./E-KGr.Ju 88 /Gen.d.Fl.Ausb. was reported shot down by a night fighter shortly after take-off from Athens/ Tatoi and crashed in flames. Fw Anton Rauch and all bar one of his crew were killed. Since there appears to have been no night fighter claims by North African or Cyprus-based Beaufighters, the Ju 88 may have been the victim of an RAF intruder from Italy or friendly fire. On 22 November, 4U+NK failed to return from Cyprus in which Uffz Karl-Heinz Riecken and crew were lost.

Several of the squadrons awaiting re-equipment by Spitfires were based along the Egyptian and Libyan coastlines for convoy-escort duty, a mundane task not appreciated by the fighter pilots ever eager for action. Action came the way for a fortunate few on 29 November when six Ju 88s and five Do 217s attempted to attack a convoy off Benghazi comprising twenty-five ships plus escorting destroyers (codename *GUS23*) and smaller naval craft that had sailed from Port Said heading westwards. Two Hurricane 2Cs of 33 Squadron were scrambled to assist Hurricanes of 3SAAF Squadron joined by one of 41SAAF to repel the bombers. The RAF Hurricanes, flown by Canadian Plt Offs. F. J. Bateson (HV511) and J. S. Hodgson (KX958), claimed one shot down and a second fell to Capt. Robin 'Pinkie' Yeats of 3SAAF and the lone 41SAAF pilot, Lt William 'Shorty' Dowden. Additionally, Capt. Mike Geldenhuys' section claimed a probable. Two Ju 88s were indeed shot down: L1+DR of 7 Staffel flown by Obfw Otto Piasta and L1+GS of 8 Staffel piloted by Fw Theodor Cöster. The crew shot down by 33 Squadron were seen to clamber into their dinghy, but although Hurricanes and ASR carried out a search, they were not found. There were no survivors from either crew. None of the ships was lost.

The intruders continued to harass the coastlines of Egypt and Libya into the New Year. On 14 January 1944, Flg Off. Rex Froud of 74 Squadron was scrambled in Spitfire VC MA256 after a high-flying Ju 88:

Scrambled from Dekheila and intercepted a Ju 88 at 32,000 feet. Port cannon and all machine-guns failed to fire. E/a escaped in cloud after diving to 12,000 feet, hotly and uselessly pursued by me.

While the Luftwaffe could keep an eye on the comings and goings along the North Africa coast, Cyprus was causing more or a problem. The island was now playing a key strategic role in the Eastern Mediterranean and a constant threat to the security of the Dodecanese. Regular recce flights were despatched eastwards from Crete and Rhodes but few of these went unobserved, though not all were able to be intercepted. However, on 3 February, two Spitfires IXs of 127 Squadron flown by Flt Lt Alan Boyle (MA447) and Plt Off. D. J. P. Matthews successfully engaged Ju 88T1 4U+BK of 2.(F)/123 about four miles north of Nicosia. The pilot, FjFw Lothar Röhrich, was killed but his two crewmen were rescued from the sea and taken prisoner.

Two pilots of 451RAAF Squadron, Flt Lt Wally Gale (MA418) and Flg Off. George Purdy (BS339), were scrambled at 06:58 on 21 February from el-Firdan to intercept a hostile plot 150 miles north of Port Said. When at 28,000 feet they sighted a Ju 88 1,000 feet above:

> Gave Tally-ho! and attacked. Enemy aircraft went into a dive but Red 1 was slightly below him and fired a burst which turned the aircraft and made him climb again. Enemy aircraft entered cloud bank and Red 2 followed, Red 1 still waiting slightly below. Enemy aircraft finally came through the cloud bank in a steep dive and both Red 1 and Red 2 made four attacks each. Strikes were observed on all attacks. Enemy aircraft was finally forced down to about 300 feet, when it crashed into the sea. Both pilots reported no return fire was encountered throughout the attacks. One partially inflated dinghy was seen on the water after the enemy aircraft had crashed. No parachutes were seen to open.

The Ju 88T-1 was 4U+RK of 2.(F)/123 flown by Fw Adalbert Langer. There were no survivors. On 29 February, 2.(F)/123 lost yet another Ju 88T-1 to Spitfires, 4U+WK falling south of Derna to Lt H. T. R. 'Bob' du Preez (MH612) and Lt Howard Geater (MH971) of 3SAAF Squadron who reported:

> 08:26, I "Tally-hoed" hostile 5 miles ahead, about 500 to 1,000 feet above. Continued climbing straight ahead. Left No.1 behind. Hostile crossed my line of flight flying south and level. Approached him from astern, port side... and identified him as Ju 88. Hostile commenced making turn to port. Overtook him steadily and he commenced medium turn to starboard. I then crossed over his line of sight, approaching from behind, out of the sun. Opened fire, range 300 yards ... and stopped firing at 200 yards when I broke away to port. White smoke was emitted from both engines. Return fire from rear gunner in several short bursts. Not accurate. I then pulled up and lost sight of the hostile. When I next dipped my wing I saw No.1 breaking off his first attack.

Red 1 Lt du Preez added:

No.2 broke off attack. Hostile took no evasive action. I then attacked from quarter astern, same level as hostile. Opened fire at 350-400 yards, closing in rapidly. Fired two short bursts. Hostile continued turning starboard, into my fire. Took no evasive action. Observed strikes starboard wing and return fire from rear gunner. I felt an impact on my port wing and fired one further long burst.

One partially inflated dinghy was seen on the water after the enemy aircraft had crashed. No parachutes were seen to open. There were no survivors of Fw August Fastenrodt's crew. A Ju 88 of 1./LG1 wandered too close to Cyprus during a recce on 3 March, L1+JR falling to the island's heavy AA guns. Fw Georg Messerschmitt was killed together with his crew bar one who survived to be rescued and taken prisoner.

Greek Spitfire pilots scored a rare victory on 21 April when Plt Off. Dimitrios Soufrilas (JL352) shot down Ju 88D 4U+FK some seventy miles north of Mersa Matruh at 13:25, shared with his No.2 Flg Off. Georgios Tsotsos (LZ807). The two pilots were patrolling over a convoy when they were vectored onto the Ju 88. Soufrilas dived to attack and as he pulled away saw smoke pouring from its starboard engine. Tsotsos followed and the damaged engine burst into flames, following which the doomed aircraft (4U+FK) exploded in mid-air. Uffz Helmut Arndt's 2.(F)/123 crew were all killed. There was an odd twist to this successful action as recorded by 603 Squadron's CO, Wg Cdr Foxley-Norris:

At Mersa Matruh we were honoured with the appearance of two squadrons of lifelike Liberator heavy bombers [these were dummies made out of wood and cardboard to fool the Germans into believing that the Allies were preparing for an invasion of Greece rather than Southern France]. The enemy activity against us at this stage was confined as a rule to a weekly visitation from a special reconnaissance Ju 86P [*sic*] which came over at very high level and photographed our airfields. Our massive 'Liberators' sat there waiting to be photographed and strict instructions were given to the defences to make sure the photography was not interrupted.

A day or two later we received a report from Air Defence Centre of an incoming track. All would soon be well and the deceptive photographs duly taken. Alas! In a moment of mental aberration, carried away by the lust for battle, or merely through lack of linguistic communication, one of our gallant Greek allies managed to shoot down the intruder. Amid yells of Hellenic enthusiasm and bellow of British fury, the Junkers crashed into the sea in flames a mile or two [*sic*] from the airfield. By what must have been a unique statistic, this one sortie achieved for the pilot at the same time a Greek DFC and a British court martial!'[102]

Yellow Section of 41SAAF Squadron was scrambled from Idku on 24 April on the approach of a bandit, Lt Johannes de Klerk (MA407) and Lt John Silberbauer (ME786) encountering a Ju 88 flying low over the water. De Klerk closed to 250 yards and believed he silenced the rear gunner with his first burst. Silberbauer followed and also saw strikes but the aircraft kept flying. The two SAAF pilots having expended all their ammunition trailed it for several miles willing it to ditch but it apparently managed to return to base. Silberbauer was in action again on 25 April, this time with better luck when Ju 88D from 2.(F.)/123 was shot down north-west of Idku. On this occasion he was flying No.2 to Lt Mauritz Hartogh (MA257/X) who reported:

> 1730: Scrambled after e/a. Vectored to target and saw it about 5 to 6 miles ahead at approximately 200 feet, own height 50 feet. E/a sighted us and turned northwards at high speed with rear gunner firing. Closed in to about 200 yards, did quarter astern attack and fired on port engine. Saw pieces fly off and engine burst into flames, burning fiercely, then fired on starboard engine and fuselage. Broke away to avoid flying debris. Red 2 closed in firing madly. E/a was by then burning rapidly and crashed into sea. No survivors. Returned to base and landed. No damage to my aircraft.

Lt Silberbauer (LZ894/V) added:

> The e/a turned into me when I made my attack and I laid off approximately 20 degree deflection, when the engine exploded, bits of cowling flying off and I had to break away to avoid this. When I next saw the aircraft it was on fire and flying erratically. It then crashed into the sea, which was covered in burning petrol.

Fw Joachim Lüdtke and his crew of 4U+HK were lost.

It proved to be a bad month for 2.(F)/123, the PR unit losing a third aircraft on 29 April, Ju 88 4U+BK (300134) being shot down ten miles south-west of Cape Greco, Cyprus, during the early morning. Four Spitfire XIs of 213 Squadron scrambled on the approach of the intruder, Sgt E. A. Stringer (MA526/V) being the first to see it. He carried out five attacks exhausting his ammunition and left it trailing smoke from its port engine. Flt Sgt K. A. L. Ford (MH590) of the second section then came across it and made two attacks whereupon it ditched in Epishopi Bay, the crew apparently thought they were over Rhodes! Obfw Helmuth Jonas and crew were safely rescued and taken into captivity. On 7 May, Sgt Stringer was again in action, on this occasion with Plt Off. J. M. Dixon when a Ju 188 was intercepted but escaped with minor damage.

Capt. Ray Burl DFC, who had featured prominently during the fighting on Kos, was now a flight commander with 41SAAF and in charge of the Cyprus detachment at Lakatamia with Spitfire IXs. These included four HFIXs (MH931, MH933, MA504, MA792) in natural metal finish sans roundels and fin flashes primarily for operations against Ju 86s.

On 24 June, Burl (LZ894/V) and his No.2 were scrambled to intercept yet another intruder, climbing to 30,000 feet, but were then ordered to land since the Ju 88 was heading for Syria. Once refuelled, the Spitfires were ordered off again it the hope of making an interception of the Ju 88 on its return journey. This was achieved as Burl's report testified:

> I gradually gained on the bandit, who was losing height. When I was some 500 yards astern he saw me and commenced corkscrewing. I identified the bandit as a Ju 88. I came in to 200 yards on the starboard quarter and gave him a short burst, then crossed to port and closed to approximately 150 yards. I gave another short burst and observed strikes on fuselage. I went back to starboard quarter as bandit tried to get into the sun and gave him a final burst at about 100 yards. He turned completely over, and a long white cloud of smoke trailed from him as he spiralled in an inverted position. The white smoke changed to black and became denser till he eventually exploded in mid-air, and disintegrated. I observed one of the crew only to bale out.

There were no survivors from the Ju 88T, 4U+KK of 2.(F)/123. Uffz Fritz Schmitt and crew were swallowed by the insatiable Mediterranean. Burl was involved in the next interception off Cyprus three weeks later (11 July), he (again in LZ894/V) and Lt Peter Brokensha (MA257) engaging another recce Ju 88. Burl reported:

> Bandit was flying east-west, but having sighted me he turned north and flew straight into Turkey. I closed very slowly and when about 60 miles inland over Turkey I identified bandit as a Ju 88. As I closed to firing range, bandit turned into the sun and black smoke came from both engines. I closed to 300 yards and gave him a short burst from the port side. Bandit took violent evasive action by corkscrewing. Red 2 and I attacked six times alternately from port and starboard, and I observed return fire on two occasions, once directed against myself and once at Red 2. Return fire ceased after third attack. I saw pieces fly off the Ju 88 but, as my fuel was becoming short, I had to return to base. Whilst I was still over Turkey on my return, my engine began to splutter and cut. This, however, righted itself after three minutes and I returned to base without further incident.

Lt Brokensha added:

I saw Red 1's fire effecting strikes on the fuselage of the bandit and saw pieces
fly off from my own fire. I claim with Red 1 one Ju 88 damaged.

The 41SAAF Squadron detachment at Cyprus had been joined by a newly
formed unit, 9SAAF Squadron, also equipped with Spitfire IXs that received
a few pilots from its host unit. It was one of these, Lt Dan Joubert, who
brought down one of the recently introduced Ju 188F recce machines of
3.(F)/33 on 29 July. Uffz Eberhard Hübner's 8H+IL fell into the sea about
forty-five miles west of Limassol, south of the island, and all were lost.
Joubert had scrambled with Lt Rietief, Joubert making the initial attack
and scoring hits on the intruder. He climbed to regain height and carried
out a second following which the port engine gushed black smoke before
the doomed machine made a slow roll into the sea. The Spitfire received
minor damage from return fire, the ground crew finding three holes in its
tailplane. Meanwhile, although Lt Rietief had carried out a single attack, he
observed no hits and the victory was credited to Joubert.

One of the last, if not the last, Luftwaffe reconnaissance machines
to be shot down in the Eastern Mediterranean fell to a Beaufighter on 5
September. Ju 88D-1 4U+KK of 2.(F)/123 went into the sea off Alexandria
killing the Staffelkapitän Hptm. Helmut Weixelbaum and his crew apart
from the observer who was rescued from his dinghy and made prisoner.

CHAPTER XIII

The End in the Aegean and Eastern Mediterranean

The German evacuation officially commenced on 30 August 1944, both by air and by land. By air, some 106 Ju 52s of the Luftwaffe succeeded in evacuating to the Greek mainland 30,740 military personnel in 2,050 flights. Likewise, from 30 August to the end of October, the Kriegsmarine evacuated a further 37,138 with the loss of 380 men and twenty-nine out of the fifty-two ships/boats involved. Therefore, within two months a total of 67,878 military personnel were evacuated. Thus, left on the Aegean islands by the time the evacuation ended were:

Crete – 11,828 Germans and 4,737 Italians
Rhodes – 6,356 Germans and 4,097 Italians
Kos – 3,228 Germans and 611 Italians
Leros – 1,102 Germans and 809 Italians
Melos – 620 Germans
Tilos – 266 Germans
Kalymnos – 193 Germans

From late September began a flurry of Allied activity, mostly landings of the Free Greek Sacred Battalion, but culminating in two larger, mixed Allied landings in late October. During the month leading up to it, the Greeks rapidly liberated/occupied six islands: Mykonos (on 30 September) after some initial fighting with the German garrison that suffered six dead, seven wounded and six prisoners before withdrawing to Syros; Chios and Lesbos (on 10 October) immediately after the Germans had left without fighting; Samos was occupied on 14 October, which resulted in the surrendering of the Italian garrison consisting of about 1,000 men; Naxos was next, on 15 October, which resulted in the death of one German and the capture of 69 others; finally, Lemnos was assaulted on the night of 16/17 October that resulted in the capture of 250 Germans and 60 Italians, mainly on ships blockaded inside the port of Moudros by the British fleet.

The arrival of British forces on the Greek mainland in September saw a number of RAF air units arrive. The airfield at Araxos became the first foothold being captured on 23 September and many airfields around it were secured within a month including Megara taken by parachute landings. Near Athens, Kalamaki (from where the Bf 109Gs of 5./JG51 had been ousted) ultimately became the centre of RAF activity and became home for 337 Wing (OC Grp Capt. George Pedley DFC), which operated a number of squadrons: 32 (soon to move to Salonika/Sedes), 94, 335 and 336 all now with Spitfire Vs, 108 with Beaufighters and two transport units. Wg Cdr Pat Woodruff DFC, former CO of 252 Squadron, was appointed Wing Commander (Flying). On 8 October, three Spitfires of the Greek 335 Squadron (flown by Sqn Ldr Konstantinos Margaritis, Flt Lt Nikolaos Volonakis and Flt Lt Mitrakos) arrived at Araxos, having flown from Biferno in Italy via Brindisi (for refuelling) and on to Greek soil for the first time since 1941. Meanwhile, 680 Squadron continued to operate its PR Spitfires and also maintained a flight of PR Mosquitoes, although the latter were based in Italy. On occasion the Mosquitoes were called in to carry out sorties over the Greek mainland, Flt Lt Ulf Christiernsson (one of the few Swedish volunteers in the RAF) flying one such mission over the Corinth Canal on 13 October.

Sqn Ldr Russ Foskett led sixteen Spitfire XIs of 94 Squadron on 19 October to take up residence arriving to a rapturous welcome. Events were marred, however, when Sgt Henry O'Keefe, impatient to land JG839, touched down before Lt Dickie Dummett's aircraft (LZ823) had cleared the runway. An unforgivable collision occurred as O'Keefe's aircraft ploughed into the unfortunate South African's Spitfire and both aircraft caught fire rapidly developing into an inferno. Sgt O'Keefe managed to extricate himself from his cockpit but Lt Dummett perished.

Kalamaki airfield now became the scene of considerable fighter activity, 94 Squadron flying recces for the mounting of strafing and bombing attacks on retreating German road and rail transport. Four days after their arrival on 23 October, two sections of 94 took-off at 13:25 for a low-level check on airfields in the Larissa area. Wg Cdr Pat Woodruff led in BR253 with W/O Bill Dorman (ER501) as his No.2., Flg Off. John Anderson (ER867) led the other section with Flg Off. Jock Maxwell (JL365) as his No.2. The Salonika airfields were found unoccupied. A wide circle enabled the sections to approach Gorgopi airfield, near Kilkis, from the north. Directly ahead, two He 111s were sighted on the ground. Each section strafed one and both were set on fire. Accurate light flak hit Maxwell's aircraft that climbed, banked right over Anderson's Spitfire and crashed in flames on the airfield, Maxwell losing his life. Within minutes, Woodruff located a long train in steam, stationary beneath a mountainside awaiting a 'line clear' signal.

The three remaining Spitfires attacked, Woodruff and Anderson blasting the locomotive and Dorman raking the carriages and wagons responsible for the inevitable flak. Another train received similar treatment on the way home and Volos harbour was reconnoitred.

The islands of Melos and Tilos were invaded on 26 October, but the operations were not successful. 152 soldiers of the Sacred Battalion and thirty of the SBS landed on Melos. This small force was supported by artillery of the cruiser HMS *Black Prince* and aircraft from the escort carrier HMS *Emperor* (see Chapter IX). Spitfires of 336 Squadron from Kalamaki led by Sqn Ldr Margaritis dive-bombed Melos. Flt Lt Pangalos' aircraft was hit while at 6,000 feet, a shell bursting beneath his seat, but he was not seriously hurt and able to return to base. Sqn Ldr Margaritis' aircraft was hit in the elevators and Plt Off. Takis Sakellariou's in coolant tank. Both managed to return safely. Sqn Ldr Lambros Parsis returned with a hung-up bomb which, to his horror, fell off as he touched down. Fortunately it had not been fused. Two days later, up to 300 Royal Marines landed on Melos. The fighting raged until 5 November, and on the evening of 7 November, the allied forces left the island, leaving a disabled LTC behind.

On the night of 26/27 October, sixty-one soldiers of the Sacred Battalion and a small party of British soldiers landed on Tilos and overwhelmed the small garrison, but on a following night German reinforcements arrived. After four days of heavy fighting and in spite of support from a Greek destroyer and HMS *Emperor*'s aircraft, which sank a German landing craft, the Allied forces were driven off the island. A second, successful, attempt was made on the night of 1/2 March 1945 that resulted in two Indian dead and two Greek wounded as well as twenty Germans killed and 142 prisoners (including 8 wounded). Two raids were made on Nisyros in February 1945 before the island was finally captured. Three Greeks were killed and ten wounded in the two operations for a total of thirty-three Germans killed, forty-four wounded and captured plus twenty unwounded/captured.

94 Squadron was to suffer the loss of its CO on 31 October, Sqn Ldr Russ Foskett (ER489) experiencing engine problems over the Aegean after strafing trains near Prokhama, compelling him to bale out between the islands of Skiathos and Skopelos, but was too low for his parachute to open. The navy despatched HMS *Emperor*'s Walrus (L2238) to search for him and discovered his body, which was recovered and returned to the sea. Sqn Ldr Hugh McLachlan DFC briefly led 94 until his repatriation to Canada, Sqn Ldr Jack Slade DFC assuming command on 29 November.

By mid-November, the Germans were beyond the range of 337 Wing's Spitfires and Crete once again became the focus of their attention. During November and December, a number of large anti-communist operations took place on Crete with German tanks and mountain artillery supporting the British in these operations. On 20 November, Grp Capt. Pedley flew to Kastelli in his Hurricane for a meeting with local partisans and, next day, Flg Off. John Anderson and Flg Off. David Jackson of 94 Squadron flew recces over the island. The same pair landed at Heraklion (now in British hands) to refuel on 27 November and on 5 December led two sections to attack an ammunition dump at Alikianov. Greek Spitfires of 336 Squadron also participated in this action dive-bombing communist positions, the five aircraft involved also refuelling at Heraklion before carrying out the raid led by Flt Lt Nikolaos Volonakis. Early in the attack, Flt Lt Emmanuel Tingos' aircraft plunged straight into the sea with its bombs intact.

The war in the Aegean was effectively over, but not quite. Newly commissioned Paddy McAughtry and his pilot RAAF Plt Off. John Bates were called upon to carry out a photo-recce of Rhodes harbour in daylight prior to a bombardment by the cruiser HMS *Black Prince*:

> It was hair-raising, the more so because we were almost finished with operational flying. [John] flew lower on the approach to the strongly-defended harbour than I ever thought possible. He operated the nose camera and I took a couple of shots with a hand-held model out of the back window. We rocked and weaved out of the harbour area, took about two stone of lead on board, and made it to the quiet country beyond the town. We suddenly came upon a large party of soldiers bathing on the beach. They scattered, but there was nowhere for them to go. We raked them with cannon fire and as we left I opened up with my single rear Browning.
>
> I kept thinking that there was no need for it. Those soldiers didn't pose a military threat ... though somebody suggested they posed a considerable threat to the Greeks on Rhodes. Maybe so, but I'd rather not have seen the men so clearly as they died.

On 29 December, Flt Lt O. P. Olsen RNZAF took-off in his 680 Squadron Spitfire to carry out a recce over Crete and Greece only to be shot down and taken prisoner. A mid-air collision on 26 February 1945 took the life of Wg Cdr Pat Woodruff DFC who was leading a flypast of over twenty-four Spitfires over Thessaloniki when his Spitfire IX (MA507) and that flown by Flt Lt Sophocles Baltatzis of 336 Squadron collided. Baltatzis survived but Woodruff's aircraft went straight down in an unrecoverable spin and splashed into the sea.

Regular Luftwaffe supply flights to Rhodes and Crete had begun in late September, transport aircraft departing from Wien-Aspern and Wien-Schwechat, initially via Athens-Tatoi (Kdo.Süd.). Due to the constant RAF fighter patrols, most sorties between Crete/Rhodes and Athens were flown under the cover of darkness. Among the early arrivals were Ju 90 G6+AY of 14./TG4 that landed at Heraklion on the night of 5/6 October. However, next day, while landing at Athens-Tatoi, the aircraft suffered two tyre blow-outs. Repairs were impossible and the aircraft was set on fire by the crew to prevent capture by British forces. At about the same time, Piaggio G6+FY was destroyed at Salonika by a low-level fighter attack. On 2 November, two Ju 290s of I/KG200 arrived at Skopje, Yugoslavia: A3+HB (Hptm. Heinz Braun and Ltn Pohl) and 9V+FH (Hptm. Emil Sachtleben and Oblt Adalbert Freiheer von Pechmann). A3+PB flown by Oblt Siegfried Wache also joined the small fleet for these operations. Every fortnight from 7 November onwards, an aircraft from KG200 landed on Rhodes carrying field post and urgent supplies. On the return trip they would take wounded soldiers back to Germany.

British intelligence reported: 'German radio beacons on Crete, Rhodes and Kos were active during the night of 27/28 November and there are indications that Ju 290s [A3+HB and A3+PB] flew from Zagreb to Rhodes during the night.' On that same night Hptm. Braun and Ltn Pohl, having landed at Rhodes to refuel, continued their clandestine journey in A3+HB towards a position just south of Mosul in Iraq where they successfully air-dropped five Iraqi parachutists in the bright moonlight and returned to Rhodes. After minor engine problems were rectified, they successfully evacuated some thirty casualties, reaching Vienna two nights later.

In December, two Fw 200s, GY+AY and G6+FY (Oblt Stanke), were assigned to 14./TG4 and these began flying supplies to Rhodes (as *Sonderkommando Condor*) from Wiener-Neustadt on 28 January 1945. Wounded and sick personnel were flown back to Austria on return flights. These flights continued until a lack of fuel put a stop to them. G6+FY was abandoned at Rhodes and its crew was eventually captured. At the end of January 1945, a British Intelligence intercept revealed: '...a Ju 90 (sic) from Germany arrived at Rhodes with a load of mouth organs and song books, football bladders and drums to boost the morale of German troops – the comments of the majority of the troops were unprintable.'

Crete (partially), Rhodes, Kos and Leros remained in German hands until the war's end, but only because it seemed senseless to waste British, Greek and German lives when the islands no longer presented a threat. After Allied ships had sunk three important supply ships during November and December, the Germans stopped supplying the islands by sea. On 1 March 1945, a small but heavy armed German force left Rhodes in a few landing craft for the coast of Turkey that had finally declared war on Germany on 20 February. They stole sheep, goats, grain and any other foodstuffs they could find. But the war was not over for the ragged and hungry men on Rhodes since six Beaufighters of 252 Squadron attacked Calato airfield on 31 March. There followed a commando raid by Sacred Battalion forces on the night of 2/3 May that resulted in three Greek wounded and sixteen German dead, one wounded and thirty prisoners, plus one Italian prisoner. Kos was visited by three Baltimores of the Greek 13 Squadron on 27 March 1945, the crews with instructions to bomb German craft evacuating the island. Sadly, bombs fell wide of the mark and killed twenty-two Greeks and a few Germans in Kos town.

On 8 May 1945, GenMjr Dr Otto Wagener arrived at Symi to sign the surrender document.

Civil War Erupts in Greece

On 2 December 1944, tensions over the role of the EAM partisans loyal to King George II of the Hellenes, who had returned in October with his government to Athens from exile in England, and ELAS communists in post-war government resulted in demonstrations during which Greek police and British forces opened fire, killing at least twenty-eight demonstrators and wounding 148 more.

The response were attacks on police stations and thus RAF units began operations against both ELAS and EAM targets, mostly around Athens. 73 and 94 Squadrons used their Spitfires on strafing runs, the latter unit losing Sgt Dickie Andrews RAAF who hit trees in ER663 while attacking ELAS motorised transport and crashed. Light bombing and strafing was undertaken by 108 Squadron's Beaufighters. Additional options were gained when a flight of rocket-armed Beaufighters of 39 Squadron was attached to 108 Squadron. These were considered very effective and over the span of two weeks 105 targets were struck by these aircraft, while 108 Squadron flew a further 265 sorties during December alone. Wellingtons of 221 Squadron were primarily used in supply flights to the Sedes facility as well as various leaflet and illumination missions, but two nocturnal bombing raids were carried out. The Greek Spitfire squadrons did not participate in the attacks, although the Greek 13 Squadron did assist in leaflet operations.

The RAF suffered a major blow on 19 December with the attack by ELAS forces on the facility at Kifisia that was home to Allied Headquarters Greece. Two 94 Squadron Spitfires flown by Flt Lt Anderson (ER222) and Flg Off. Dan Tolkovsky (MH590) had successfully strafed ELAS troops attacking AHQ the previous day and several had surrendered to the army. The RAF Regiment's No.2933 Squadron defended strongly but was ultimately overrun with the capture of many British prisoners.

221 Squadron's Wellingtons conducted supply drops to these personnel during their march north. 94 Squadron received a batch of Spitfire IXs upon moving to Sedes from where surveillance sorties were flown in support of British Army columns disarming the remaining ELAS troop outposts with reconnaissance flights over Thrace and Florina. In the six weeks it took to defeat the ELAS communists, the British Army had suffered more than 2,000 casualties. By 7 January 1945, Athens was secured and a ceasefire negotiated on 11 January. While some fighting continued, British fighter squadrons were withdrawn by summer 1945.

But the civil war did not end with the British withdrawal. 1946 saw the official transfer of Greek-manned RAF squadrons into the Royal Hellenic Air Force. Meanwhile, government opposition was on the rise and the formation of the Democratic Army of Greece led to the loss of control of much of rural Greece. March 1948 saw the RHAF enter the action with attacks on landing strips set up by communist forces to receive aid from Albania and Yugoslavia. Involvement by the United States led to the launch of Operation *Dawn* in April 1948 and was supported by RHAF units with a total of 641 sorties with the loss of one Spitfire plus damage to ten more. Dakotas were utilised for leaflet and supply operations. The operation was successful but the withdrawal to northern border regions limited RHAF effectiveness due to a five-mile-stop line to avoid an international incident.

A fresh offensive was launched in July 1948 against communist forces in the Grammos Mountains with the support of 335 and 336 Squadrons operating from Yanina and Kozani. Additional aircraft included AT-6 Texans and Austers. The offensive saw anti-government forces withdraw across the border to Albania. A new Spitfire IX unit was formed, 337 Squadron, giving the RHAF three Spitfire units. For heavier bombing, Dakotas were fitted with bomb racks and it was rumoured that RAF Mosquitoes flew photo-recces for the government. The RHAF flew 3,474 sorties during the operation, suffering the loss of a Spitfire plus a further twenty-two damaged.

Operations in September 1948 centred on the Vitsi Mountains area and were supported again by the RHAF. They were marked by better co-operation with army units and the first use of napalm, although this was not used heavily. These operations lasted to the end of the year, bringing the grand total of combat sorties for 1948 to 8,907. A major attack at Florina by guerrilla forces was defeated with significant air support by the RHAF. On 21 January 1949, Lt-Col Selden Edner DFC DFC (US) of the US Air Force, a Second World War fighter ace, was captured by communist troops when the AT-6 Texan of the RHAF in which he was flying as an observer was shot down. The Greek pilot, Lt Panayiohi Tsoukas, was killed and Edner injured. It transpired that Edner was brutally tortured and beaten before being executed by hanging. His body was later recovered by government troops.

August 1949 marked the final series of operations against the guerrilla forces and again the RHAF played a large role in supporting government forces. In particular, during the final portion of the month, 336 Squadron swopping its Spitfires for newly acquired SB2C Helldivers, of which forty had been supplied by the United States Navy. This operation resulted in the final destruction of opposition military resistance and resulted in a final ceasefire being signed. During August, 826 sorties had been flown dropping 288 tons of bombs and firing 1,935 rockets. Napalm was used again with 114 such strikes being made.

Peace of a kind may have returned to Greece but unrest remained, and remains, under the surface.

Beaufighter Operational Losses – 1943-44

26/04/43	Sgt R. A. Harvey	†	227 Sqn	JL639	Struck mast
	Sgt W. H. Fisher	†			
	Flg Off. A. G. Deck	Interned Turkey	227 Sqn	EL431	Flak
	Plt Off. G. W. Ridley	Interned Turkey			
28/04/43	Sgt J. H. Harrison	Rescued from sea	227 Sqn	JL644	Engine problems
	Sgt J. R. Sloper	Rescued from sea			
01/05/43	Flt Lt T. St B. Freer DFC	Interned Turkey	227 Sqn	JL519	Flak
	Flg Off. C. Holman	Interned Turkey			
16/05/43	Sgt E. Havnar	POW	227 Sqn	EL500	Flak
	Sgt D. Galley	†			
	Flt Lt J. E. Atkins	†	JL514	Ar 196	
	Flg Off. R. L. Wellington	†			
04/06/43	Sgt J. A. Lewis	†	227 Sqn	EL460	Flak
	Sgt J. A. Roff	†			
02/09/43	Flt Lt W. Y. McGregor DFC RNZAF	†	227 Sqn	JL552	Struck mast
	Flg Off. C. Turner	POW			
17/09/43	Flt Lt C. T. H. Delcour (Belg)	Unhurt	252 Sqn	V8335	Ar 196
	Flt Sgt T. R. Lumsden	†			
20/09/43	Flt Sgt W. D. Webster RNZAF	†	227 Sqn	JL642	Flak
	Flt Sgt E. S. Taylor	†			
21/09/43	Flt Sgt R. S. Neighbour RAAF	†	227 Sqn	JL640	Flak

	Flt Sgt C. G. Hoskin RAAF	†			
24/09/43	Flg Off. D. M. Anderson RCAF	†		227 Sqn JL915	Ground collision
	Plt Off J. Timmons	†			
	W/O G. Grennan RCAF	†		227 Sqn JM239	Ground collision
	Sgt S. Palmer	†			
	Flt Sgt W. C. Budd	†			
03/10/43	Plt Off. P. F. Glynn RCAF	†		227 Sqn JM710	Flak
	Sgt T. J. Barrett	†			
	Wg Cdr G. A. Reid	†		46 Sqn JM238	Flak
	Flg Off. W Peasley	Interned Turkey			
	Sqn Ldr W. H. Cuddie	†		46 Sqn JL907	Flak
	Flg Off. L. E. M. Coote	†			
	Plt Off. E. J. Ledwidge	Interned Turkey		46 Sqn JL903	Flak
	Sgt J. Rowley	Interned Turkey			
	Flt Sgt L. Holmes	Interned Turkey		46 Sqn JM264	Flak
	Flt Sgt M. Bell	Interned Turkey			
06/10/43	Plt Off. B. J. Beare RCAF	Rescued from sea	227 Sqn JM648	Engine problems
	Sgt C. E. Humphreys	Rescued from sea			
	Sgt R. H. Carter	Rescued from sea	227 Sqn EL516	Engine problems
	Sgt H. J. Harris	Rescued from sea			
17/10/43	Flt Sgt J. Hey	†		603 Sqn JL761	Bf 109
	Flt Sgt E. Worrall	†			
	Flt Sgt R. Reid	Rescued from sea	227 Sqn JL735	Engine problems
	Sgt H. L. Seymour	†			
18/10/43	Flg Off. J. S. Holland (US)	Rescued from sea	46 Sqn JM249	Bf 109
	Flt Sgt H. E. Bruck	†			
23/10/43	Flt Sgt T. C. Mofitt	†		227 Sqn JM277	Engine problems
	Flt Sgt J. J. Jackson	†			
29/10/43	Flg Off. J. Dixon	†		47 Sqn JM225	Ar 196
	Flg Off. G. A. Terry	†			
30/10/43	Flg Off. J. E. Hayter RNZAF	Rescued from sea	47 Sqn JM317	Flak
	W/O T. J. Harper RNZAF	Rescued from sea			
05/11/43	Flt Lt J. P. Tremlett	†		227 Sqn JL900	Bf 109
	Flt Sgt R. E. Jobling	†			
	Flt Sgt J. A. Swift	†		227 Sqn EL478	Bf 109

	Flt Sgt G. F. Austin	†		
	Flg Off. W. Yurchison RCAF	†	227 Sqn	JL939	Bf 109
	Flg Off. P.M. Wroath	†		
	Flg Off. A. P. Mazur RCAF	†	227 Sqn	JM276	Bf 109
	Flg Off. K. Stakes	†		
	Wg Cdr J. A. Lee-Evans DFC	POW	47 Sqn	47/D	Flak
	Flt Lt D. A. Heden	POW		
	Flt Lt T. C. Graham	POW	47 Sqn	47/B	Flak
	Flg Off. J. H. K. Langdon	POW		
06/11/43	Flg Off. L. Rossner	†	47 Sqn	JM403	Bf 109
	Sgt H. K. Levy	†		
	Sqn Ldr C. A. Ogilvie	Evaded	47 Sqn	JM352	Bf 109
	Flg Off. M. O'Connor	Evaded		
	Plt Off. K. I. E. Hopkins RAAF	Rescued from sea	47 Sqn	LX998	Ar 196
	W/O K. V. Roget RAAF	Rescued from sea		
10/11/43	Flg Off. J. Hayden	†	47 Sqn	LZ148	Bf 109
	Sgt J. McMaster	Rescued from sea		
	Plt Off. W. A. Eacott	POW	47 Sqn	LZ275	Bf 109
	Plt Off. W. B. F. Pitchard	POW		
12/11/43	Flg Off. A. G. Greentree RNZAF	†	47 Sqn	LX912	Flak
	Sgt G. H. Freeman	†		
13/11/43	W/O F. M. Cox RAAF	†	603 Sqn	LX977	Acc
	W/O N. S. Ferguson RAAF	†		
	Flg Off. E. L. Clary Jr RCAF (US)	†	603 Sqn	LZ127	Bf 109
	Sgt W. E. Finbow	†		
	Sqn Ldr S. Muller-Rowland	Interned Turkey	47 Sqn	LX928	Ju 88
	Flt Sgt J. D. Anderson	Interned Turkey		
14/11/43	Flg Off. J. A. Horsfall RCAF	†	46 Sqn	JM248	Bf 109
	Flt Sgt J. R. Colley	†		
	W/O R. Lindsey	†	46 Sqn	JL894	Bf 109
	Flt Sgt A. C. A. Gardener	†		

16/11/43	Flg Off. W. W. Thwaites	†		47 Sqn	LZ125	Bf 109
	Flg Off. J. E. Lovell	†			
	Flg Off. J. B. Fletcher	†	47 Sqn	LX923	Bf 109
	Sgt J. Dale	†			
	Flg Off. A. D. Bond	†	47 Sqn	LX883	Bf 109
	Sgt A. R. Cottle	POW (esc.)			
26/11/43	Flg Off. F. J. Gregory RCAF (US)	†	47 Sqn	LX987	Engine problems
	Flg Off. A. G. Wood	†			
07/12/43	Flt Sgt P. J. Martin RCAF	†	252 Sqn	JL898	FTR
	Flt Sgt J. Hamilton	†			
	Flg Off. D. Nichol	POW	47 Sqn	LX898	Flak
	W/O G. Ball	POW			
03/01/44	W/O R. J. Barrett	†	47 Sqn	LX919	Bf 109
	Sgt W. H. Fairfield	†			
13/01/44	Flg Off. L. F. Morgan	POW	227 Sqn	JM274	Flak
	Sgt R. A. W. Ferguson	POW			
16/01/44	Flt Lt G. W. MacDonnell	†	47 Sqn	LZ138	Flak
	Flg Off. S. W. Piner	†			
22/01/44	Flg Off. D. B. Hume	†	47 Sqn	LX863	Flak
	Flt Sgt E. W. Peggram	POW			
23/01/44	Flg Off. R. B. Hutchison RCAF (US)	†	227 Sqn	JL905	Flak
	Flt Sgt L. Sawle	†			
	Flg Off. K. S. Judd	†	227 Sqn	EL270	Flak
	Sgt A. G. Thomas	(injured)			
26/01/44	Flg Off. A. H. Will RAAF	†	227 Sqn	JL708	Flak
	Flg Off. B. Findley	†			
27/01/44	Flt Sgt A. H. Rooks	†	603 Sqn	LZ144	Ar 196
	Flg Off. M. J. R. Thom	†			
30/01/44	Flt Sgt C. A. Melling	POW	47 Sqn	ND203	Flak
	Flt Sgt I. L. Davies	POW			
31/01/44	Flg Off. D. A. L. Hall	†	252 Sqn	LZ341	Bf 109
	Sgt A. K. Cowie	†			
	Flt Sgt H. A. Stevenson	Interned Turkey	252 Sqn	LZ377	Bf 109

	Sgt C. Thompson	Interned Turkey			
02/02/44	W/O K. F. Wright	Rescued from sea	227 Sqn	T5170	Engine problems
	Flt Sgt G. L. Jones	Rescued from sea			
04/02/44	Lt J. S. Ogilvy SAAF	†	16SAAF	LZ332	Mid-air collision
	Lt E. R. Scherer SAAF	†			
06/02/44	Flg Off. C. H. Mason	Interned Turkey	252 Sqn	LZ345	Flak
	Sgt J. R. Smith	Interned Turkey			
09/02/44	Plt Off. F. P. Stanger RAAF	†	252 Sqn	LZ141	Bf 109
	Flt Sgt J. S. L. Reynolds	†			
	Flt Sgt A. W. Squires	†	252 Sqn	LZ271	Bf 109
	Flt Sgt W. H. Boon	†			
	Flt Lt R. H. R. Meyer	†	252 Sqn	LZ287	Bf 109
	Flt Sgt P. Grieve	†			
11/02/44	W/O K. F. Wright	†	227 Sqn	JL585	Flak
	Flt Sgt G. L. Jones	Interned Turkey			
13/02/44	Flt Lt J. Unwin	†	47 Sqn	LZ240	Bf 109
	Sgt K. R. Farmer	†			
16/02/44	Wg Cdr J. K. Buchanan DSO DFC	†	227 Sqn	EL467	Flak
	W/O R. C. Howes	Rescued from sea			
	LAC E. Eliav (Bulg)	†			
	Lt W. P. Ridley SAAF	POW	16SAAF	LZ333	Flak
	Lt J. A. S. Louw SAAF	POW			
18/02/44	Lt T. J. Simpson SAAF	†	16SAAF	LZ481	Flak
	Capt. J. F. A. Steyn SAAF	†			
22/02/44	Flt Sgt S. B. Appleton	†	227 Sqn	X8103	Ar 196
	Flt Sgt J. Fenton	†			
	Flt Sgt R. F. Scarlett	†	227 Sqn	EL228	Bf 109
	Flg Off. G. S. Hartley	†			
	Flg Off. J. C. Corlett	†	227 Sqn	JL731	Bf 109
	Flg Off. G. Williams	POW			
25/02/44	Flg Off. R. S. Euler	Rescued from sea	47 Sqn	?	Flak
	Flt Sgt C. A. Boffin	Rescued from sea			
27/02/44	Flg Off. W. M. Davies DFC	†	227 Sqn	EL509	Flak
	Flt Sgt G. A. Brown	POW			

6-7/03/44	Flt Lt A. Taylor DFC (SA)	†	46 Sqn	LZ335	Flak
	Plt Off. R. Peace	†			
12/03/44	Maj. J. E. Bell SAAF	†	16SAAF	NE248	Bf 109?
	Lt N. H. Stead SAAF	†			
30/03/44	Sgt P. E. Davies	†	227 Sqn	JL915	Engine problems
	Sgt R. W. Beach	†			
	Flt Sgt L. Hibbert	Rescued from sea	227 Sqn	JL626	Flak
	Flt Sgt H. Parker	Rescued from sea			
03/04/44	Flg Off. R. W. Densham	†	252 Sqn	LZ464	Flak
	Flg Off. D. C. Rooke	Rescued from sea			
	Flt Sgt V. Lacey	†	46 Sqn	LZ369	Flak
	Flt Sgt R. E. Brown	†			
05/04/44	Flg Off. R. J. Owen	†	227 Sqn	JL730	Struck mast
	Flt Sgt L. A. Everett	†			
08/04/44	Sgt H. Lacey	†	603 Sqn	NE282	Flak
	Sgt J. Foster	Evaded			
11/04/44	W/O E. T. Lynch RAAF	†	603 Sqn	NE421	Flak
	Flt Sgt C. C. Sykes	†			
13/04/44	Sgt R. Gosling	†	603 Sqn	LZ370	Bf 109
	Sgt S. A. West	†			
15/05/44	Flt Sgt J. E. Paddison	†	603 Sqn	LZ404	Flak
	Flt Sgt J. Rhodes	†			
	Flt Sgt E. G. Harman	†	603 Sqn	LZ281	Flak
	Flt Sgt L. E. Hopkin	†			
16/05/44	Plt Off. D. C. Lendrum	†	252 Sqn	NE579	Flak
	Flg Off. D. C. Rooke	†			
25/05/44	Flt Lt E. A. T. Taylor DFC RCAF	†	252 Sqn	LZ518	Flak
	Flt Sgt D. C. Dick	†			
01/06/44	Wg Cdr B. G. Meharg	POW	252 Sqn	NE293	Flak
	Flt Lt E. H. G. Thompson	POW			
	Flg Off. J. W. A. Jones	POW	227 Sqn	JM235	Ar 196
	Flg Off. R. A. R. Wilson	Evaded			
	Flt Sgt R. M. Atkinson	†	603 Sqn	LZ517	Flak/Ar 196
	Flt Sgt D. F. Parsons	†			
	Capt. E. A. Barrett SAAF	POW	16SAAF	NE641	Ar 196

	Lt A. J. Haupt SAAF	POW			
6-7/06/44	Flt Sgt A. Lord RAAF	†	46 Sqn	ND273	Flak
	Flt Sgt T. Dawes	†			
15/06/44	Lt F. W. Begbie SAAF	†	16SAAF	LZ397	Ju 88
	2/Lt Phipps SAAF	Rescued from sea			
17/06/44	Capt. K. G. Muir DFC SAAF	†	16SAAF	NE551	Flak
	Lt J. H. Strydom SAAF	†			
	Capt. R. Munton-Jackson SAAF	Rescued from sea	16SAAF	NE???	Flak/Ar 196
	Lt ?	Rescued from sea			
19/06/44	Plt Off. W. Davenport DFC	POW	252 Sqn	NE546	Flak
	Flt Sgt C. P. Grainger	POW			
05/07/44	Sgt C. H. Dean	†	603 Sqn	NE579	Hit sea
	Sgt D. W. Taylor	†			
19/07/44	Sgt H. E. Yorke	Evaded	603 Sqn	NE595	Flak
	Sgt J. G. Shaw	†			
21/07/44	Flt Sgt D. Joyce	†	603 Sqn	NE465	Flak
	Flt Sgt K. F. Thomas	†			
	Flg Off. K. Jenkinson	Rescued from sea	603 Sqn	NE610	Flak
	Flt Sgt J. K. Rogers	†			
	Flg Off. C. A. de Bounevialle	Evaded	603 Sqn	NE494	Flak
	Flt Sgt A. E. Potter	Evaded			
	W/O L. F. Sykes RCAF	Rescued from sea	603 Sqn	NE340	Flak
	Sgt W. H. Foxley	Rescued from sea			
28/07/44	Flt Lt C. A. Whyatt	†	252 Sqn	NE255	Flak
	Flt Sgt R. A. Barrett	†			
01/08/44	W/O C. G. Davis RCAF	Evaded	252 Sqn	NT895	Flak
	Sgt G. N. Waller	POW			
	Plt Off. J. D. Clarke RCAF	†	252 Sqn	LZ530	Flak
	Flt Lt E. A. C. Young	†			
30/08/44	Flg Off. H. W. Soderlund RCAF	POW	603 Sqn	NV213	Ju 52
	Flt Sgt I. L. Nichol	POW			
13/09/44	Plt Off. A. B. Woodier	Rescued from sea	603 Sqn	NE367	Flak
	Sgt H. Lee	Rescued from sea			

16/09/44	Sqn Ldr A. G. Deck DFC	Interned Turkey	603 Sqn	NV215	Flak
	Flg Off. C. A. Heide DFC RCAF	Interned Turkey			
23/09/44	Flt Sgt S. E. Skippen	†	252 Sqn	LZ456	Flak
	Flt Sgt J. A. Truscott	†			
01/10/44	W/O R. Knight	†	108 Sqn	ND???	FTR
	Flt Sgt L. Harwood	†			
03/10/44	Sgt D. Harrison	†	603 Sqn	NT893	Flak
	Sgt D. V. Bannister	Evaded			
	Flg Off. C. A. de Bounevialle DFC	POW	603 Sqn	NV205	Flak
	Plt Off. A. E. Potter	POW			
09/10/44	Plt Off. C. E. Baldry	Rescued from sea	108 Sqn	ND???	Hit sea
	Flg Off. J. Watson	†			
12/10/44	Flt Sgt J. McEwan	†	256 Sqn	(Mosquito HK509)	FTR
	Flt Sgt S. Coles	†			

Plt Off. Sam McAughtry, prior to undertaking the first of his thirty-seven ops with 252 Squadron in 1944, was dramatically informed:

> Flying a Beaufighter in daylight, attacking enemy harbours and shipping convoys … they're being shot down like fucking flies. (see *McAughtry's War*)

The losses listed above proved sadly prophetic.

Shot Down and Captured

W/O Sotirios Skantzikas (see page 17)

Wt Off. Skantzikas was transferred to Stalag Luft III. On 25 March 1944, he took part in 'The Great Escape' but was captured near the Czech border with his co-escaper Plt Off. Jimmy James and was executed by the Gestapo on the 29 March 1944. Jimmy James wrote:

> After joining my group in the woods, we were led off round the camp by a Sqn Ldr [J.E.A.] Williams. It was a freezing cold night and we must have walked about ten miles before we reached our objective, which was a country station called Tshiebsdorf where we knew we could take a train south. I was feeling terribly excited. The plan was that we would get down to Czechoslovakia. After a short wait we got on board a train and travelled south to another country station – just north of the Czech border. We expected a check at the station but it was nine o'clock in the morning and obviously the alarm had not reached the station yet. At this point the group split up and I went off with my partner Skantzikas, a Greek fighter pilot.
>
> We proceeded to climb over the Reisengebirge - or giant mountains - with snow up to our necks. Not only was it tough but we knew that if we had another night in those conditions we would probably freeze to death. Rather than proceeding on we walked into Hirschberg West Station secure in the knowledge that we had good passes and some money. At the ticket office we were intercepted by a civilian policeman who asked us for our papers. We presented them airily and he looked at them and put them in his pocket. "Hey, what's going on? I'm German and I'm just off to see my old mother in Belgrade," I told him. "We'll talk about it in the station," came his reply. We were taken down to the police station, where there were already four other members of our party locked up. Two more came in later. By the end eight of us had been caught in the local area and all eight of us were interrogated and then taken to the civilian jail in Hirschenberg, where we were each thrown into a cell.
>
> It was only twelve hours since our escape. We were prisoners again and it was shattering. We didn't have any idea what was going to happen. After a couple of days four of our names were called out – Skantzikas, a Canadian [Jim Wernham] and [Kaz] Pawluk and [Toni] Kiewnarski, two Poles. They were told to pack up their things and go. Our natural reaction was that we thought they were going to be taken back to the camp. In fact they were taken off to be shot.

Sotirios Skantzikas was murdered on 30/03/44 by Brealau Gestapo agent Lux who was responsible for at least twenty-seven of the executions. Lux allegedly died fighting near Breslau towards the end of the war.

Shot down 3 October 1943 – Plt Off. Edward Ledwidge 46 Squadron – Interned Turkey (see page 60)

Immediately on landing water streamed into the fuselage port side, putting out what flames were left, and the aircraft appeared to go under the water with the top hatch closing – and everything went dark and green. I undid my harness and parachute straps and pushed the escape hatch open with a great heave. As the sea gushed in I forced myself up through the opening, surprised to find myself in bright sunlight. The aircraft was still moving forward, nose down, at a fair speed and the sea was washing up over the nose. By then however it was sinking rapidly and I jumped over the leading edge of the starboard wing into the water as the front end started to disappear. I'd left my dinghy in the seat, still attached to my parachute, as the top escape hatch was too small to get through with them. However, I had my Mae West and I could swim – and more important than anything else at that moment was that I'd survived the flames and the ditching and was comparatively safe. I then tried to inflate my lifejacket by pulling on the small lever on the CO_2 bottle at its base. Unfortunately for me, when the bottle had been attached, the fabric of the garment had been damaged, allowing all the contents of the bottle to escape into the water in a mass of bubbles. There was a tube attached to the Mae West so that it could be inflated by simply blowing into it, but this merely created more bubbles.

I watched the Beau rapidly sinking. Then, as the rear part and the tail started to slide down into the depths, the rear canopy opened and the navigator [Sgt John Rowley] seemed to pop out like a cork into the water. He didn't say anything but kept gesticulating to me, so I swam over to him and asked whether he had his dinghy. He nodded assent and pointed to his backside to indicate that it was still attached to his parachute harness. Whilst I was trying to unclip his dinghy, I remembered the pigeon we carried in the aircraft for emergencies, which was in the nav's charge and kept in the rear of the fuselage. "Did you bring the pigeon?" I asked. He then uttered his first words, "Fuck the pigeon!"

After several hours, their dinghy drifted towards the Turkish coast where they found refuge for the night before being taken to the military authorities and to eventual safety.

Shot down 10 November 1943 – Plt Off. Wally Eacott 603 Squadron – Prisoner of War (see page 95)

Bob [Pritchard] wasn't far off, and neither was the dinghy. The only good luck that day was that we had obtained an advance model Beaufighter, with an automatically ejecting dinghy. There the luck stopped. The bloody thing was upside down and only partly inflated. Every attempt to turn it right way up met with failure. It collapsed upon itself, time and time again. We couldn't get at the inflating pump, naturally, until we were able to right it. I think it took about 45 minutes, and by that time poor old Bob (he was 28, and granddad to me) was thoroughly exhausted. Eventually, we were in it. We were both stained bright yellow from the sea-dye marker, which had also operated automatically, and we sat uncomfortably in several inches of water. The sea-dye, by the way, was a pack of concentrated colouring, tied to the dinghy by a piece of cord, and designed to leave a bright trail of yellow dye in the water that could be seen from the air by potential rescuers. It was 15:00 hours when we were shot down, and the next 18 hours were very miserable. The torn-off starboard wing floated for a long time, about a hundred yards away, and we lost sight of it when it got dark.

All through the night I kept starting up from a fitful doze, looking for signal flares. I felt sure we would be rescued by some magical allied submarine which would pop up nearby. (This had actually happened to one of our mates only three weeks before, in similar circumstances). Although I thought I saw coloured flares several times in the distance, the miracle didn't happen for us. Daybreak was a relief from the very cold night. Heartened by the light, and by some of our emergency rations, (mainly Horlicks tablets and chewing gum) we started to paddle eastward, in the direction of Turkey (it was only 60 miles away). We kept up the paddling for a long time, and were doing quite well, I seem to remember, when, at about 09:00 hours on 11 November, a most appropriate day, two Arados hove into view. Our air-sea rescue service. These blokes did something else other than act as fighter escort to supply ships. I felt distinctly disappointed that we were about to be saved, after all. I had begun to place high hopes on surrendering to a neutral country, and tasting some Turkish delights.

Both kites landed, and taxied slowly to our dinghy. The observer of one climbed out on to the float, and threw us a rope. "How long you shvim?" he called. "Since yesterday", I replied. "Since yesterday, hah!" he said, (as if he didn't know!) "For you, Ze Var iss over." I have since learned that Jerry said this to almost every captured airman I have ever heard about. It was a bit of a relief, after all, to sit in a dry aircraft, and be flown, courtesy of the Luftwaffe, to the western end of Crete. I didn't like the smell – all German aircraft had a typical smell that was quite unlike the exciting, familiar smell of Allied aircraft.

Stiff and sore from our overnight experience in the Aegean Sea, we were each given a blanket to wrap around ourselves, taken to a small building under guard, and fed a plateful of pasta each, with a mug of water to wash it down. After a few hours of fitful sleep, we were flown off the next morning at 03:00 hours to Greece in a Ju 52, the big troop transport aircraft that we had been hunting. Now I knew the reason we were usually unable to find the troop carriers in these waters. We often did sweeps, hoping to pick up a Ju 52 or two. We flew first to Athens, to offload some of the military passengers who were also travelling on the aeroplane. Bob and I were closely guarded the whole time by two escorting soldiers, and we were accommodated in a large drill hall, filled with other German soldiers, where we stayed for two nights, sleeping on a couple of blankets on the floor. One of the soldiers who tried to converse with us made it fairly plain that many Germans did not approve of Hitler, who he hastened to tell us was not really German at all, but Austrian! Our first inkling that the Great Leader was not the cat's whiskers with all of his people. On the third day we were again loaded into a Ju 52, and taken to Salonika. I spent 10 days in a cooler there, being interrogated and pining for the Squadron.

Shot down 1 June 1944 – Flg Off. Ernest Thompson 252 Squadron – Prisoner of War (see page 130)

Flg Off. Thompson was Wg Cdr Willie Meharg's navigator:

Looking away from the convoy, we simultaneously sighted a small yellow object about 40 yards away and recognised it as the dinghy pack. What luck! Willie kicked off his shoes and swam towards it. He brought it back and together we opened it without a word, though each of us was thinking of that precious Very pistol and its three cartridges. It was our only hope.

The gun was quickly assembled and now we settled down to wait for the circling aircraft to be in the most favourable position for observation. Three cartridges meant three chances. Willie held the pistol aloft and at what he thought was the right moment fired it into the air. A red star sped 100 feet skywards and then descended leaving a trail of smoke. We waited with our hearts beating but it was soon obvious that our God-sent effort to claim attention had gone by unobserved. The pistol was reloaded and again we waited. A few minutes later two Arado 196s made a very wide orbit and approaching close to us. This was it. Please God make them look this way.

Again the little red distress star sailed through the air and this time our prayers were answered. Almost immediately they turned and came in our direction. One of them did a tight turn directly over our heads and I watched the gunner closely but his guns did not move. A few minutes later, the second aircraft flew directly over our heads, very low and dropped a smoke float. Smoke billowed forth and our position was obvious for all to see. Every one of the aircraft came over to have a look … their crews seemed to be enjoying themselves immensely.

Then we saw the Arados land and taxi towards us. While Willie hastily threw the gun away just in case our saviours came alongside. Willie made for one machine and I went to the other, where the gunner was standing on the starboard float. "Climb on the float," he ordered, surprising me with his very good English. But I found it impossible to obey. My leg seemed paralysed and my arm and head so tender that I couldn't bear to touch anything. Somehow he managed to haul me out of the sea and into the aircraft and I took his seat in the rear, chilled to the bone. The air was now at my burns and it was incredibly painful. The engine of the other plane roared and I looked round to see it take off. We were turning into the wind and the gunner told me to sit on the floor. I did so and he began to unwrap a first-aid dressing but the aircraft began to leap forward and after a number of bumps it suddenly became smooth. Never was I so glad to be airborne.

A POW camp awaited but for the meantime they were safe.

Shot down 30 August 1944 – Flg Off. Harry Soderlund RCAF 603 Squadron – Prisoner of War (see page 138)

In the late evening of the day of our capture we were placed aboard a Junkers 52 with German soldiers being evacuated from Crete. The plane took us to Athens fortunately without any encounters with 603 Squadron aircraft.

After a week I and other prisoners were placed aboard a train bound for Salonika, Greece. The train travelled at night without lights. At one point when the train was travelling slowly I decided to try to escape through a small window near the top of the carriage. As I was getting up to the window a shout from some Russian prisoners alerted the guard. I quickly dropped back down and I heard the click of a rifle bolt. No light came on and the incident passed. I often wonder if I had made it out how this story may have changed. At the prison compound at Salonika we were joined by several P-38 Lightning pilots who were shot down while attacking aerodromes in the vicinity. The German guards said they were Chicago gangsters.

The forward compartment of a transport truck was our accommodation for the next leg of a journey which took us to Skopjle. Bulgaria. We arrived at an aerodrome in time to see several Junkers 87 Stuka dive-bombers dive on the aerodrome and drop their bombs. The guards had taken us outside the aerodrome as the sirens sounded. It was an encouraging sign. We learned that the planes were captured from the Germans and flown by Romanian pilots who had by this time been liberated.

The aerodrome at Skopjle, Bulgaria, was quickly repaired after the Stuka dive bomber raid and after sunset I was placed aboard a Junkers 52 again with German soldiers and the plane took off. The journey was not without excitement. At one point the plane was rocked by bursting anti-aircraft fire. The flight landed at Zagreb in Yugoslavia and I was put in a holding room. Later that same day I was put aboard a passenger train, which took me to Budapest, Hungary. There was a tourist aspect to this journey because I could observe the scenery in the lovely countryside. Crossing the Danube River it was noticeable that some repairs were done to the bridge. I soon found myself in a narrow cell at the Budapest penitentiary. On the way in a guard relieved me of a shirt I had under my arm.

After a few days I was place aboard a 40-man or four horses carriage along with other prisoners and the train headed westward. In a couple of days the train arrived at Frankfurt, which was the interrogation centre for aircrew prisoners. I saw at this time the rubble of bombed-out buildings first hand. The interrogation officer suggested that since I had no identification that I could be turned over to the Gestapo. After getting only my name rank and number I think he decided he knew more than I did. He told me that my flight commander had been promoted to squadron leader. Silently I was impressed. After a week I found myself aboard another train headed for Stalag Luft III.

I arrived at Stalag Luft III about a month after I was shot down so that would be sometime around October 1st. The camp had a library of sorts and one could exercise within the camp grounds. Food consisted of dark, heavy bread and thin soup once a day. The International Red Cross was allowed to bring in concentrated food parcels approximately 10 inches square by 3 inches deep once a month and this was a godsend. As I recall we could send out one letter a month. Showers were cold water; our beds were straw mattresses on wood slats.

A clandestine radio procured by some ingenious prisoners provided news which was passed around in a book. We knew of the crossing of the Rhine at Remegan. In February the Russians were approaching Stalag Luft III and so prisoners marched to various destinations. The group I was with spent about five days to reach Luckenwald, a city south of Berlin. We could hear the bombing of Berlin. About the end of April the Russians were nearing Luckenwald and soon a Russian tank came and knocked down the gate and we were able to get out in the countryside. An American convoy of trucks came to take us away but the Russians refused to let us go. It was not till a week or so later that agreement by the Russian and Allied generals allowed our return to western Germany and evacuation to Britain. The war was over and the next move was back to Canada!

Reminiscences

Karl-Heinz Lüdtke, SeenotStaffel 7

The Italians changed sides in [September] 1943 and were now our enemy. As most of the islands in the Mediterranean were occupied by them we had to re-occupy them as quickly as possible. During the night we were ripped from our dreams and had to report to the Staffel immediately, where we arrived early in the morning. Soldiers were all around the building and as we later found out they were the famous Brandenburger, an elite regiment. We didn't know what was going on and didn't even know that the Italians had switched sides. During the briefing we were told what was going on. The British had to have acted very quickly as most of the islands were now occupied by them as we found out around noon on the first island. Without the Do 24 the quick retaking of the islands could not have happened. We were not in action every day and there was ample time to do things for oneself. There was more than enough to view in and around Athens but we were never able to see everything as most of these sights were too far away, though they could be reached by train or bus. We of course visited the Acropolis and also the palace of the Greek king. The harbour of Piräus was an important one as the ferries to the islands all started there. Around 1943 these had all been stopped and for the average Greek it was very difficult to get to one of the islands. The Olympic stadium was also worth a visit. There was so much to see and write about Athens.

My pilot, Flugzeugführer Lange, one of the best pilots, knew the Do 24 like the inside of his pocket. He knew how to take-off and land without any difficulty and that wasn't easy as he had to judge the waves, which were always different. Lange, and he was not alone in this, was fond of the drink, not only when he was thirsty but also when he was flying. In the evening when we were hanging around, Oberfeldwebel Lumpi called me over. He said he had something for me; of course he referred to his Dröpkes, this while he knew I didn't like alcohol. He convinced me to taste it; the Greek wine was disgusting, but you had to have fun and there was plenty of that. But he was able to fly under any circumstance, he was a pilot through and through, he was the best. That was even mentioned in a paper by Hauptmann Gorican [sic], who deserted with a Do 24 to Turkey, and he mentioned this fact to the English.

In our neighbourhood was an elderly German lady, and she was a real lady. As we later found out she was the widow of a brewery owner from Athens. She lived in a small house and cooked for us. We brought something to eat back with us, as food was in short supply in Greece. Oil and eggs were ours in bringing and with a little negotiation she supplied the rest and cooked for us. Those were happy times I will never forget, sitting on her porch in the evening with a lovely wine from crystal glasses. We looked like the Count of Luxembourg. It was like there was no war. We had our barber, of course a Greek. When we supplied the food he would cook for us. All the bars were situated on the sea, the beach right beside it. So when you had too much to drink you could cool down in the sea. Among our men was a dark haired guy from Hannover who was much loved with the Greek women. He often came too late on service and was often punished for this. His name was Helmut and he was a good friend. From the training as mechanic we were together and also travelled to Athens-Phaleron together. What became of Helmut I don't know, our stations were far apart. His name was often spoken off in the Staffel when he (again) was arrested for being too late.

My initiation as mechanic was to the crew of Oberfeldwebel Wilhelm Lange, who lived in a small house, to which I would move. There were two crews in the house, so in total 12 people. It was situated in the middle of the village of Phaleron, a suburb of Athens. To the left and right were Greeks and we lived in good harmony. Next to us was a shoemaker who put our shoes in good order in trade for food, because there was not plenty around of that. I almost forgot that he made boots of goat's leather for the women; they weren't bad and fair in price. Back to the house, it didn't have an actual roof, just half a metre thick walls. We lived peacefully if there just hadn't been a war going on. As flying personnel we had good provisions and to get through the situation better we helped ourselves to some olive oil and eggs, actually we were doing a sort of black market.

We flew back and forth to the islands where supplies were plenty, especially cigarettes. My friend was the purest black market trader around and traded everything with the Greeks. Lesbos, with its capitol Mitilini, was mainly an olive tree island, where even before the war a German olive oil company was present. The soap was mainly produced from oil, as was the margarine. The name of the firm has slipped my mind. As we needed olive oil, to bake eggs and for my speciality, mayonnaise, and to make potato salad, yes we knew what was good for us, and the Greeks needed oil too. So we traded. That was just the island with the oil, then there was an island with the precious wine. When you drank a glass of this wine, if you could stop there, you had to be very careful, that alcohol percentage was enormous! The German company I mentioned offered some paid labour, but there was little else around.

Crete was a major destination for transport flights from Athens, the Do 24Ts frequently being used for such flights:

Whenever we flew to Crete we went via Monk Mountain where the monks had a monastery in a mountain range. We passed very close and could recognise the monks. On Crete we even slept under the olive trees or walked at night from Chania to Suda. The people of Crete were actually very different from the Greeks. The Cretans had been conquered many times in the past by the Romans, the Turks and finally the Greeks. Crete is the biggest island in the Mediterranean and the outpost of Seenotstaffel 7 was Suda, where there was always one Do 24 ready for take-off in case of an emergency. We were often in the capital Chania. Crete was the only island with an airfield and all the other islands were dependant on the Do 24 or ships. So besides flying SAR we made many transport flights, we even transported a general once; he was an infantry general who wanted to look at the islands from above.'

The Lange crew got orders to pick up a Do 24 in Kiel-Holtenau, a welcome job for any crew. We flew in a Ju 52 from Terteu to Vienna and from there on by rail to Kiel. When we arrived there the Do 24 wasn't frontline ready yet, so we had some time for ourselves. The trip back was wonderful, always magnificent views from the plane. It took us four weeks due to the weather. Our Feldwebel Lange was promoted during this flight to Oberfeldwebel. Leutnant Kemp [Kämpf], our observer and former teacher from Vienna, was a very fine gentleman. The promotion was made official by Kemp [*sic*] in a small tavern somewhere in Yugoslavia. He told the rest of the crew outside the tavern and Lange had to report to him in full military style after which he promoted Lange to his surprise and to the surprise of the rest of the crew. As we were in a tavern this had to be celebrated.

During the first period I didn't even notice the war, everything was so peaceful. The understanding between the Germans and the Greeks was very peaceful, nowhere was there an insult or assault in any way. In the Staffel we had a young Greek to whom Oberfeldwebel Lange was like a second father. He was part of an Albanian group that worked around the base and when not at work was always to be found in our group. He spoke perfect German and when we eventually had to leave Greece in front of the Allied troops we took him along, even all the way to Germany.

The Lange crew were shot down on the night of 1/2 October by a 46 Squadron Beaufighter (see Chapter X). Karl-Heinz Lüdtke continued:

The next morning we started walking and saw a shepherd in the distance. He told us that he hadn't seen any German soldiers for a long time. He was a friendly man who was armed, so he could have shot us at any time. We even got some bread, cigarettes and fresh milk from the sheep. We told him where the dinghy and the other stuff was and told him he could have it, it was the only thing we could offer in return. The island where we were was named Poliagos and was part of three islands located close together. The shepherd brought us to Kimolos in his small sailing boat; the weather was awful and there was a fierce storm blazing. Lange and I were very happy when we reached land. On Kimolos was a small village where we were greeted by the mayor with red wine, raison marmalade and bread. The bread was so hard we had to scrape it with our teeth.

For the journey to the next island, which was Melos, he even provided us with medication and sent along a young man to help us. When we approached Melos we made ourselves known by a flare and the German Navy who was still on the island sent a boat to pick us up and later we driven by car to the HQ there. Later Meissner also arrived there; he had also landed on Kimolos. He brought the sad news that Oberfeldwebel Führmann passed away shortly before he reached dry land. He approached a cliff coast and wasn't able to grab hold of the cliffs when the wind pushed him in high waves on the rocks. He fell and hit his head on the rocks with the next wave. It all happened so fast that Meissner wasn't able to rescue him. We reported by radio to our base and were picked up by a Do 24 from Phaleron, flown by Feldwebel Sommer. Without an enemy encounter we were back at Phaleron where we were greeted by Staffelkapitän Oberleutnant Karlheinz Dähn with a glass of sect. He was happy to be able to greet at least three of the original six members back on base. I heard that our crew was reported missing so I can understand the way Dähn was feeling.

In Athens many things had changed during our three days absence, our house had been cleaned out and our stuff was packed in a local school, ready for evacuation. The ground crew was ready for the retreat and still missions were flown with the Do 24, getting Germans off the many islands. Many an aircraft was shot at and even shot down. I, Lange and Meissner were no longer on active duty. I got a dry pleurisy that hurt badly which I encountered the first night on Kimolos. I stayed in my bunk and hoped to be cured by the time we had to evacuate. I was ordered as support for the last train, packed with material that left Athens for Saloniki. I was very disappointed in the staff of Seenotstaffel 7 as to why they could have let me go on this train in my state of illness, but as they say I had to follow orders. I wanted to stay to the last day and be there when the Seenostaffel 7 was disbanded.

Fw Alfred Jobst 7./KG27

My squadron, 3rd Group combat-squadron Boelcke, 7th Squadron [7./KG27], had already been withdrawn from the Eastern Front at the beginning of August 1944 because of lack of fuel (airfields Mielec and Biala Podlaska) and transferred to eastern Prussia, where the occupants were sleeping in the straw-filled barn of a manor by Schippenbeil, 60 km south of Königsberg. Our remaining aeroplanes were surrounded with protective banks of earth and covered with camouflage nets at the edge of the nearby airfield.

On 27 September, five air crews were unexpectedly chosen with the command to be ready for a special assignment beginning in the morning on the next day, without any information about the goal and order of the mission. Take-off was set for 6 o'clock in the morning with the temporary destination of Wiener-Neustadt. I remember a hazy sky covered with low scraps of clouds and take-off under blind-flight conditions. After a few hundred meters of ascent, however, the morning heavens opened to show the horizon and the rising sun.

A strange ritual at take-off left me feeling conflicted. Beside the start-block, someone had posted a standard bearer, framed by two soldiers, who saluted each of the planes as they took off by sinking the squadron standard, the existence of which I had never known until that moment. Since we didn't yet have any real idea about our actual destination, the deeper sense of such an emotional gesture was lost on me – honorary tribute or writing on the wall (or both) – puzzling. The only thing that counted was to finally be sitting back behind the wheel of my Heinkel after so many long weeks of aeronautical abstinence, ready to prove myself in the service of the Fatherland, an attitude, that I myself can scarcely understand today, but is an example of the abused idealism of a youth trimmed on heroism and martyrdom according to the Latin motto that I learned in high school: *Dulce et decorum est Pro patria mori*: 'How sweet and honorable it is to die for the fatherland.'

In Wiener-Neustadt other than a succinct statement of our destination Belgrade, we didn't get any information about our forthcoming mission. The confusion was complete the next morning when we received our orders to fly to Athens with a stopover in Salonika. Hellas! This prospect made me almost forget the war and the coming mission, as it promised the fulfillment of a long-tended dream of my youth.

Since reading the sagas of the Greek gods and heroes as a child I had felt magically drawn to this country. However it was only much later, as student of philology, that I found an adequate expression for it in Iphigenia's words: 'Seek the land of the Greeks with your soul.' I would get to see Athens with my own eyes, the acropolis, for me the quintessence of Greece, the Aegean, the fateful sea of Odysseus, and maybe even Mount Olympus, the mysterious seat of the antique gods, if only from the cockpit of a German bomber: already quite an outlandish educational trip.

The flight from Salonika to Athens has remained in my memory as the emotional and aesthetic high point of my life as a pilot. It was a sunny autumn day. For safety reasons we flew low over the Gulf of Saloniki, smooth as glass and gleaming in emerald tones, with an occasional view of the almost 3,000 metre high Mount Olympus on the starboard, then over the virtually uninhabited island Euboea, whose scant mountain landscape, covered in mild pastels and peacefully grazing sheep brought to view for me the imaginary, poetically fixed concept of Arcadia and for a moment made me forget that this idyll only actually existed in the eye of the beholder. And then Athens lay at our feet, the Acropolis illuminated by the mild late-afternoon sunlight. And against all commands and instructions, we circled twice at an altitude of approximately 150 metres.

After landing on the airfield in Athens-Kalamaki and being shown our quarters, the comfortable villa of the former Finnish ambassador in Athens, now only spartanly furnished with cots protected by mosquito nets, we were finally filled in on the orders for our forthcoming mission: the evacuation of German soldiers from the island of Crete. At first glance a business that appeared rather harmless. The reality meanwhile, was quite something else. The evacuation process had been going on for several weeks under extremely dramatic circumstances. British, mainly with Beaufighters were in almost continual deployment against the transport formations of the German air force from Peloponnese and Crete's east by day, but primarily by night. The Germans, with the placid Ju 52 had no chance against the superior night hunters, who were armed with four 20mm cannons and six MGs and a speed of approximately 500 km per hour. After disastrous losses the Germans had finally been withdrawn. Now we, as clueless as we were, with the admittedly faster, but still far inferior He 111 were supposed to close the gap and bring this hopeless business to a different conclusion.

At our disposal was the Heinkel [1G+MR], a specially built model originally made for an invasion of England, with two bench seats opposite each other for eight to ten people instead of the bomb bay. Moreover, the aeroplane was equipped with a rubber dinghy that was placed as a package behind the bow cockpit under the sheet metal of the fuselage. In an emergency, the pilot could operate a mechanism from his seat that opened a compressed bottle of air, whereby the rubber dinghy was inflated within a few seconds; the cover separated in the fuselage at the predetermined breaking point and fell out of the hatch that had been created. The dinghy was connected to the fuselage with a security rope that would prevent the boat from drifting away at sea and could be cut easily. On the floor of the boat were four constructible paddles, a rudder, a compass, a receptacle with emergency food: cookies, chocolate, some packets of 'Dextro-Energen', a few cans with beverages (including can openers) and a first aid kit. Hardly conceivable, the scenes that might play out and actually did play out during the free-for-all over one of the five places in the rubber dinghy after an emergency splashdown on the return flight with a full aeroplane.

Fw Jobst and his crew were shot down by a Beaufighter on the night of 1/2 October. His story continues:

We tried to arrange ourselves in the 'nutshell' as well as the circumstances would allow. Four people sat, two on each side, astride the sides of the boat, with one leg almost up to the knee in the water. The fifth sat as helmsman on the stern, trading places in the coming hours lying before us with a rower to get a breather. Meanwhile, the moon stood over the horizon as a gigantic disk and brilliantly poured forth its silvery light over the still virtually smooth as glass, infinitely wide sea. Our odyssey had begun!!

According to the last position-reckoning, the crash site lay about 35 km north of Heraklion. So we steered in a southerly direction. After some hours, it may have been around 3:00 in the night, the distant outlines of rocky land rose before us. With fresh courage, we paddled on, until after approximately 12 hours (it must have been about 9:30) we reached the Heraklion offshore island of Dias, under a sunny sky. Just before that we had a traumatic experience. We recognised a British aeroplane, brilliantly silver in the blue of the sky, and feared that we would be shot in the rubber dinghy. However, the aeroplane didn't take any note of us. With effort, we found a place to camp on the jagged slope, which crashed steeply into the sea. We tried to catch our breath a little bit after we had spread our still moist shirts and shorts (the pilot's summer-uniform in the tropical south) to dry in the sun. Meanwhile I climbed the rocky slope to a flat plateau, overgrown with all sorts of foliage. From there I saw the harbour and airfield of Heraklion lying in almost tangible proximity before me. The actual distance from the south coast of Dias to Heraklion is somewhat more than 3 kilometres.

Shortly after returning to camp, the story took an unexpected turn for us all. To our left in close proximity to the coast, a Greek fish-cutter with its chugging support-motor appeared, heading out to the open sea. Shouting, signalling and wildly gesticulating, we succeeded in getting the fisherman's attention. He stopped his boat and steered it as near to us as the cliffs would allow. We tried to make the fisherman understand with all sorts of signs and imaginative expressions like 'Germanski', aeroplane broken, etc., and by making sounds that were supposed to sound like machine-gun fire and trying to show two aeroplanes flying one behind the other with our hands, that the five strange figures he had found perched on the cliffs of a god-forsaken isle was a shipwrecked German air crew. The sight of us on the ledge of the beached rubber dinghy finally made a comprehensible story out of all the confusing details.

There was also a 15- or 16-year-old boy on board with the fisherman, apparently his son. The fisherman was a man of about 60 with a full beard and a badly creased, suntanned face. The boy eyed us, intimidated, as though we had appeared from another world. With great respect and spontaneous helpfulness, the five of us, for the captain actually nothing more than hostile occupying forces, were heaved on board, and the cutter headed toward the Heraklion's harbour with its strange load. There we had already been routinely written off, and so the mystification and joy were all the greater as we entered the port like the erstwhile Odysseus and his men on a Greek barque. That was it, *our* odyssey, even if it was pretty modest: without Polyphemus, Circe, Calypso and the sirens and without Scylla and Charybdis, thank God without Poseidon, the cruel God of the storms.

We thanked the Greek fisherman, our captain, by compensating him for not having brought in a catch, with a box with food, cans, cigarettes and all sorts of spirits. I will never forget how the old man, a bit helpless and sheepish, but obviously delighted and thankful, accepted the gift, humble compared to his unselfish effort. This report is dedicated to the old Greek fisherman from the distant country of the Minoans, who has long since gone to join the 'round dance of blissful spirits' in the Elysium, as a late memory of a noble gesture of humanity in the middle of a merciless, dark war.

Plt Off. George Eley, 255 Squadron

Not every sortie was a success. Although not tasked with patrols over the Aegean, single Beaufighters of 255 Squadron based at Grottaglie on the Italian eastern coast were sometimes despatched to this area as was Flt Sgt B. C. Dinham-Peren and his navigator Plt Off. George Eley who wrote:

This is an account of just one ordinary sortie, written within a few hours of the trip, whilst the details were fresh in my memory. It was the night of September 14/15th 1944. The Germans were in a fix in the Balkans and 255 Squadron was trying to add to their difficulties.

With Flight Sergeant Dinham-Peren as pilot (called D-P for short) I set off from Grottaglie aerodrome, near Taranto, at 8.45pm in Beaufighter C for Charlie, on an intruder operation in the Gulf of Salonika, 300 miles from base, hoping to intercept German transport planes evacuating the Dodecanese Islands.

We had a little difficulty starting the starboard engine but, otherwise, the take-off was uneventful. It was a clear starlit night but there was no moon and it was slightly misty. As we left the flarepath, rising into the inky blackness of the night, we circled the airfield once and then climbed on an easterly course to 10,000 feet. We were then passing over the brightly lit towns of the heel of Italy, now bothering no longer about blackout. Gradually, our eyes were becoming accustomed to the darkness, though we could only just discern the Italian coastline as we crossed it. We were due to reach the Albanian coast south of Valona at 9:22pm, but as we approached the land, the small patches of cloud below us merged into one complete cloud mass, and we could see nothing but an endless greyish-white carpet beneath us and the stars above.

As we crossed the 8,500 feet high peaks of the Balkans, the cloud became denser and soon we were completely enveloped. We climbed in bumpy conditions to 12,000 feet, where we emerged at intervals between towering cumulus cloud tops which rose to about 14,000 feet. The air temperature was just at freezing point - not really cold, but chilly after the warm September night at Taranto. We could see, far away to the south-east, violent white flashes and reddish glows from the aerodromes around Athens which we knew were being bombed heavily by our Wellingtons.

Then as we approached the east coast of the Greek peninsula the cloud became thinner and the cloud-tops lower. Here and there we could see odd lights from scattered buildings as we passed gaps in the cloud, but no well-lit towns like those of Italy. Once, I saw, some miles away to the south and a little behind and below us, a reddish glow, brightening and dying away every few seconds, which resembled the light from infra-red detection apparatus used by German night fighters. If it was a night fighter it must have passed well away from us, but for the next five minutes I kept a very good look-out behind us! Perhaps it was on the prowl waiting for our returning bombers.

Due to reach the east coast at 10:14pm, we actually passed over it at 10:15pm but found ourselves over the Gulf of Volos, 40 miles south of our track. The large town of Volos itself, on the shore of the Gulf, was in complete darkness. We turned due north into the Gulf of Salonika, losing height to 2,000 feet. The sky here was practically clear of cloud but the night was still very dark and we could only just discern the coastlines. On our intercom we could hear the familiar crescendo wail from ground radar stations, which indicated that the enemy were 'sweeping' us and plotting our track.

We stooged back southwards down the Gulf for some 40 miles and had just turned north again when, at 10:45pm, I picked up radar contact on an aircraft 4 miles away to starboard flying at about 3,000 feet above the sea. We were then at about 4,000 feet altitude, so we went down to our target's level, only to find that it was climbing hard. I warned my pilot that the range was closing so rapidly that it might be approaching head-on, but it proved afterwards to be on a north-westerly course, crossing our proposed track from right to left.

We turned in behind it, and when it was two miles ahead D-P said he could see its lights. I assumed that it must be showing navigation lights preparatory to landing. I told D-P to throttle right back but, being engaged in my radar, I did not bother to examine the lights myself. He told me afterwards that there were three lights, bluish-mauve in colour, so obviously they were not navigation lights at all, but exhaust flames from a three-engined transport plane. As we closed in, I realised the enemy was roughly on our own course climbing hard and only flying at about 100mph, whereas our speed had only fallen off to 160mph. We passed right underneath the enemy aircraft so that we were then ahead of it, but about 1,000 feet below it. I looked back, expecting to see the lights which D-P had mentioned but, of course, saw none, as the exhaust flames would only be visible from behind the enemy machine. We were a little too far below it to discern its outline against the starlit sky. D-P began to orbit, but I did not realise he still thought the enemy aircraft was travelling in the opposite direction to us (i.e.

south). He was under the impression that, having passed us, it would have been going rapidly away from us behind, whereas in actual fact it was now following behind us.

Having a moment to spare as we were commencing the orbit, I thought I would switch my radar momentarily over to beacon range, which would enable me to see how far we were from the north shore of the Gulf. As we turned, I saw we were six miles from this shore. Then I switched the radar back to interception range, but for some unexplained reason it switched right off. I quickly pushed down the HT switch to put it on again, but only the first stage of HT would come on. Previously, during the evening, I had experienced this trouble but did not imagine it could possibly happen in the middle of an interception, unless I switched off the HT. So there we were, having lost contact with the Hun, and without the use of our radar. It was then that I first realised D-P had stopped his orbit on south, so I immediately told him to turn to north.

At the same time, I scoured the northern sky again for any sign of the enemy. Just at that moment, as he approached the coast, the Hun aircraft switched on and off twice (like the letter 'i' in Morse) two powerful landing lights which threw beams down to the water. Behind these lights lay the star constellation Plough, so I saw at once he was still roughly north of us. As the enemy was then just off Salonika, I thought the flashing of the landing lights was a signal to the nearby aerodrome to put on its flarepath, so we decided to stooge around for a bit, waiting for the lights to come on. However, nothing happened.

A few moments later the 2nd and 3rd stages of HT on my radar came on again, but there was no sign of the Hun. I realised later that he must have continued on his northerly course, up the Vardar valley towards Hungary. Too much time had elapsed to give chase, and in any case I did not know then whether he was still in the vicinity waiting to go into land at Salonika. The lives of, perhaps, fifty German officers [*sic*] had been saved by - what? A faulty electrical relay? A whimsical decision of an over-enthusiastic navigator to ascertain his exact position in the middle of a chase? A lack of imagination by a pilot who thought German planes might use blue navigation lights in place of the usual red and green?

When again would I be likely to get such a prize as a Ju 52 full of Germans?

We then decided to climb up to 10,000 feet over Salonika to see if we could see any lights further afield, but we found none. Down we came again to 3,000 feet and made three more patrols across the Gulf, but nothing of interest happened. Continually, after this, the HT of my radar would not come on beyond the first stage until about five minutes after switching on. On our way back, we found the cloud tops much lower than on the outward journey and we were just clear of cloud the whole way. We left the Balkans mainland at ten minutes after midnight and commenced to descend to 3,000 feet. At 12:25am, not having sighted land or any coastal beacon, we called up Base. They asked if we wanted a vector home so D-P accepted the offer, but just as he had done so I saw the Cape St. Maria de Leuca navigation light ahead, bearing 325 degrees, so we headed for it. The wind had evidently maintained its high velocity for we were well south of track. Shortly afterwards, Base told us we were 15 miles SE of St. Maria de Leuca, which we could now see, was an accurate 'fix'. We proceeded up the East coast of the Gulf of Taranto, arrived over base at ten minutes to one, and called up aerodrome control for permission to land.

Then the fun started. On the approach to the flarepath, having put down wheels and 10 degrees of flap satisfactorily, D-P proceeded to put down more flap, but the flaps suddenly went up, instead of down. So he pushed the throttles forward and started to climb and go round the circuit again. The wheels went up all right but, as we came round to make another attempt to land, he again proceeded to lower the wheels, but they then unlocked and hung loose and would not go up or lock down. The flaps would not operate at all, either. He then tried the emergency hand pump for pumping down the wheels and flaps but, after fifty 'pumps', this still showed no build-up of hydraulic pressure. I then crawled forward behind the pilot and tried to pump for him. I gave about 350 'pumps' but still no pressure had built up. So D-P came to the conclusion that the fluid had leaked out of the hydraulic system. The aircraft would only climb with difficulty now the wheels were hanging loose. We decided to go into a dive to try and lock the wheels by swinging them forward with a jerk.

We were using the last of our petrol very fast. We had now been circling for twenty minutes and the gauges showed we had hardly any petrol left. Then the red warning light came on, showing tanks nearly empty. Quickly D-P switched over to his other tanks, but these too showed the red warning light 'empty'. Then suddenly the port engine cut, the plane swung violently to port on its one engine and lost a lot of speed. D-P put the nose down to regain speed, whilst he switched back to the few gallons of petrol left in the inner tanks. We were heading to earth and I was still standing behind the pilot not knowing whether we would be able to reach the airfield, or not. I asked D-P if I had time to get back to my seat (where I could strap myself in) and at the same moment the engine coughed and picked up again. We were able to climb once more - though very slowly. So I crawled back, whilst D-P called up to control to stand by for an immediate emergency landing. He was heading for the flarepath so I suggested he avoided using it as other planes were coming home. As we did not know where other aircraft were parked on the field, D-P called control again for instructions where to land and was told to come in on the east side of the flarepath.

The hanging wheels and empty petrol tanks must have altered the trim of the plane, for we touched down tail first and then flopped forward onto our engines. There was a grinding and crunching of metal and the machine shook and shuddered and stopped dead from 100mph in a few yards. I did not stop until a fraction of a second later! My forehead struck the cupola and I smashed my goggles, cut my eyebrow and my left hand, and bruised my right elbow. The starboard engine broke away from the machine, the main frame was twisted and D-P's emergency hatch would not open. Fortunately there was practically no petrol left, or I am sure there would have been a bonfire. D-P smashed the Perspex of his emergency exit with a hatchet and crawled through the jagged hole, unhurt. It was 1:15am. We had been airborne just four and a half hours. The ambulance was quickly on the spot and took me off to sick quarters where my wounds were dressed. F/Lt Binns, the 1435 Squadron doctor, came and stitched my wounded eyebrow. He finished at 1:45am. The five hours had ended in nothing but a battered Beaufighter and a bedraggled and disappointed aircrew. It takes greater skill and initiative, better judgement and quicker decisions to win DFCs.

Examination of the wreck next day revealed that two hydraulic pipes had rubbed together during prolonged engine vibration and had worn a hole in one of them, through which the hydraulic fluid had leaked. A tiny hole less than a quarter of an inch in diameter had caused the destruction of an aircraft.

Secret Mission – Kommando Süd

The dropping of agents in Allied territory was carried out by I /KG 200, which operated by means of outlying detachments, there being seldom more than a few crews and aircraft at the base. One of these detachments – Kommando Süd – was set up at Kalamaki aerodrome, near Athens, in September 1943 with the purpose of establishing a chain of wireless posts in North Africa and eventually of dropping agents there.

Following the Axis surrender in North Africa (May 1943), the Germans had little knowledge of the Allied build-up or where the landings on the Mediterranean coast might be expected. In an endeavour to acquire such information Kommando Toska (part of KG200) was formed at Kalamaki (Athens) to carry out long-range reconnaissance sorties into the North African interior and specifically Tunisia where the abandoned former Italian airfield at Wadi Tamet was known to be available for the clandestine operation.

The initial plan was to set up a W/T station from where intelligence could be transmitted back to Kalamaki by German and German-trained Arab agents. The more ambitious plan called for a series of supply dumps and landing grounds to be established for use as bases for paratrooper assault troops who were to be flown in using captured B-17s from where they would carry out attacks on Allied airfields in Tunisia and Morocco.

To set the operation in motion it was necessary for a small aircraft to be located at Wadi Tamet to enable agents to be flown to Sierra Leone, Monrovia and Durban. Initially, a Fi 156 Storch was earmarked for this task but having established its range to be insufficient, a four-seater Bf 108 Taifun was made available. The audacious plan called for the Taifun to be towed by a He 111 across the Mediterranean to the Gulf of Sirte (Libya) where it was known there was a 'gap' in the Allied radar network. Upon release, the Taifun's engine would be started and it would fly under its own steam to its destination.

On 12 November, with Oblt Paul Karger at the controls, Heinkel T9+NK lifted off from Kalamaki with Taifun T9+XK on the end of the towline, onboard of which were Oblt Horst Dümcke and his observer Ltn Kussmal, plus two W/T operators. Once over the Gulf, the Taifun was released and the Heinkel turned away to distract Allied radar. Dümcke eventually landed safely and radioed his arrival. A supply drop was planned for the next day but both Heinkel supply aircraft were damaged during an American bombing raid on Kalamaki. No further flight was undertaken until 17 November when Oblt Klager returned with the Heinkel. Having camouflaged the Taifun, the whole party returned to Athens, leaving just the W/T operators at Wadi Tamet. The primitive W/T station operated only for a few weeks and was closed down when it was feared that its whereabouts had been compromised. However, a second station had been established some eleven miles from Wadi Tamet and the original station reopened in January. Two B-17s (including A3+BB), two Heinkels and SM75 AI+AZ were involved in the nocturnal supply flights, successfully evading Allied night fighters, but not British intelligence. At dawn on 14 March, the base was attacked by a force of the LRDG. The only aircraft on the landing strip, the SM75, was destroyed and four personnel captured. As detailed in Saul Kelly's book *The Lost Oasis*:

> …an armoured car platoon reached the site El Mukaram [Wadi Tamet] … some 60 miles SW of Sirte, and found there an SM82 [sic] aircraft and a dug-out in the side of a hill nearby. The party opened fire on the dug-out. Fire was returned from the aircraft itself, which was engaged. Two men left the aircraft, two more came out of the dug-out, and all were captured. The aircraft was burnt out, but a W/T transmitter and traffic tables were secured. There were 2,000 gallons of aviation petrol on the site.

During the afternoon, the Heinkel and Taifun arrived; however, when the British arrived the Heinkel had been refuelled and the Bf 108 rendered unserviceable. Both crews were able to return to Athens onboard the Heinkel. The subsequent British ADI(K) report revealed:

> This SM75 was captured when already burnt out. Four prisoners have been taken, one, the W/T operator [Fw Hubert Schultz], belonged to the flying crew, another [Uffz Martin Olhoff] is a ground W/T operator, and the two others [Obgfr Witte and Obgfr Fleckner] are ground mechanics. The four P/W belonged to a detachment which they called Kommando Sud. This is under the command of Oblt Duemke and operated from Kalamaki, Greece with the object of maintaining a W/T channel from North Africa. Oblt Duemke is already well known for his work dropping agents.
> A W/T station was started near El Mukaram [Wadi Tamet] last November. This station communicated through Kalamaki, code name *Toska*, with a station near Berlin, code name *Burg* and with a Rangsdorf W/T station in the south of France, code name *Rigaletto*. El Mukaram station has been supplied regularly since November 1943 by air from Kalamaki. W/T traffic to date has been almost certainly confined to weather reports and arrivals of aircraft from Greece. The code name for the whole enterprise is *Etappenhase* [Bunny-Hop]

That was not quite the end of the story. On 15 May, Oblt Dümcke attempted to resurrect the operation when he flew to Wadi Tamet in one of the B-17s. Having landed safely, the aircraft came under heavy machine-gun fire and was badly damaged. Despite being wounded in a hip, Dümcke managed to take-off only to eventually ditch the large bomber in the sea off Kalamata on the southern Greek coast. All were rescued including a seriously injured Uffz Günter Harlos.

The Discovery of Two Abandoned Ju 86Rs

Ju 86 R-1 modified from Ju 86 P-2

Two aircraft of this type were found on Tatoi airfield. Unfortunately, both were very badly damaged, particularly as far as the fuselage, cockpits and engines were concerned.

Markings Aircraft A:

T5 in small black letters, VH large black letters. Painted on the fin were the figures 9454.

Two main plates were recovered from the leading-edge of the port mainplane which gave the following information:

MUSTER UMBAU JU86P-2

Wk Nr 0860454 1940

Ju86R-1

UMBAU 1942

Wk Nr 454

From this is will be seen that this machine modified once in 1940 was again modified in 1942 to the sub-type R-1.

Engines – Jumo 207 B3V – Only one engine plate was recovered, that being from the port engine that gave the Works Nr. as MSD 84. Both engines were very badly damaged.

General Remarks – Unfortunately, the pressure cabin was so badly damaged that very little information could be obtained. Entrance is by means of a circular hatch that is internally controlled by the lever operating two-geared lever arms in the belly framework of the cockpit. The cabin was constructed with two skins of dural and Perspex. The Perspex portions were fitted to T section steel frames. The tail portion of the T section in most cases had been lightened by drilling.

In shape, the nose was somewhat like the He 111. Where the skin joined the framework it was noticed that close double rows of rivets had been used. The controls passed through the cockpit bulkhead through gland boxes while the electrical leads are connected to a Bakelite panel, the sockets of which appeared on either side. No guns or gun mountings were found. No de-icing devices for the main or tailplanes could be found. It was noticed that the petrol tanks carried in the fuselage were metal without the self-sealing covering. Camera fittings were found in the aft end of the fuselage.

Markings Aircraft B:

This machine was, if possible, in an even worse state than the one described above, but the main data plates were recovered and read as follows:

MUSTER

JU 86R-1

Wk Nr 086 - 0285

BAUJAHR UMBAU 1941

This aircraft thus appears to have been modified in 1941 direct from a standard Ju 86 into the high-altitude sub-type R-1.

Markings:

5 (small black) + W8 (large black). On fin in white 285.

No difference in construction or fittings could be found in this aircraft with the one previously described.

Information via Andy Mitchell

Acknowledgements

First and foremost my thanks to Val for her everlasting support, understanding and encouragement. My old and trusted friend Bruce Lander for his invaluable contributions; the late Capt. Harold Kirby SAAF, and his son Robin, for logbook entries and photographs; Roy Butler DFC for permission to include his account of 46 Squadron's operations from Gambut; Grp Capt. Dougie Barr, 46 Squadron Association; Peter C. Smith for permission to use information and extracts from *War in the Aegean*; Byron Tesapsides, author of *Die Deutsche Luftwaffe in Griechenland*, and Efthymios Serbis (Greece); author Sqn Ldr Bruce Blanche (603 Squadron historian, for photographs and documents); Brian Bines, Leendert Holleman (Holland), Ludovico Slongo and Gianandrea Bussi (Italy), Steve Darlow (author); Ian Westworth, Col Bruggy, Bruce Vinicombe and Matt Freckelton (Australia), Jim Perry and Frank Olynek (USA); Bertrand Hugo and Alexis Rousselot (France), Jim Routledge, Andy Mitchell, Alex Smart, Andreas Brekken (Norway), Bjorn Hafsten (Sweden), Matti Salonen (Finland), Stig Jarlevik (Sweden), David Pausey; Doug Stankey (Canada); Andy Fletcher, Ian Simpson. Tinus le Roux and author Mike Schoeman (SA). I also wish to offer thanks for the support received from Ruy and Ross of Twelve O'Clock High (TOCH) and RAF Commands forums, respectively; and to forum members not previously acknowledged above. Last but not least, my thanks go out to Alan Sutton, Jay Slater and Jasper Hadman of Fonthill Media for enabling this project to come to fruition.

Endnotes

1. The Dodecanese Islands comprise twelve islands of which Rhodes, Kos and Leros are the largest. Although Crete is not part of the Dodecanese, this large island effectively straddles the gateway to the Aegean.
2. Newly promoted Grp Capt. Aitken, son of Lord Beaverbrooke, had recently commanded 68 Squadron (Beaufighters) in the UK and had raised his score to twelve destroyed, having earlier commanded 601 Squadron on Hurricanes in 1940.
3. See the author's *Gladiator Ace* (Haynes Publishing) for further information about the RAF at Crete in May 1941. Also *Air War Yugoslavia, Greece and Crete* (Grub Street, 1987).
4. See *Escape to Live* by Wg Cdr Edward Howell OBE DFC (Grosvenor, 1981).
5. Damaged were Wk Nr. 5577, 5578, 5556, 5558, 5572, 5213, 5225 of LG1 and, among others, Ju 88Ds 430054 and 430093 of 2.(F)/124.
6. See *Spitfires over Sicily* by Brian Cull, Frederick Galea and Nicola Malizia.
7. The Ar 196s were 7R+BK, CK, IK, GK, HK and MK. Armed with two 20-mm cannons in the wings, one 7.92 heavy machine-gun in the starboard fuselage and another in the rear cockpit, it proved to be an effective opponent when defending convoys against striking Beaufighters. Although designed primarily as a shipborne reconnaissance aircraft, it found its niche operating from the islands in the Aegean. While 4./126 remained at Suda Bay, 1 Staffel (Hptm. Kurt Kroll) and 2 Staffel (Hptm. Otto Hörnig) were based at Scaramanga (Athens) with 3 Staffel (Oblt Barth) at Volos (north of Athens in the Gulf of Pagassetikos).
8. General Bräuer was later charged with war crimes by a Greek military court, found guilty and was executed on 20 May 1947.
9. Following the Italian armistice, General Carta, a Royalist, was smuggled out of Crete, together with some members of his staff, by the SOE and reached Egypt safely.
10. See Air 23/6739.
11. See *Five of the Few* by Steve Darlow.
12. Extracted from *Flying in Foreign Skies* by Ilias Kartalamakis, translated by Themis Serbis.
13. See Air 23/6739.
14. *Ibid*.
15. Grp Capt. Wheeler had spent most of his early flying career in India with 39

Squadron before transferring to RAF Intelligence. He died from his injuries on 21 September 1943, aged 37.

16. On release from internment, Morganti and Berti returned to Italy and were later assigned to 9°Gruppo, 4°Stormo, of the Co-Belligerent Air Force. Morganti was subsequently released from service in September 1944. Another of the Kos detachment's pilots, Loris Baldi, joined the NRA, retrained on the Bf 109G and was credited with five victories by the end of the war.
17. See *Eagles Victorious* by H. J. Martin and Neil Orpen.
18. Extracted from reminiscences of Ray Burl to Don Lilford of the *Weekend Argus Magazine*, dated 14 May 1977.
19. Correspondence with the late Capt. Harold Kirby.
20. 7SAAF Squadron ORB.
21. *Ibid.*
22. See *War in the Aegean* by Peter C. Smith and Edwin R. Walker.
23. See *One of the Few* by Grp Capt. J. A. Kent.
24. See *War in the Islands* by Adrian Seligman.
25. See 7SAAF Squadron ORB.
26. *Jagdgeschwader 27* by Hans Ring.
27. See *I Fear No Man* by Doug Tidy.
28. See Air 23/6739.
29. *Ibid.*
30. *Weekend Argus Magazine*, dated 14 May 1977.
31. See Air 23/6739.
32. *Ibid.*
33. *Ibid.*
34. *Ibid.* Sqn Ldr John Morgan DFC was a Spitfire pilot with at least eight victories to his credit. He was currently on the staff of 219(F) Group.
35. See *Tigers.*
36. *Ibid.*
37. The wreck of D1+EH was discovered by Greek fishermen in 1982 at a depth of ninety-one metres and transferred to the shallow waters of a bay on the island of Herakliea.
38. See *War in the Aegean.*
39. See *The Greatest Squadron of Them All.*
40. Flg Off. John 'Tex' Holland was an American volunteer in the RCAF. He had won his DFM flying Wellingtons with 70 Squadron before requesting a posting to Beaufighters.
41. See *Beaufighter at War* by Chaz Bowyer.
42. The Ju 88, from II/KG6, was officially credited to 2/Lt RE Williams.
43. Extracted from an account by S/Sgt George Underwood who flew sixty-nine sorties with 310thBG but not over the Aegean.
44. These included 42-32464, 32487, 32488, 32489, 42-64501, 64531, 64579, 64580, 64587 and 64668.
45. Several sources erroneously 'credit' B-25Gs and Beaufighters with the sinking of the *Sinfra.*
46. On 8 February 1944, RN submarine HMS *Sportsman* torpedoed the 4,785-ton German freighter *Petrella* off Suda Bay. She had onboard 3,173 Italian POWs destined for Greece. 2,670 were drowned.
47. The wreck of JM225 was discovered in 2007.
48. Three of the Z.506Bs were allotted RAF serial numbers HK977, HK978 and HK979 while a Z.501 became HK976. It is not known if any were used operationally by the RAF but one unidentified Z.506B flown by RAAF pilot Flt

Lt Cyril Kissner and carrying Wg Cdr Richard Outfin was lost off Fredonia, Italy, on 29/04/44, possibly while on a clandestine operation.

49. Account of Major Hans Dochtermann's attack on the troopship *Rhona* (1,179 lost) on 23 November 1943 off the Algerian coast. The attack was carried out by Hs 293-equipped He 177s of II/KG40. Extracted from *Warriors and Wizards* by Martin J. Bollinger.
50. *War in the Islands.*
51. See *Long Road to Leros* by Marsland Gander.
52. See *Churchill's Folly* by Tony Rogers.
53. *Ibid.*
54. See *Long Road to Leros.*
55. *Ibid.*
56. See *Churchill's Folly.*
57. See *The Second World War Volume V Closing the Ring* by Winston Churchill.
58. 227 Squadron ORB.
59. See *No Hero, Just a Survivor* by G. R. T. Willis.
60. Jochen Prien.
61. The B-25Gs flew fourteen missions during the month. On 14 November, a B-25G crashed during local flying killing 2/Lt John C. Minord and his crew.
62. See Bruce Blance's article *Beaufighter Rocketeers* (*FlyPast*, May 2004).
63. See *A Lighter Shade of Blue* by Air Marshal Sir Christopher Foxley-Norris.
64. See *McAughtry's War* by Sam McAughtry.
65. See *No Hero, Just a Survivor.*
66. See *A Lighter Shade of Blue.*
67. See *McAughtry's War.*
68. Combat Report Air 50.
69. See *McAughtry's War.*
70. See *75 Eventful Years* edited by Tony Ross DFC.
71. See *Coastal Strike* by Colonel John Clements DFC.
72. See *The Greatest Squadron of Them All.*
73. See Bruce Blance's article *Beaufighter Rocketeers* (*FlyPast*, May 2004).
74. See *McAughtry's War.*
75. *Ibid.*
76. *Ibid.*
77. *Ibid.*
78. See Chris Goss article *Convoy Attack* (*Britain at War*, July 2011).
79. See *McAughtry's War.*
80. *Ibid.*
81. This was Sqn Ldr Tommy Deck's fifth confirmed (two shared) kill making him the top-scoring day Beaufighter pilot of the campaign.
82. See *Whispering Death* by Lee Heide.
83. See *A Lighter Shade of Blue.*
84. 3K+HM was used as a minesweeper. The large degaussing ring was an electrified metal ring built in sections that were supported with bracings under the fuselage and wings. Low voltage current was fed through the ring while the aircraft was flying over the water suspected of being mined by the Allies. The electromagnetic field generated by the minesweeping ring would explode any magnetic mines encountered.
85. See *McAughtry's War.*
86. W/C Hugh Eliot DFC had flown Hurricanes in France (1940) and Malta (1941). His two victories in October 1944 raised his score to at least seven with one shared. He and his navigator were shot down and killed by flak over Italy on

04/03/45. His DSO was Gazetted in May 1945.

87. See *Straight and Level* by Air Chief Marshal Sir Kenneth Cross.

88. *Ibid.*

89. *Ibid.*

90. Extracted from *RAF Middle East: The Official Story of Air Operations Feb 1942-Jan 1943* (HMSO).

91. *Spitfire – The Story of a Famous Fighter* by Bruce Robertson.

92. *Ibid.*

93. The Ju 86 was deemed irreparable and destroyed by German forces on their departure from Bir-el-Abd as confirmed by ULTRA intercept HW 5/145: 'From G.A.F. Station Command 6/IV to 2(F) 123 Castelli on 12/10/1942: Ju 86 Works No.5101 was destroyed by fire on 11/10. Pressure-cabin entirely destroyed.'

94. *Spitfire – The Story of a Famous Fighter*.

95. *Ibid.*

96. PFC Charles F. Cline of HQ Squadron may also have been lost in this aircraft.

97. See *One of the Few*.

98. Air 28/9.

99. *Ibid.*

100. *Ibid.*

101. *Ibid.*

102. See *A Lighter Shade of Blue*.

Select Bibliography

Air Historical Branch, *Operations in the Dodecanese Islands, September-November 1943*
Blanche, Bruce, David Ross and William Simpson, *The Greatest Squadron of Them All* (Grub Street, 2003)
Bowyer, Chaz, *Beaufighter at War* (Ian Allan, 1976)
Brown, David, *Seafire* (Greenhill, 1989)
Carr, John, *On Spartan Wings* (Pen and Sword, 2012)
Churchill, Winston, *The Second World War Volume V Closing the Ring* (Cassell, 1952)
Clements DFC, Colonel John, *Coastal Strike* (Clements/Gibson, 2005)
Cossey, Bob, *Tigers* (Weidenfeld, 1992)
Cross, Air Chief Marshal Sir Kenneth, *Straight and Level* (Grub Street, 1993)
Darlow, Steve, *Five of the Few* (Grub Street, 2006)
Foxley-Norris, Air Marshal Sir Christopher, *A Lighter Shade of Blue* (Ian Allan, 1978)
Gander, Marsland, *Long Road to Leros* (Macdonald, 1945)
Heide, Lee, *Whispering Death* (Trafford, 2000)
Kartalamakis, Ilias (translated by Themis Serbis), *Flying in Foreign Skies* (Kartalamakis, 1993)
Kent DFC AFC, Grp Capt. J. A., *One of the Few* (Kimber, 1971)
Martin, H. J. and Neil Orpen, *Eagles Victorious* (Purnell, 1977)
McAughtry, Sam, *McAughtry's War* (Blackstaff, 1986)
Nesbit, Roy C., *Armed Rovers* (Airlife, 1995)
Rogers, Tony, *Churchill's Folly* (Cassell, 2003)
Schoeman, Michael, *Springbok Fighter Victory* (Freeworld Publications, 2010)
Seligman, Adrian *War in the Islands* (Sutton, 1997)
Smith, Peter C., *War in the Aegean* (Stackpole, 2008)
Tesapsides, Byron, *Die Deutsche Luftwaffe in Griechenland* (Byron Tesapsides, 2011)
Tidy, Douglas, *I Fear No Man* (Macdonald, 1973)
Willis, G. R. T., *No Hero, Just a Survivor* (Willis, 1999)

Britain at War, July 2011 (Chris Goss article)
FlyPast, May 2004 (Sqn Ldr Bruce Blanche article)
Weekend Argus Magazine, dated 14 May 1977

Air 23/6739 Operation *Thesis*
Air 27 Squadron Operations Records Books
Air 28/9 No.103 Maintenance Unit Aboukir
Air 50 Combat Reports

Many excellent websites, too numerous to record.

Flying Personnel Index